GARZ

England:

The Land and the People

England:

The Land and the People

By Donald Cowie

South Brunswick and New York: A. S. Barnes and Company
London: Thomas Yoseloff Ltd

© 1972 by A. S. Barnes and Co., Inc.
Library of Congress Catalogue Card Number: 70-146750

A. S. Barnes and Co., Inc.
Cranbury, New Jersey 08512

Thomas Yoseloff Ltd
108 New Bond Street
London W1Y OQX, England

Photographs in this book are by courtesy
of the British Travel Association,
239 Old Marylebone Road, London, N.W.1

First Printing February, 1972
Second Printing October, 1972

ISBN 0-498-07827-2
Printed in the United States of America

For
RUTH
again,
and perhaps decisively

Contents

England:

The Land and the People

1

Why?

On the shores of Lake Léman in Switzerland, late at night while the sickle moon above was being encircled by astronauts, a Mexican said: "I have just arrived in Europe for the first time. And most of all I want to go to England."

"Why?"

"Because I know it will be a different country at last."

"Different in what way?"

"Oh, just different. Filled with fog, and strikes, and so many people rushing about in your wonderful London, hippies and city workers, very short skirts, under Big Ben, the Houses of Parliament, Buckingham Palace, your Queen and Royal Family. How old is London exactly? Do you know?"

"Now that is a difficult question. Very, very old, much more so than we think. But you could perhaps say for practical purposes, some two thousand years."

"Oh, surely, not so old as that!"

"Probably much older, but scholars would say that it mostly began during the last century before Christ. A Celtic tribal leader now known as Cymbeline (because of Shakespeare's play) developed some sort of port amid horrible swamplands towards the tidal waters of the river Thames."

"Horrible because of the fogs?"

"That's a good point. England has had this bad reputation for weather right from the beginning. Julius Caesar had never before known anything like it. The real reason England was never properly

11

civilized like the rest of western Europe was that the open-air Romans couldn't enjoy themselves there thanks to the unpredictable, continually moist climate. And a lot of that moisture came from the imperfect drainage of the land that continues even to this day. Nearly every year there are floods around cities such as Gloucester, and still nothing is done about it."

"But they must have done something about those swamps on which London was built."

"Well, there were two small hills of more or less solid land, about thirty-five feet high. Cymbeline built a wooden fortress on one, and on the other rose eventually a typical stone forum, basilica and administrative offices of the Roman invaders. When you get to England yourself you must visit the old City of London on a typically quiet Sunday. Little will be there but the occasional red buses and the pigeons. On either side will rise the cliffs of head offices and the time-bleached towers of Wren churches. Right in the middle of this little commercial enclave, between Cornhill and Lombard Street of the bankers, with Leadenhall Market and Fenchurch Street on the east, is the site of the original Roman forum. You won't see much of it, if any, save in the Guildhall Museum not so far away."

"But you still haven't explained how they drained those swamps."

"They didn't. The whole point about England, which makes it different from most other countries, is that it prefers to evolve rather than innovate. Not for nothing was Darwin an Englishman. He worked out that extraordinary theory of evolution because that is the English way of life. There used to be a catch-phrase: 'Like Topsy it growed.' So with London. The streets today are far above the level of the swampy land when the Romans arrived. It so happened that the place became important and gradually rose above the water line, only not deliberately, not like Venice or Amsterdam. Eventually it rose right above the little tributary rivers which flowed into the Thames, and today those run far underground. It rose on its own rubbish."

"So your wonderful London is just a rubbish dump."

"You could call it that. But a more accurate description would be 'a crossroads.' The Romans failed completely as civilizers in ancient Britain. You can see that when you study the so-called 'pop' culture of London today. No thoroughly Romanized people could behave in that disgusting way. The same applies to those unfortunate parts of America that have been ruined by English influence. All the Romans left behind in Britain was Christianity and a few long straight roads with potential city sites where they intersected. London arose upon one of the most important intersections, which also had an outlet to the sea, regularly flushed out by such a strong river that it could always be navigated by deep ships. When the Romans had to retreat from their colonies they left behind a demoralized native people of Iberian-Celtic origin who were good at the arts but hopeless at large-scale warfare, rather like the Italians today (strange somersault of history!). These unfortunate creatures in Augusta, the old Roman London, just fled into the neighboring swamps and forests when the sea-rovers from Scandinavia and Germany arrived. The old Roman London never fell. There is no record of any battle. It was just abandoned. Its native inhabitants probably found eventual sanctuary in the distant mountains of Wales. So if we want really to be fair we should give back London today to its original owners, the Welsh."

The Mexican grinned. "I have heard," he said, "that London has been controlled by the Welsh for a long time, the Welsh, and the Scots, and the Jews, and other foreigners."

"Yes, London is not an English city. It never has been. It is not England."

The Mexican spread his hands in distress. "I am sorry. I did not mean to say that. Besides, when I think of England I think first of London. I see the Beefeaters at the Tower. The Old Curiosity Shop of Charles Dickens. Your Carnaby Street. That is why I must go there, to see those things."

"And what else do you expect to find in England?"

"That I do not know. Perhaps I might just visit London and then go away, or visit Scotland and Ireland. I do not know."

"You cannot think of anything very English outside London?"

"Well, I have heard of the rain in your Manchester. And castles and cathedrals in a countryside which is very green because of the continual storms that sweep over you from the Atlantic. Shakespeare, Rolls-Royces, all the time strikes in factories. Not much else. I don't think I would like the fog, which is why I might prefer to stay in a big hotel in London and then go."

"I am sorry, you know, but you have got it all wrong."

"How have I got it all wrong?"

"I will try to tell you. It is probably about time that somebody made the effort, before it is quite too late."

"How do you mean, too late?"

"Oh, something has happened to the English in our time. They have lost so much that they have nearly lost hope, and consequently they and their ideas and their institutions might disappear altogether (as that Roman civilization disappeared). This might happen as the result of a sudden atomic war, under which a comparatively unprotected Britain would just become a steaming heap of radioactive ashes. Or it might be the product of this 'don't care' attitude on the part of the people, which could allow native ideas and institutions to be submerged under alien ways of life. I think it is very likely that in fifty years' time a book about the England we know today would be like a book about the world before the Flood."

"Perhaps you should write that book now."

"I shall try; and along the way you might learn at least two things— first what is different about England which should attract you there as a tourist, and second, what this little country has contributed to our western world which is worth remembering when her own propagandists and those of other lands so frequently conspire to run her completely down."

2

Counties

May hill in Gloucestershire, England (pronounced "Glostershir"),
rises only some 973 feet above the fertile plain that surrounds the
river Severn. But it is like a Fujiyama or holy mountain to the local
inhabitants. It dominates the land from all angles, especially because
it is crowned by a kind of toothbrush moustache of trees.

A poet once sang about "the coloured counties," and May Hill
perfectly explains what he meant. It rises softly with the molding of
a feminine breast to that toothbrush summit, and is patterned all the
way up with fields divided by hedges and diversified by occasional
clumps of elm trees, like an old-fashioned patchwork quilt. The hues
range from the bright greens of pasturage to the infinitely various
red-browns of ploughland, from the white of daisies to the yellow of
mustard.

Once on a midsummer's night not so long ago the rough grass at
the top of May Hill was occupied mainly by strange people with
much hair and with dolorous eyes, some modern religious sect out
celebrating, and continuing to use that pretty eminence for a purpose
that goes right back to primeval times and the horrid rites of Baal.

The savage ancestors of the English apparently learned from visiting
Phoenician tin-seekers or traders how to get a kick from slaughtering
chosen babies on a stone altar upon a hilltop. Also something went
on with maidens, a privilege of the priests; and such hilltops became
known as Beltiens or "places for making the fire of Baal."

It is curious that the crankier of religious organizations still pay
their periodic visits to the place; and that should remind the inquiring
stranger that one of the points of difference between England and his

15

own land is that the people of England have lived in the one place for such a very long time compared with the people of the world's new lands. They are a true "native" people, like the indigenous populations of other still primitive places, Borneo and China, Japan, black Africa, and Siberia.

The ancient British are still the modern British even though the Romans came, and the Saxons and Vikings and Normans and Huguenots, and, latterly, refugees from Germany, Poland and Hungary, as well as a few millions of colored immigrants from the former British imperial possessions in the West Indies, Africa and India.

The immigrants have always tended to swirl around in the drab parts of cities, whereas the true England has sturdily and obstinately remained—May Hill.

There are thousands of acres of still unspoiled countryside like that of May Hill, with similar histories and almost identical, craggy inhabitants, as for example the Mullocks with whom the writer of this book used to drink rough draft cider in a small inn just under the toothbrush summit.

The Mullocks were a family of farmers; they owned several farms, and were so shrewd that it was quite impossible to outwit them in anything. Old Mullock the father had been to school but had wisely refused to learn, and found it difficult to sign his name on a check, but had a multiplicity of undeclared bank accounts.

A watchdog in the dirty farmyard was continually chained up and half-starved, to "keep him bright and snappy, see?" And the numerous cats that subdued the rats and mice were leaner and more nervous even than those of the Capitoline Hill in Rome, because old Mullock insisted they be given no food from the house. "Let 'em forage" was not only his stern command but also his philosophy.

He certainly knew how to forage himself. His family of three sons and four daughters were held down hard. A few of them got away, to become self-governing Mullocks elsewhere, but most were like the two leading brothers who at the age of forty still slept together in a narrow bed under the sloping attic roof. Their father gave them a few dollars a week, and they had to work for him like the Egyptians who built the Pyramids. What they did for sex was nobody's business, but it did become obvious as the years passed that they were just waiting for the moment when the old man faltered and then they would swiftly do the equivalent of killing him and taking over—and main-. taining the same regime forever and ever.

The so-called city civilizations never last. They always generate

cancers that eventually consume them. They are fundamentally unnatural. Even when guided by the best brains that can be assembled
in Washington and Moscow they must inevitably destroy themselves.
After which there will just be the Mullocks left again, to carry on.

Thus the real England is the land of these colored counties, because
it is the part that has endured comparatively unchanged in its mental-
ity since the earliest times. The Romans came and built roads and

Thatched roofs and roses round the doors.

forums, then went soft and ran for their lives when the Mullocks
turned up at night with hayforks and scythes. Later the Mullocks took
the fine-fashioned stones from the roads and forums and used them
for the making of dry walls and crude barns.

It was exactly the same, if rather more protracted, with the Normans. They built castles and country houses and temporarily gave
England an aristocracy, but in the country districts today the manor
houses are being converted into farms again, and the last scions of
the nobility are long-haired in London and working for the foreigners
who have largely taken over that socalled capital.

We would drink the rough cider as it was drawn from large wooden barrels in the cellar-like interior of our May Hill inn. Old Mullock would sit with gaitered legs apart, his shrewd blue eyes continually darting in their obvious effort to squeeze some financial advantage from the occasion. And invariably he did, but less than if we had been true strangers and not ourselves of his own sharp blood.

The cider was drunk in cool pints, three of which were enough to floor a softie like a tap on the skull from the butt of a Colt Woodsman.

"What's this 'ere Common Market?" old Mullock would ask. "They wants us to join up with these frogs and Germans and Eyetalians. It won't never work, it won't."

And: "These 'ere dancing fancy boys they puts on the telly. Send 'em down 'ere and we'll larn 'em, eh?"

Nothing would disgust and annoy old Mullock more than a display of wealth on the part of a neighbor or stranger. He would literally dance on his old gaitered legs with violent emotion.

There were stories of how he would go to bed with a daughter or even with an aged horse, and altogether he was a nasty, unwashed old man, but the true England beside which the suburban commuters to sad cities were as stupid ants who would surely destroy themselves and leave the sweet land to those who knew how to handle her again.

The most notable English military achievement of modern times was that of the Gloucestershire Regiment, who did a little to help in Korea. The crude conscript from the shires has always been the backbone of the country in a military sense. Wellington, who beat Napoleon with them, said they were "the scum of the earth, enlisted for drink," but had to add "it really is wonderful that we should have made them the fine fellows they are."

Much of the trouble with modern England is that the children or Mullocks have been attracted to the towns and cities as factory workers for higher wages and drink and holidays, and have been quite out of their true rural element there. Their native hardness, envious natures and independence of character have made them impossible to discipline. Machines aren't cows and factory floors aren't broad acres. The continual strike is the essentially intractable countryman's way of asserting himself when he is out of place in town. And perhaps his way of putting the clock back to where it should and will ultimately once more be.

So the true England is organized in counties as the U.S.A. is in states and Switzerland in cantons. The visitor who wants to enjoy the best of the place will realize this and get out of London as soon as possible. For that he will need to travel swiftly from the center of

Buckland, a typical Devonshire village.

the metropolis, and then leave the main roads to twist about in the
feathered lanes, always surfaced better than rural roads anywhere
else, and take his night's lodgings in a cool pub, where with any luck
he may still find chintz furnishings, and eat bacon and eggs for breakfast, and enjoy the privilege of local talk. Should he by chance know
how to shoot and fish he may even be given a chance really to know
the local landscape and its lore and its people. ("Bill, here's a gentle-

man from America who wants to get a few rabbits. What about taking him out in the marning down Bleak Bottom way?")

Each county differs from the next—in dialect, farm architecture, even shape and color of the fields and little, rolling hills. There are 43 true, ancient counties, ranging from Cornwall in the southwest to Northumberland in the northeast, from Kent in the southeast to Cumberland in the northwest. Some of them are also known as shires (the word "county" is an invention of the Norman conquerors). The modern English language is frequently a similar amalgam of the old and the aristocratic Norman "new." "Sheep" is old but "mutton" is the flesh of it which only the noble invaders were privileged to eat. "Woods" are English but "forests" are French. The foreigners have "ancestors" but the true English have "forebears."

Much of this may be sentimentality, and many people visit England without once encountering what is being written about here. But they should try, because foreign travel means looking for differences, and these are among the matters that truly differentiate England from other countries.

Some of the countries are relics of old distinct kingdoms. Cornwall is to this day almost the separate nation that it often was in history. Northumberland was once the ancient kingdom of Northumbria under the mighty Edwin. East Anglia formerly had two nations, those of the North Folk and those of the South Folk, now the counties of Norfolk and Suffolk. Sussex was the land of the South Saxons, and Essex of the East Saxons, and many of the Midland counties formed part in the old days of the now-forgotten great kingdom of Offa the Dane called Mercia.

To know the most perfect rural county of all England at once the visitor should go over to Herefordshire past Gloucestershire. Save for a few factories spewed down there by the wars it is red soil and green fields all the way, with magpie villages of half-timber work, and with hops for beer, and still the basic stock of the docile red-brown cattle with white faces that originally made pioneer fortunes in the Wild West.

But it is always unnecessary to go too far in England. Parts of Essex, one of the London counties, are still decent; while even Sussex of the commuters has its moments; and one of the most unlauded counties can be explored immediately by the visitor who may still arrive at Southampton, that Hampshire which is as rich and rural at its heart as it is unpleasantly suburbanized at the edges. Alton, a typical country town of Hampshire, is only a short 49 miles from London. It has some red brick houses of the 18th century and earlier, and a very stately 15th-century church with much antique woodwork and a south door that still shows bullet-marks from *England's* Civil War between Cavaliers and Roundheads of over three hundred years ago. Outside are hop gardens that help to make a good local beer.

It is necessary to get used to this beer. It will seem flat at first, and, worst of all, lukewarm, but is one of the most outstanding of English experiences eventually. Like much of England it takes some knowing and is an acquired taste, but when that taste is wisely acquired then it will be realized that the brew perfectly suits a palate conditioned by moisture-laden air and a complete absence of climatic extremes.

England is exposed to the constant caress of a warmish water and air current that comes across the Atlantic from the so-called Gulf Stream. The Deep South belches and England eventually gets the aftermath. She should have a very cold climate, like Russia, parts of Siberia and northern Canada, because she lies between the same lines of latitude as those, but the Atlantic current keeps her average temperature comparatively high in winter as it prevents her from becoming too hot in summer. There is a continual seaside climate almost everywhere in England, and the palate is conditioned by it to prefer the medium taste in everything. The beer in the big cities can be positively hot, a peculiar affront always to the North American. Do not, however, linger in the big cities or drink much beer there. Take your ale in the country inns, where its temperature will suddenly seem just right, as slightly chilled by the thick stone walls and floors of cellars. And what may at first seem flat and heavy may be found at last to be perfectly suited to the tastebuds as changed in their nerve-ends by rich breakfasts and other meals that are always "different" by Transatlantic and European standards.

The true Englishman drinks his peculiar draught beer ponderously and in pints until gradually he becomes human. Then he may suddenly sing.

The hop gardens of Alton in Hampshire point green fingers upwards at old, old chalk downs, the English name for largely treeless undulating uplands used mainly throughout the ages for raising sheep and exercising soldiers. The historian must be an archaeologist here, for traces of prehistoric man can suddenly turn these nice bare hills into mysterious fortresses and burial places of the remotest past. But he can also be a literary man and pause a mile or two out of Alton on the swift Winchester road at Chawton. The remarkable figure who once lived and worked here was Jane Austen, the sheltered spinster who wrote such perfect English that she was enabled thereby to elevate gossip into an art form to endure forever. Her house and personal relics can be inspected. It is all so pretty and peaceful that one quickly understands why the poor girl had to develop such a sharp tongue.

In Hampshire alone a man could spend weeks of fertile exploration if he sought the true England. It is not so much a county as a country, with a proud old capital at noisy Winchester, and an ugly great industrial region around Southampton, and an ever-expanding city on the western coastline where Bournemouth, dear old Edwardian lady, now reproduces herself continually like an automatic mother of modern architectural mediocrity. But in the hinterland is still the New Forest.

It is typically English in that it is called new because it is so old, being given its name by William the Conqueror around 1066. He decided on arrival in England from France across the water that the 100,000-odd acres of indigenous woodland would make an excellent playground for himself and his knights and ladies in intervals of holding down a new subject land. But the forest itself went back to the days, thousands of years before proud William, when England was truly wild with sabre-toothed tiger and neanderthal man, and although the Conqueror could enclose it and make it out of bounds to the native inhabitants, he was unable to make it safe for his family. It is still possible to visit the spot where his brutal son Rufus was accidentally or deliberately killed, while hunting, by an arrow from the bow of Sir Walter Tyrrel (August 2, 1100). The "Rufus Stone" stands there now.

And all around the ancient trees proliferate. Here are what used to be the true English oaks. The ships of the Royal Navy were formerly constructed from their timbers. Here are also giant beeches and yews from which the weapons of Agincourt bowmen were made. The whole is diversified by many varieties of fern and gorse and broom and by the kind of steely tarns and stagnant pools that stood beneath houses of Usher. Although Edgar Allan Poe was probably never there, it is still a region haunted by his kind of dreams or nightmares; and there are many people who still find it an uneasy, even a horrid place, as primeval prints in their subconscious minds take them back to days when danger actually did lurk in every rough thicket.

This wonderful New Forest is still for the fearless and nature-loving. There are wild ponies to this day and foxes and squirrels and three species of deer, also a regular "Swainmote," a semi-democratic institution of Crown officials and local "verdurers" mixed, which partly administers the region—and dates back to pre-Conquest and Saxon times if not earlier.

That is superficially one county, just Hampshire. And there are so many others. Right away in the north is as a contrast, for example, Northumberland with relics of the Roman wall that once divided England and Scotland, also bleak, gaunt castle keeps from seven hundred years ago and more, and walks upon the Pennine hills, backbone geologically of the country, that could be in deep space so silent are the wide skies save for the cries of curlew, peewit, ascending larks, and, quite often, girl students in love. The heavy old 19th-century industries of coal and iron only sometimes bruise the horizon with the furnace color at night or smoke the blue of sky in daytime. It is the same in great Yorkshire and royal Lancashire, two very large counties that still provide England with much of her industrial wealth. Although man has done his very best to ruin the superb natural landscapes of hills and dales here, a large part of both counties is nevertheless green and tranquil. Even in the slums of factory towns the grass begins to grow between Dickensian cobblestones. Painters like Lowry start to detect charm amid the already crumbling relics of Victorian England's commercial might. Moorlands rise far above the tattered chimneys everywhere, and from the purple heather in summer arise grouse with the curious sound of awkward wings.

That sound must often be detected derisively by the gigantic antennae of the steel towers at Fylingdales Moor in Yorkshire, where America has one of her "early warning" systems against intercontinental ballistic missiles. At least she has such a system there at this time of writing.

Some of these counties will be described later in proper tourist detail, but the moment's purpose is to give a spaceman's view of the land, Northumberland in the north, Sussex in the south, Cornwall with its gnarled old foot in the cruel Atlantic Ocean. Cornwall is the legendary land of King Arthur of the Knights and the Round Table, and its place names are among the most beautiful in the world. There is a prehistoric stone circle at Trippet Stones, and there are some of the actual ruins of what could have been King Arthur's Castle at Tintagel on the wild coast above the fabled sea that once supported sable barks from final Lyonnesse. Bolventor village on Bodmin Moor has the original of Daphne du Maurier's *Jamaica Inn,* and Dozmary Pool nearby may have been where Arthur was laid by Sir Bedivere after his

last battle against the wicked usurper Sir Modred (Arthur was probably a Celtic chieftan, who, after the departure of the Romans, used
their code of living and method of fighting to keep the Saxon invaders
of England at least out of Cornwall. Modred's name sounds suitably
Saxon to the etymologist).

Camelford in Cornwall is a quiet old town today but might originally have been Camelot; and two miles out of the town is what the
natives still call Slaughter Bridge, because, they say, Arthur fought
that last famous battle there (and the memory of the bloodshed is
still bright in their minds after some 1900-odd years).

In Cornwall there are Constantine and Creed and Lostwithiel and
Marazion. Sweet Mawgan-in-Meneage is one village and Mousehole
is another. Pixies' Hall is a curious subterranean tunnel near Constantine; and such names as Giant's Hedge, for a remarkable prehistoric causeway, and Giant's Quoit for a strange, legendary stone,
support the theory that in these parts once there did indeed dwell a
mighty race of men, compared with which all moderns are pygmies.

Cornwall has Portwrinkle, and Crafthole, and St. Anthony-in-Rose-
land, not to mention St. Just-in-Penwith, St. Tudy, Tresillian and
Washaway: and so many others that the full list would make a dic-
tionary of verbal delight.

Rutland is England's smallest county. Great efforts have been made
by central government to destroy its administrative identity, and it
has only 152 square miles and some 25,000 largely agricultural inhabitants, right at the center of the British island like an insignificant
but vital heart. It has a county town called Oakham, proud with about
5000 people, and a hosiery factory that links it with the neighboring
big county, Leicestershire, where since time immemorial the folk have
been chiefly interested in hunting and knitting. (Also on the border
of Rutland is Northamptonshire, where the historic sports have been
hunting and bootmaking, significantly lower in the subtle English
social scale.

(England has many mysteries but the all-important social grada-
tions are the most profound. It is quite impossible to understand and
appreciate the country without an understanding of snobbery also. English people can detect superiority or inferiority in each other by accent
alone or by type of automobile used—not its size but its quality—
and among the counties there are those which rate high and those
which are socially low indeed.

(The London commuter is a better man if he lives in Surrey or

Kent than Middlesex or Essex. To come from Shropshire is something but to be a Staffordshire man is almost nothing at all.)

Leicestershire is one of the most industrialized of English counties, but, at least since William the Conqueror cut it up in neat parcels for his friends, it has always come nearly at the top in the social register. Towns with names like Ashby-de-la-Zouch (of the medieval tournaments) and Melton Mowbray (of the crisp round pies with holes in the top for insertion of gravy that turns to nice jelly) recall the knights of old always, and in this county are some of the most important "hunts." What are those? They have of course been transplanted often in good American soil, but have never taken root there in this remarkable English way. The strong men in the old English days banded together as knights to repel invaders and kill dangerous wild animals. The chief bands still remain, under such names as the Quorn, Pycheley, Cottesmore, with traditional Masters, Huntsmen, Hounds, Horns (and even foxes in boxes for chasing). The heart of the matter is Leicestershire, which makes its money from mass-production knitting of stockings, socks and cotton undergarments (with a new fortune recently thanks to the mini-skirt and necessity of tights) but has a landscape outside the factories that is peculiarly suitable for chasing on horses after little animals, neatly-patterned and soggy fields with live hawthorn hedges and always perspectives that enable shrewd eyes and noses to follow the course of tawny tails. Also some very strong aristocratic families developed here thanks to that original Norman carve-up of England, and a few of them have remained relatively vigorous and comparatively solvent, with castles and abbeys and manor-houses still.

Nevertheless that huntin', shootin' part of old England is not so vigorous today as its antithesis, the do-gooders who organize campaigns against what they call blood sports. When the hunt turns out the passionate opponents of the hunt gather also, and it is the hunt which is on the defensive. England, as will be demonstrated to the visitor always, is soft in its old age, but exceedingly hard in its softness. The middle-aged female with umbrella rampant is one of the most formidable animals produced by this country since St. George killed the dragon. Will England eventually need a good St. George again? (He, of course, was not English at all, but a Levantine from Cappadocia, true heartland of our civilization, who was martyred by the Romans for going to church at a period of history when *that* was anti-social.)

Or the Lake District of Westmorland and Cumberland counties in the cool, mountainous northwest: that is something entirely different again. Short of real desert and tropical jungle this strange little country of England certainly has nearly everything geographical, a microcosm of the larger world. The mountains of that Lake District are only low hills, and the lakes themselves are no larger than the Thoreau ponds of Massachusetts. But by some strange trick of perspective and lighting combined those hills often look like peaks in the Rockies or Swiss Alps, and the glistening stretches of Windermere, Ullswater, Coniston, Derwentwater and the rest of the fifteen main pools can frequently, by a small stretch of the imagination, bear a remarkable resemblance to the real lakes of Switzerland and even some of the Great Lakes of North America.

The green here, in a predominantly green country, can be so vivid as to afflict the eye, extending from the grass and the reflections in the water to the color of the local dour stone from which not only the squat houses and walls and their roofing tiles but also quite a lot of the human inhabitants seem to have been fashioned. It is beautiful; it is bleak; and when the daffodils come out it is like the smile on the

The traditional sport of wrestling at Grasmere in Westmorland, the county of Wordsworth.

face of an elderly spinster when someone has, out of charity or mischievousness, accorded her a sudden sexual compliment. It is also like the verses of the indigenous poet William Wordsworth, a bleak sheep of a man who didn't mind breaking the heart of a French girl he had met in Europe, and took public money as a typical bureaucrat without earning it, but could sing like a bird at the sight of a flower suddenly before sinking back into metrical banality and pseudo-metaphysical portentiousness. He wrote:

> Continuous as the stars that shine
>   And twinkle on the Milky Way,
> They stretch'd in never-ending line
>   Along the margin of a bay:
> Ten thousand saw I at a glance,
> Tossing their heads in sprightly dance.

There is Brantwood by Coniston, bought by a schoolmaster as a permanent shrine to Ruskin, another English writer whose literary skill similarly redeemed his pomposity in very occasional flashes; and they still remember in Keswick that Hugh Walpole who lectured so remuneratively in America in intervals of writing novels about this England which are still readable in spite of what the critics' jealousy said about them; and there is Caldbeck village where that John Peel once lived who wore the coat of gray and, in nursery rhyme for some reason or other typified the John Bull kind of Englishman forever after. (The real John Bull was naturally something of a fraud, a long-haired musical man who is chiefly remembered now for his perpetration of the British national anthem *God Save the Queen*.)

Six Jacobites were hanged in 1746 from the Capon Tree on the road from Brampton to Gelt Woods; and it is possible to remember Charlotte Brontë's "Lowood School" from *Jane Eyre* in Casterton of the Old Hall, Westmorland. A disused quarry near Windermere is haunted by the legendary "Crier of Claife"; while cosy Cockermouth has not only the birthplace of the great Wordsworth but also that of Fletcher Christian, leader of the *Bounty* mutineers, and of John Dalton the pioneer nuclear chemist. The noble painter Romney is buried at Dalton-in-Furness; and, deep in a lake, not so far away, lies the remains of Donald Campbell, fastest man in the world on land and water at the time of his sacrificial death amid a final speed run.

Quakers from all other countries come to the original Firbank (in

Westmorland) where George Fox, founder of their cult, once preached to thousands of the local dalesfolk assembled.

Grasmere has not only the tourists surging around Dove Cottage where the ubiquitous Wordsworths lived, but also memories of that Thomas de Quincey who was the first literary man to go on regular psychedelic "trips". The churchyard has both Wordsworth's and Hartley Coleridge's graves.

Kendal, a shoe-making town where most of the men still wear greenish suits, produced that remarkable Catherine Parr who became Henry VIII's sixth and surviving wife—and it has the "Kendal Brown House," once supplier of tobacco snuff to half the world, and still with its ancient machinery and trade secrets intact.

Not only Hugh Walpole but also Robert Southey died in Keswick; and Greta Hall, a girls' school there, has by poetic justice become that after once being the home of Samuel Taylor Coleridge.

"Long Meg and her Daughters," near Little Salkeld, consists of some 66 enormous stones arranged in a circle, with "Long Meg" as a kind of phallic symbol in the centre, the chief of many such prehistoric monuments in these parts that again recall the possible race of giants that once owned England before the little men came.

Not far away is a village, part of which was left to the nation at her death by Beatrix Potter. Those who are interested can see exactly where and how the Peter Rabbit stories were written. Others might prefer to see Netherby Hall in Cumberland, where once lived the "Young Lochinvar" of Walter Scott's poem *Marmion*. Or Sizergh Castle by the Kendal–Milnthorpe road where one English family, the Stricklands, lived continuously for over 700 years.

Yet a connoisseur might say that no English county is more typical —or nearer the English ideal of rural beauty—than Somerset in the southwest (past Gloucestershire and lying alongside the Bristol Channel almost lasciviously in places, where the pink cottages rise from the blue sea and the hillocks mount like tree-titted breasts of the land).

Somerset nudges the big city and port of Bristol at its northeast corner; and they were sturdy men from this county who sailed merchant and pirate ships from the Bristol Channel across the Atlantic to Virginia, Carolina, Georgia for the tobacco, the cotton and the slaves. Robert Louis Stevenson in *Treasure Island* immortalized the breed, whose toughness seems part of England's past now (but continues in the wildcat striking workers of nearly every industry).

The county is, nevertheless, little more than a garden museum

Original drawings for one of the Beatrix Potter children's books.

today. It lies asleep, exhausted from its riotous history, and consists largely of splendid rolling hills, the Quantocks and the Mendips, divided into outwardly idyllic farms by hedgerows and trees, and of valleys bisected by slumberous, leafy lanes that lead to villages of white-washed, pink-washed and thatched cottages, all neat and ship-shape, "Bristol fashion"; villages such as the almost too-perfect Stogumber (with its medicinal spring from which one of the world's best beers has been made), and Bruton in the Brue valley with its relics of a 12th-century Augustinian priory, and its 17th-century, aptly-named Sexey's Hospital (an almshouse), and its 16th-century grammar school, and monastic dovecote, and its "Bruton Bow," the old pack-horse bridge over the river.

The farm people and the sharp-eyed villagers talk with a burr and a soft lilt that will remind the American visitor of what happens in his own country when the Potomac River is crossed southwards. The agriculture is at once primitive in the shape of the patchwork fields and paddocks, and in the sheer age of the buildings, the hedges and the walls, and yet modern as it can be when the scarlet and blue machinery comes out. There is real money here in spite of the apparent cessation of history and the overgrown lushness of a land that is constantly exposed to the enervating Gulf Stream air currents. It would probably be more satisfying and even financially rewarding to farm in Somerset today than almost anywhere else in the world, because the good soil and climate of the valleys produce rich crops and the life of the old inns and sports events and other meetings with neighbors is an organic life, a natural growth of the good earth.

The visitor should choose an ancient but modernized hostelry in a village preferably and allow himself to be absorbed in the atmosphere of the countryside, for several weeks preferably; and that would be a better cure for the ills of mechanical life than any expensive clinic could provide.

Somewhere near Athelney could be chosen, where formerly a swamp enabled King Alfred the Great to hide from the Danes (878 A.D.). A stone obelisk marks the site of the peasant's cottage where Alfred burnt the cakes in intervals of planning the historic comeback that decided the future of his England. Or somewhere on Exmoor, under Dunkery Beacon, much of it an untamed high wilderness of bracken, fern and grassy moorland, where the local people can still resemble the characters in R. D. Blackmore's *Lorna Doone,* a novel that sprang from the land like a native plant.

Down by the cliffed coast, above the craggy bays of red sandstone that is remarkably veined with iridescent alabaster, is such a village as Dunster, laid out exactly like Gruyère in Switzerland with its single broad street and market building all under the medieval castle that was the seat of one strong family, the Luttrells, for 400 years. The cottages are mostly tourist shops now; but at least the visitor gets what he wants here, including splendid teas still with Somerset cream and magnificent local strawberries in season. The church, like most of those in the country, typifies England's major contribution in ecclesiastical architecture, the so-called Perpendicular style, whose upright, delicate lines, particularly of towers, lead the eye if nothing else to what could, in the imagination at least, be heaven.

The village names, as ever, are pure poetry, yet so often represent the beginning of world-wide events. Dowlish Wake, for example, has the serpentine tomb of the man who discovered not only the source of the River Nile but also Lake Tanganyika and Victoria Nyanza. He was Captain John Hanning Speke. East Coker not only gave the Bostonian expatriate T. S. Eliot some portentous poetic ideas, but was the birthplace, 1652, of that William Dampier whose original circumnavigation of the globe was the 17th-century equivalent of the Apollo moon landing.

Anywhere in or near Glastonbury can be magical still, although as yet not even physicists can explain the phenomenon. The legend is that St. Joseph of Arithmathea and his eleven disciples in the year 63 A.D. not only brought the Holy Grail temporarily here, but also built a church whose site is reputedly under that of St. Mary's Norman chapel, and planted a hawthorn tree that might have sprung originally from the staff he plunged into a local hill, a tree whose offspring still yields blossoms in the spring. Also there is the legend that Arthur's fair Isle of Avalon arose from the marshes hereabouts (where primitive baskets are made from the osiers).

It is all rather bogus in its modern manifestations perhaps, but the legends contain sufficient truth to create a strange atmosphere that affects even the most cynical observers. This is a place where great events took place, and their psychic imprint is still sharp for the sensitive.

Glastonbury Abbey is a perfect demonstration of the architectural or aesthetic principle that age redeems all. The toothy ruins are more beautiful than ever the original edifice could have been.

Believe it or not, the Monk's Cemetery in Glastonbury is traditionally the burial place not only of St. Joseph, but also of St. Dunstan, St. Patrick of Ireland, King Arthur, Queen Guinevere, and the ancient Kings Edmund, Edgar and Edmund Ironsides.

In the garden of Glaston Tor School is the Chalice Well or Blood Spring, which might once have concealed that Holy Grail brought from Palestine after containing the life essence of Christ: the Holy Grail that was for the knights of Arthur's period a search-object transcending all human ideals. It meant more to them than even a million dollars to modern man.

Once the strongest man in history lived in Somerset. He was Sir John Hautville; and under Maesknoll Camp, an earthwork erected by the ancestors of the English perhaps thousands of years ago, is a gigantic boulder, called Hautville's Quoit, that the brave Sir John reputedly hurled down from the hill.

It can be seen already that the English might be famed for their phlegm and their dislike of exaggeration, but deep inside their own country they can indulge their flights of fancy like the natural poets most of them are.

Comfortable in the arms of the soft Quantock Hills is the very typical Somerset village of Holford, where the actual poets Wordsworth and Coleridge once tried to live together in Alfoxton House, and were historically interrupted in their work or their world-shattering discourse by the arrival of "a person from Porlock."

Porlock is itself a village of considerable thatched charm down by or at least near the glitter sea (with its extraordinarly small port called Porlock Weir). Arising hereabouts is the 1 in 4 gradient of that Porlock Hill which, in the early days of motoring, was a test which very few internal combustion engines could endure (and is still quite a terrifying experience, but of basically miniature proportions in a miniature land).

Church-lovers must never omit to visit Huish Champflower and Huish Episcopi, the one for a church of the rare "Decorated" period, 1272 to 1380, and the other for a building that subtends perhaps the most beautiful "Perpendicular" tower in the county (with a Norman doorway, a Jacobean pulpit, and a Burne-Jones window).

Somerset slumbers today, and will often arouse the contempt as well as the love of a visitor from a more recently successful land. It is farm-rich and lovely but half-dead. That makes it good for a holiday, maybe based on the former main town of Ilchester. In Roman times this was one of the most important centers in all England. The great Roman road known as the Fosse Way still runs through the principal shopping district.

In the year 1214 Roger Bacon was born in Ilchester. He became a Franciscan friar, but also the founder of experimental science. Maybe he invented gunpowder, but certainly his work in optics, explosives, engineering and theoretical flight laid the basis of what has been going on at Cape Kennedy in more modern times. In his day, of course, Friar Bacon was regarded as a sorcerer.

The most famous of all English actors, Sir Henry Irving, was a Somerset man, from Keinton Mandeville.

Another Somerset village is called Nempnett Thrubwell.

Henry Fielding, the author of *Tom Jones,* was born at Sharpham near Glastonbury.

The church of St. Peter and St. Paul at Shepton Mallet has perhaps the finest carved oak roof in existence. It is adorned with 350 panels and 350 bosses (exactly). But Shepton Mallett, an old market town of narrow streets, is the center of the Cheddar cheese industry. A few people still know how to grow and manufacture fine food and other articles in Somerset. The visitor who would like to combine business with pleasure should visit leather and boot and shoes factories at Street, and a glove factory at Stoke-sub-Hamdon, and glove, shirt, collar and silk factories at Taunton, busy but neat town with much 18th-century red brick and white-pillared porticoes, as well as Vivary Park with old monastic fish ponds, and Wilton House, birthplace of Alexander Kinglake, the historian of the *Crimean War* and author also of *Eothen.*

Yeovil has been manufacturing fine gloves and cheese products probably from time immemorial, but, more lately, has become strangely adept at the making of helicopters and other aircraft.

This is altogether an English county. The visitor may stop at the old Virginia Inn near Henstridge for some good local cider—the characteristic drink of these parts, very good when made from genuine Somerset "black apples"—and may inquire what is the precise connection of this picturesque place with the southern state back home. He will be told that when Sir Walter Raleigh returned from the colony in Elizabethan times he sat in the inn and made so much smoke with a pioneer pipe of tobacco that a servant rushed for a bucket of water and drenched him with it. But if the traveller continues his peregrinations in Somerset and neighboring Devonshire he will be frequently told the same story in other "authentic" places.

The best blue serge as worn by hicks on Sundays was always made at Wellington, which also gave its title to the "Iron Duke" victor of Waterloo, and accommodates a great public school, which in England means, of course, a private school of the type that can still give the best form of education devised by man since the ancient Spartans first realized that you should catch them young, treat them rough, and teach them nothing.

Wells is not only the perfect small cathedral city, but has a Bishop's Palace surrounded by a moat, with a bell-rope outside the Gatehouse which is pulled by the local swans when they are hungry. Some famous hymns were written by a Bishop Ken in the summerhouse of this Palace.

The last battle fought on English soil was that of Sedgemoor. The Duke of Monmouth, a bastard both actually and literally, rose against his kinsman James II and was supported particularly by the townsfolk of Taunton and the peasants of Somerset, who mistakenly thought they could challenge the tax-gatherers, whoremongers and near-Catholics of

London who ruled their land. These deluded people fought to the death and, when they did not die, were slaughtered and dispossessed afterwards by "Bloody" Judge Jeffreys and the Royalist soldiery in such numbers that to this day the hedgerows and village people remember the gibbets and the blackened bodies hanging. Weston Zoyland is the place to visit for specific memories. The stately Perpendicular church there was once crammed with hundreds of the rebels after their defeat.

John Locke, the 17th-century philosopher, one of the founders of the so-called "Age of Reason," was born in Wrington (rather ironically, as the "Perpendicular" church there has the finest high tower in England, rising 140 feet); and another child of this remote, quiet village was Hannah More, an original 18th-century "blue stocking" and authoress of so many books that are now quite unreadable.

But Somerset still has wonders that could occupy pages of highly readable description. The Mendips are the hills south of Bristol. First the traveller comes to Burrington Combe and that curiously-named Toplady's Cleft which was the original *Rock of Ages,* and then he descends into Cheddar Gorge, which, like the moon, is far from being made of green cheese. Indeed it is, in its miniature way, one of the geological marvels of the world—England's version of a Grand Canyon, with silence, overbearing cliffs, silence.

The cliffs and the rocky ground underneath contain vast subterranean caves, so beautiful and fantastic that their typically English nomenclature is scarcely believable. One is Cox's cave, consisting of many cathedral chambers of stalagmites and stalactites, grottoes, pools and vivid pillars, all lit by electricity. The other is Gough's cave, reached by an immensely long tunnel, eventually like a limestone city of the dead (and perhaps one day to be the last refuge again of the surviving English).

Wookey Hole is a short distance on. Three vast caverns with their own private river present limestone marvels again, deep underground; and the archaeologists say that ancient Britons lived down there for at least 700 years. Bones of prehistoric animals have been found, and Roman coins, and a genuine hyena's den. Local legend has it that once a bad woman lived there, known as the Witch of Wookey. She cast evil spells on the local villagers, until a Glastonbury monk assaulted her with bell and book and candle and she was turned to stone, a great stalagmite now dutifully gaped at by the tourists after they have paid their proper entrance fee.

And so to Bath. Architecturally this is one of the finest cities in the world, and there is no nonsense about it, no Williamsburg pastiche or Italian and Swiss faking. Most of the squares, crescents and circuses were built in the 18th-century from the local, light-brown stone to the order of Ralph Allen (a supreme example of private enterprise as he owned the actual stone quarries) and according to the designs of two John Woods, father and son. This is the apotheosis of English good taste in building, with no gaudy and stupid admixture of styles, just the plain classical motif everywhere (as reintroduced into England by the Scottish brothers Adam, one of whom, Robert, beautifully decorated the Guildhall in High Street, and designed the Pulteney Bridge, which is still rarely shop-lined for England).

But the wonder of Bath does not just derive from its 18th-century unity of architecture. It goes back to strange, radioactive hot springs that first attracted the voluptuous Romans to the place. In 1775, during the building of the modern city, the original Roman Bath was found, altogether one of the most splendid Roman remains in northern Europe. It was carefully disinterred. It helped to attract ever-increasing numbers of gapers to the city. There were two great periods when all society had to go to Bath at certain seasons of the year. A dandy named Beau Nash in the time of Queen Anne reigned as Master of the Ceremonies over people of the type who have always, most oddly, been popular in otherwise sober England, people just like the long-haired, fantastically-dressed habitués of modern Carnaby Street in London. It is as if the English are naturally so strait-laced that they must occasionally go to such extremes.

Then towards the end of the 18th-century the newly constructed city again became seasonally popular with the kind of people written about in the novels of Jane Austen, Charles Dickens and many other simple-minded but highly talented authors. After which it slowly died away, was momentarily blasted out of its lethargy by the bombs which Hitler threw in revenge for Rostock (the renowned Assembly Rooms were gutted) and today the city has a wealth of antique dealers, but little else save its memories.

3

Seaside

"I Do like to be Beside the Seaside" was the title of a very popular song at the beginning of the 20th century in England; and, at the time it was true folk art in that it expressed a strong emotion among the common people.

That song half a century later was just one more relic of the different past. The English by then had learnt about Continental travel and, even the poorest of them, found they could get cheaper and more interesting holidays abroad than they could in the numerous resorts that, throughout their grandparents' lives, had mushroomed round the long, long coastline of their watery land.

At the time of writing this book it is as nostalgic to visit those resorts as to read Marcel Proust's *A la Recherche du Temps Perdu.* They have the quality of a vintage car or a film like Bergman's *Wild Strawberries.* They not only represent much of the England that was great in the childhood of today's old men, great, and odd, and exasperating, and nice, and so obviously containing the seeds of its own imminent decay. They are also a strange, rare experience like a long-lost wine from some dim cellar, or a browse through old volumes of *The Illustrated London News* or *Punch.*

The English cathedrals and churches, the castles and country houses, the museums and art galleries have always been unique, but today priority should be given by the intelligent visitor to Brighton and Margate, Skegness and Scarborough, Southend, Blackpool, Eastbourne, Hastings, Torquay. In these already weird places is not only a true essence of the England that came its present cropper, but also scenes

"I do like to be beside the seaside": at Blackpool in Lancashire.

and architecture and customs that are as completely different from those of Tuscaloosa and San Diego as are Rider Haggard's Mountains of the Moon. If the purpose of a vacation be mental stimulus and a complete change combined with bracing air and plenty of time in bed or in overstuffed chairs, then the American visitor should certainly make a leisurely tour of the decayed seaside resorts of old England.

They still have excellent facilities for moderate comfort—so long

"I do like to be beside the seaside": at Brighton in Sussex.

as it lasts—and from the beginning they have done their best to cushion the execrable climate (and in many ways have tried very hard to conceal the fact that, like all great businesses, they are based on an initial great swindle).

As every tycoon knows his fortune really began when he told a certain monstrous untruth, and as all honest priests and politicians (if that contradiction in terms may be admitted) realize in their innermost hearts that their prosperity really began with an illusion well-established, so the seaside resorts of England started with the false premise that they enjoyed good weather. They advertised this gross distortion of the truth widely, and still do, with rayed pictures of Old Sol, and of tanned, pneumatic females on golden sands basking. They even published statistics of comparative hours of sunshine, claiming always that theirs were the best.

But meanwhile they wisely provided covered pavilions and more-or-less windproof shelters on promenades, and copious ranks of cinemas, umbrella and rainproof shops, and they built hotels with large, comfortable lounges and playrooms, so that the visitor could for the larger part of his stay at least have some indoor fun.

Therefore the English seaside places, however deserted by the true English and by the fashionable society after some generations of hard experience, can still be extraordinarily comfortable to inhabit for a few curious days by the inquiring stranger who likes to combine aesthetic pleasure with sociological examination.

First he should run down briefly to remarkable Brighton. It is a mere fifty miles from London, almost a suburb of that vast city, with a part-population of commuters who travel thence each day and back again easily. And it is at once the great original and archetype of all the other resorts, starting towards the end of the eigtheenth century, when, after thousands of years of wisely neglected wildness, the sea coast of Britain suddenly became fashionable.

Prior to that the coast and the true countryside alike had been avoided as much as possible by all who could afford to do so. Mud and water and sand and rocks and insects, bitter winds, occasional scorching bursts of sunshine, and the necessity of always going out with the garments of an arctic explorer in case the weather turned had long since convinced English people that towns were worth building and that the true civilization was that of the city. Indeed the word "civilization" literally meant "of the city." Holidays as such consisted of a day off for a religious feast or secular fair, and when the Englishman really wanted to get away from it all he either did a Grand Tour of Europe, which chiefly meant warm Italy, or he took the waters (usually with something strong in them) as provided by miniature Londons scattered about the country like Bath and Tunbridge Wells.

Then the habits of the English in their spare time were by sheer chance changed. This chance was the liaison that George, Prince of Wales (heir to the throne) had developed with a widow named Mrs. Fitzherbert, whose misfortune at that time was to be not only a commoner but also a Roman Catholic, and so unqualified for permanent, legal residence in the royal bed. According to one story (it is by no means certain) the Prince first met his fate while visiting the Duke and Duchess of Cumberland at Brighthelmstone, the fishing village in Sussex which was the original nucleus of modern Brighton. He was so enthralled by the pretty young widow (twice a widow already) that very soon he was ready to sacrifice his very future throne for her sake, the true ancestor of the later King Edward who abdicated in order to marry the American Mrs. Simpson.

Domesday Book, a register of English lands compiled in the 11th century by order of William the Conqueror so that his French taxmen could make the most of his conquest, records that "Bristelmestune" had to pay William de Warenne, of nearby castled Lewes, a rent of four thousand herrings a year. And as late as 1724, according to Daniel Defoe, author of *Robinson Crusoe,* the place was still a poor fishing village that had lost as many as one hundred houses to the ever-encroaching sea during a few previous years.

The place was, and is, situated where the characteristic English chalk cliffs of the Dover side come down to a long stretch of shifting shingle. During the 18th century certain medical men on the make had cast about for means of making money from a new preoccupation with health that was one of the products of this "age of reason." They had rediscovered the old Roman method of making wealthy patients drink and bathe in the unpleasant waters of mineral springs. One of these savants, a Dr. Richard Russell (of commanding Lewes again), had the bright idea of plunging his victims in the sea. The idea was sufficiently outrageous to be instantly successful. And it coincided with the Prince of Wales's early visits to Brighthelmstone and his desire to keep Mrs. Fitzherbert in a place where he could periodically make the most of her charms without the distraction of too many prying eyes.

Moreover the fat lover suffered from yet another malady, swollen throat glands, and of course sea-bathing was recommended as the one certain and specific cure. (The Prince had a high collar made to hide his disfigurement, fastened with a scarf, and that is how our modern collars and ties began. The stock or cravat was indeed originally designed to mask a royal monstrosity, as were many other items of our curious clothing.)

A rather elegant Queen Anne style of house at Brighthelmstone belonged to a randy young nobleman, brother of Lord Egremont. It occupied a gardened park not far from the sea; and the portly Prince stayed there frequently. When the Mrs. Fitzherbert affair developed "Prinny" decided to buy the house, pull it down, and erect on the site a stately pleasure palace, a Xanadu indeed, to be called the Marine Pavilion. This was in 1785. The Prince personally supervised the building operations. He loved to build more than anything in life, and if born to lowly estate would undoubtedly have been a good workman and might even have become a public works contractor.

The Pavilion at what they were now calling Brighton was at first a large Italianate villa with a cupola in the middle. But there was a lot of fussy iron trellis and wood fretwork around its windows and balconies already, the first significant pointers to the quite disastrous bad taste of the coming Victorian age; and soon the infatuate Prince was experimenting quite wildly with the building (that was connected by a short garden strip with the small, green-shuttered house wherein Mrs. Fitzherbert did her homework).

Eventually the Pavilion, known now as the Royal Palace, became the complete architectural expression of the Prince's sad, sentimental and somewhat Oriental cast of mind: it was given Eastern minarets and domes and looked rather like the tawdry result of an improbable marriage between St. Peter's, Rome, and the Great Mosque of Constantinople. The wit Sidney Smith came down and observed that St. Paul's Cathedral had evidently been there before him and had had puppies by the sea.

But the combination of the Prince and his doxy and his extraordinary palace and all the talk about the revitalizing qualities of sea water soon had the effect of bringing nearly everyone to Brighton. Mr. Pitt and Mr. Fox were there, and the Duke of Chartres, and the Duke of Queensberry. Young bucks flogged horses to break the speed record down the Brighton road from London, and the stagecoaches

Brunswick Square, Brighton: the Regency best of English seaside architecture.

and post-chaises daily sped along. Mr. Sheridan the playwright devised his wisecracks among the throngs at Brighton of aristocrats, politicians, beauties and beaux. Between the Palace and the sea was a broadwalk known as the Steine, and here the world would stroll (in intervals of rushing for shelter from the rain into the numerous hostelries that had sprung up all around).

Dr. Russell had found a wonderful coadjutor in a local fishwife called Martha Gunn, who would stand with her protruding stomach and voluminous skirts, her three-cornered hat and eternally snuff-sniffing nose, and supervise the letting out of wonderful "bathing machines" to the numerous rich seekers after health and sex in the briny.

And so it all began, the cult of the English seaside holiday. It spread all around the coast, as will shortly be seen, then jumped over to France, and crept down to Spain and Italy. It took the people of England a century and a half to realize that they were actually being swindled at home—the English have always been slow to move—but at the end of that time they definitely realized that if they wanted comfortable sea bathing in the sun they would have to go at least as far as Majorca (which, at the time of writing, is enjoying exactly the same kind of desecration as occurred during the first Brighton boom, with hundreds of bus planes arriving daily from London to spill out the suckers on a ruined littoral).

Some of the more charming features of the seaside holiday will shortly be recounted as an inducement to the visitor perhaps to break the cathedral-castle routine and savor them instead. But first it must be insisted that great Brighton is still quite unique.

It is unique for its architecture. When the Prince of Wales became Prince Regent during the insanities of his father (promoted by such disasters as the Mrs. Fitzherbert affair and the George Washington affair in the remote American colony) the architects and interior designers of England honored their patron with a distinct aesthetic style, which eventually became known as Regency. The speculators came down to the infant Brighton and financed the building of what at that time amounted almost to a new London by the sea, with rows of tall houses and squares and circles and crescents and avenues all in a kind of classical, Italianate pastiche, made white and yellow with stucco everywhere to hide the crude brick of their fabric, with applied columns, urns, patera, all the mock Graeco-Roman nonsense of the age.

And yet in this place, thanks to the innate good taste of the builders (who largely followed the excellent designs of that John Nash who had made the best of modern London) the result became not only noble and pleasing but also enduring. The visitor who does not know Brighton and is fortunate enough to come across it in fine weather today will never have known such a beautiful seaside city before. On either side of the central squalor of small shops and pubs and parked cars and long-distance buses extend the high and gleaming rows of Palladian houses, many of them hotels now; and a view from the sea will show how monotony is broken by crescents with gardens and statues, so that the entire town seems to have been built according to a perfect Regency master plan.

Brighton has never been particularly good for the typical English seaside holiday as such. It does not possess the "golden" sands necessary for that exercise, and the climate is too brisk and overladen with ozone. What the town particularly possesses still is "atmosphere"—a kind of randy, semi-dissolute atmosphere that probably goes right back to that Prince of Wales and his more dubious associates. There is one pub—what the 19th-century English euphemistically called a "public house," or premises on which alcohol could be consumed by license during restricted hours—and it is not far from the Steine where the dandies minced along, and to this day it is patronized mainly by male homosexuals. The writer once entered there by accident for a pint of vulgar beer and found himself being ogled by mascaraed eyes in all directions, eyes that were lifted towards him over genteel glasses of port wine.

There is another pub not far away where the original "Teddy boys" still congregate, so-called a generation ago because they favored an Edwardian style of dress. Now they are growing old, but nicely scowl at the newcomer with their vicious, pasty faces, instantly recalling that marvellous "Pinky" of Graham Greene's local novel *Brighton Rock.*

Then the Lanes wind like woodworms through what was originally the 18th-century village, the Lanes of the so-called antique dealers. In the early 1950s there were perhaps a hundred small shops in this condensed district, ranging from those of Middle Eastern people who "specialized" in the most esoteric and expensive of early porcelains to that extraordinary bazaar on two floors with suits of armor and ancient stone urns outside, which was presided over by a dour, precise man with a Dutch name who was as bleakly rude to the visiting fools whom he could not abide as he was courteously charming to those

Perfect domestic building of the Regency period in Royal Crescent, Brighton.

who genuinely admired and understood his vast collection of colored glass and of decorated chamber-pots.

England was then in the process of selling up the happy home in order to pay the debts accumulated in two world-saving or world-shattering wars, and added to at that time by the expense of running a species of bloodless revolution called the Welfare State. The fine furniture and other household objects that the rich classes had acquired during the previous two centuries of prosperity were then being sold off by these antique dealers.

But eventually the attics, the drawing-rooms and the repositories could yield no more; and a visitor wisely counselled to traverse these fabled "Lanes" now cannot expect to find much more than memories, reproductions and other junk. Yet the visit will be worthwhile to the sentimental, especially if he stay at the Royal Albion Hotel right at the center of it all, where he will obtain at least a fleeting idea of how the real English of the upper classes once lived and loved.

Then Brighton has curious wings. One stretches eastwards and mounts the chalk cliffs to what is naturally called Black Rock (after a wonderful Aquarium and miniature railway above the waves for the children) and then to Roedean that has been able, in its time, to boast the best and most expensive girl's school in the world (past a great asylum for the blind, ironically placed so that below them is a breathtaking seascape that they can never see) and finally to Rotting-dean, which has its position but little more to commend it now, and finally to that ineffable Peacehaven, a sprawled development of bunga-lows and other tawdry houses which, after the First World War, was supposed to represent the world safe for democracy on behalf of which so many unfortunate men of Sussex had laid down their lives in eter-nally ungrateful France. Peacehaven is the final indignity done to the lovely Sussex soil by modern man in search of seaside bliss (although it is possible that its achievement may be outdone yet by a "marina" proposed by "developers" for the central seafront which could finally project Brighton into the sublime future, obliterating all recollections of youth when the millionaires strolled upon the noble Promenades in silver spats and the light ladies of fashion flounced everywhere with rolling Lily Langtry eyes).

That takes us to the other, western wing of the town, which is Hove. The name must be pronounced with a certain reverence always, because this part was promoted towards the end of the nineteenth century as a refuge for those holidaymakers and retired senior citizens who would indefinably lose caste by living in actual Brighton. There is even a subtle division on the great seaside Promenade, where the visitor steps across from Brighton into Hove as into a different land. This is something wholly and quite delightfully English, a deliberate class frontier. There is no customs post but there well could be. In Hove people try to hide their nakedness and mask their sins, and the place is of course ineffably dull (but very much safer to live in than Brighton itself). It is a place of careful children and old people who can only remember an always better past.

Such conservatives should not, however, be always mocked by the historian who knows that human history has had both its grand and its pitiful, decadent eras. Certainly the builders of the Regency terraces of Brighton were architecturally better and larger people than the perpetrators of modern buildings in the town.

Then the coast sweeps away in a broad bay of hopeless shingle, held precariously in position by thousands of wooden groins like the lateral bones of a disintegrating herring, and there are many small resorts that have unsuccessfully tried to ape the great mother Brighton in their time, places like Shoreham, and Worthing, and Littlehampton, and that prissy little Bognor Regis, which got its name because royalty went to stay there: at Hotham Park House, when Brighton had ceased to be safe from prying eyes, but which has never made the similar grade, being redolent chiefly of flimsy pink and white villas and so-called hotels, of buckets and spades, shops selling shrimping nets and candy-rock (with the name stamped all through), and of memorable childish days when to build a sand castle and to keep the cruel sea at bay for a few hours was the height of human ambition. That was the training many of the modern English had when they were young; and of course they have been metaphorically building similar sand castles ever since.

Eastwards from Brighton is eventually a dim place called Seaford, climatically adjusted to the needs of expensive private education but somewhat disturbing for those whose idea of a seaside holiday is constant sunshine and tranquil sands. The waves that bore up the English Channel frequently assail not only the Promenade and containing motor road with stones and sands but also the bordering caravanserais, which always have had the appearance of buildings that have been subjected to a hideous bombardment in some final war. But the inquiring visitor should pause here if only to understand why the English, who have been educated and exercised at holiday time in such a place, have been able subsequently to astonish the world with their hardiness in the face of militarily more numerous races.

The chalk cliffs now mount to Beachy Head, which might be described as one of the main safety valves of England in that it has always been a favorite venue for high-pitched suicides and marital murders.

The white headland stands suitable sentinel over large Eastbourne farther on, a seaside town that was mainly created, as a very sensible business proposition, by the seventh Duke of Devonshire (thus entitled because his estates were in Sussex and not in Devonshire). As a result it is still a place that can be visited almost if not quite without loss of social status in England. It combines extreme dullness with a tenacious and not unlovely respectability, also better-than-average hotels and other facilities for keeping out of the wind and rain. The period bandstand on the Grand Parade is, in particular, without compare elsewhere; and when occasionally it is possible to sit comfortably in the open air around this delight there can be no greater nostalgia than to watch the peaked conductor with his prim English flourishes, the red-faced military blowers of wind instruments, and to tap the reminiscent foot again to the strains of Souza and Ketelby, the brothers Strauss and Amy Woodforde Finden.

Or similar strains can be absorbed in the inevitable Winter Garden, in intervals of trying to watch international tennis in Devonshire Park, or county cricket, or Peter Pan boats on the model-yachting lake of Prince's Park.

Further eastwards the visitor will wonderingly come to Bexhill-on-Sea. This, even more than Eastbourne, represents the apotheosis of what used to be the English ideal. The writer in his nonage knew a by no means indigent couple with the inevitable only child who for seventeen consecutive years spent their annual fortnight's holiday from a London suburb at Bexhill-on-Sea. The resort was built and developed for such people, such miniature snobs and stick-in-the-muds, the summit of whose ambition was to be known for what they liked to describe as "select" tastes. The guide books have ever since called Bexhill "a seaside resort of a select character," which means that for generations only quiet, highly respectable folk went there, and that the place has absolutely no character save that provided by its greatest pride, the De La Warr amusement pavilion, which was the last word in modern architecture in the 1920s and is already the last word in glass and concrete bad taste, the progenitor of a thousand similar structures that have similarly ruined the coastlines of Spain, Italy, North Africa and the Middle East.

It is necessary to pronounce it the De La *Ware* pavilion in order to pass socially in Bexhill.

Thus it will be somewhat with relief that the wanderer continues along the sad, ruined coast to St. Leonards-on-Sea and Hastings, because Hastings like Brighton retains a little still of the robust atmosphere that was English in the old days before suburbanization rubbed out the spirit from much of the land. The ruined castle that dominates Hastings was built by William the Conqueror soon after he landed nearby on his way to make a Norman colony out of England. But a red-haired Jute from Denmark originally founded the town, which he called Haesten, and that was getting on for two thousand years ago, so that there are more than Victorian memories here. Also the climate is strangely milder than elsewhere along the Channel coast, and sea-bathing can be not too uncomfortable, save of course when the effluent from the sewer at least used to be swept the wrong way by the always playful waves.

The old town of Hastings can be tarry with fish nets still although Cockney with whelk-stalls, amusement arcades and the inevitable offerings of a substance that is neither ice nor cream. Afterwards the traveller will wisely continue east along rich orange and red cliffs to the little old towns of the marshes such as Rye and Winchelsea, where he can perhaps rest awhile and gain his second wind for this modern antiquarian's tour of the seaside resorts, an enthralling but admittedly an exhausting sport.

The seaside resorts of Kent, next county on the way along, are subtly as different from those of Sussex and the rest of the country as are redheads from blondes. This is partly because Kent has its own peculiar geology, based on chalk, and its special climate, exposed more to the east winds and "brisker" than that of Sussex, also a distinct history of continual conquest across the narrow straits of Dover from the Continent. The first part of England to be conquered from Europe, it was also the final settlement of the most vigorous colonizing types, longheads and redbeards from Denmark mainly (including the Angles of Holstein who gave all England its name).

But the resorts themselves have, with one or two exceptions, a vulgar flavor that is wholly derived from proximity to London. From about 1850 to 1950 they were visited daily in season by paddle steamers that could be crowded with beery excursionists. The Cockney spilled out here then: and afterwards was succeeded by similar day-trippers from French towns across the water such as Calais and Boulogne.

Folkestone, the first resort, is near enough to the Romney Marshes and Sussex to have a few "ideas" still. There are some good hotels that accommodate retired people of the better class. The ancient Britons and the Romans are not only still remembered here, through the agency of several archaeological discoveries, but can actually be encountered in the palm courts where teatime orchestras play, and along the green Leas, a clifftop promenade, that, during the first half of the 20th century, provided a regular parade ground for the fine old warriors and their formidable women. After the decline of that class, alas, these elegant walks more frequently knew the motorized and narcotized gangs of overpaid and under-disciplined youth; and Folkestone became one more coastal relic, with memories and all kinds of tucked-away architecture for the explorer, Tudor, Stuart, Georgian, Victorian, Edwardian, but for the rest, just a few minutes pause on the way to the Continental promised land. Thousands of motorists would pass through on their journey down to the Dover car ferries particularly.

Dover itself thus became, in the second half of the 20th century, just one big car ferry, although it had always possessed a certain indigenous charm, derived from the Norman archetype of all castles guarding England's entrance right on top of the celebrated white cliffs, and from the stuccoed architecture of the tall 19th-century houses and hotels that still survived round the bay between the docks. There is a sense of sanctity in the place, perhaps proceeding from the awareness every Englishman has of the extreme vulnerability of his too-rich land. During wars the great leaders such as Churchill have always come down and stood brooding here. The castle has always been perhaps the strongest in the world, built on solid masonry that is 40 feet deep and provided with walls that are 22 feet thick; and army and air force installations in the locality have inevitably given it a curious air, for England, of perpetual beleaguerment. And, by the castle on that historic cliff, is the oldest building in England, what remains of the pharos or lighthouse built there soon after the year 43 A.D. by the Romans to guide their nervous galleys across from France.

Shakespeare, another great Englishman, from far-inland Warwickshire, well knew his Dover and its great importance for its lack of size. The Shakespeare Cliff is regularly visited by old-fashioned holidaymakers who have never read *King Lear,* not the least tragic of all tragedies, that has several scenes set upon the very springsome turf where their plastic sandals now tread.

Halfway to the real Kent resorts of Ramsgate and Margate from Dover comes the special case of Deal. This is a perfect small resort for the connoisseur, because the beaches are shingle, the geographical position is peculiarly exposed, and some of the narrow streets and small houses are still delightfully 18th-century. The holidaymaker who wants only to sprawl in the sun and watch naked girls will find it undoubtedly horrid, but every wise man will be braced here by the ozone-laden winds and the period character of the place. Sea-anglers love it especially, and golfers; and there are trips to the Goodwin

Sands and lightships, and stories of Caesar who originally landed
(probably seasick) on the shingle to the north, and of Thomas
A'Becket, Richard Cœur de Lion and Perkin Warbeck, and of many
survivors from Dunkirk, who similarly came wet-footed ashore here.

But Ramsgate farther along is great and wholly artificial, a bawdy
town of day-tripping Londoners with everything that men and women
and children once wanted to give them a memorable short stay at
the seaside: blustering winds, frequent squalls of roguish rain, and
every facility for so-called recreation that could then be devised. An
entire installation facing the usually deserted sands is called "Merrie
England," with restaurants that expensively provide chips with everything, an amusement park, and what is proudly described as "the
largest ballroom on the South Coast," an American touch that is not
without its pathetic connotation. The Madeira Walk, above the scummy
old harbor of so-called pleasure boats and of freighters bringing
Volkswagens to England (a useful fruit of the last war to end wars),
has not only artificial rock formations but also a real imitation waterfall. There are the inevitable Marine Parades; and a West Cliff
Promenade that usefully presents a Model Tudor Village. Three
thousand shivering souls can sit in the arena around the Italian
Renaissance-style bandstand to listen to the martial strains, interlarded
with popular sugar, that once stimulated the English to world-shattering feats of arms (if only in the imagination) while a sporting people
are provided with every kind of spectator event, including the thrills
of the Dumpton Greyhound Racing Track.

Broadstairs is sandwiched between Ramsgate and Margate, and,
like Deal, is not quite the real thing, although some collectors might
prize it for its very differences from the norm. Thus it has never
grown, and was long despised by the roistering Londoner who found
only dullness there. Actually it grew enormously during a few years
in the first half of the 19th century, and then became almost the
personal property of Charles Dickens, the first English novelist to
make a real fortune out of American lecture tours. He decided that
it should be his shrine, so that today it is completely Dickensian, not
with stage coaches but at least with little houses of twinkle windows,
and self-conscious local fishermen, and, on high ground above the
little pier, that actual Bleak House where the genius wrote part of
David Copperfield. Down in the town at 31 High Street the *Pickwick
Papers* were completed, and at 40 Albion Street a portion at least of
Nicholas Nickleby was indited in a fine, cursive hand. Dickens was
evidently something of a dabster, starting a book here and finishing

there, but always making sure that his imprint was firm on every part of Broadstairs. The actual Dickens House, near the corner of High Street and the Parade, was supposedly the home of the original of Miss Betsy Trotwood. The great man might not, however, approve of what is inscribed on a house in York Street, the words "Dickens did not live here."

Oh, heavens, there is also Lawn House in Harbour Street, where Dickens did live for a considerable while.

In modern times Broadstairs, a town that evidently likes punishment, has been similarly honored by another public man, Prime Minister Edward Heath who has curiously combined leadership of the British Government with youthful sailing exploits and organ playing in a local church. A bachelor, Mr. Heath became increasingly noted as a political striver for consistent unpopularity in the opinion polls and consistent dignity in that anomalous position, the dignity of the true Englishman who at all costs refuses to recognize the inevitable and often, for that very reason, succeeds beyond all expectation (all going back, perhaps, to a national hero, King Canute, who firmly sat on his throne in the waves and refused to retreat, thus becoming a famous legend for his pains).

And so to Margate, seaside metropolis of Kent, and one of the only true rivals to great Brighton along all the English coastline. It boasts what the advertisements call 9¼ miles of "glorious sands," but, even more important and sensible, a whole district called "Dreamland," where 20 hitherto useless acres were eventually covered with facilities for holiday fun and games, ranging from big wheel and scenic railway to such an odor of whelk stalls and candy-floss machines as will never be forgotten by the inquiring newcomers who had previously been unused to such things. Elsewhere there is a Grotto and Sunken Gardens, and aptly-named Winter Gardens: and the architecture everywhere is so magnificently in period that it should always be carefully preserved. It is a pastiche of Brighton, imitation seaside Palladian of the most revolting type, but executed on such a grand scale that, like the baroque when coated on really thick, it succeeds by its very excess of enormity.

The visitor should, however, be careful to avoid Margate on what the English still call Bank Holidays, because it *can* be the scene of what amounts almost to civil war between raging forces of young people whom the old can no longer effectively control in this essentially anarchic land. The garish city by the sea where worthy holiday-makers took their children for a healthful fortnight's battle with the elements is now another kind of battlefield frequently, where the modish young of the so-called working classes, lacking overseas worlds to conquer anymore, take it out on each other with broken bottle and vicious slick-knife (but not guns in England as yet).

Margate, like Brighton, even has a Hove, called Cliftonville, where people once lived who wished to enjoy the best of both worlds, that of good town shopping by day and complete respectability at night.

Soon after Margate the 19th-century developers gave up. The weather and the terrain became temporarily quite impossible. Resorts were halfheartedly started at Birchington, Herne Bay, Tankerton and Whitstable, but faced north and were already near to the Thames mud. Slimy beaches and interior marshland eventually repelled all but wild birds and shrewd industrialists; and it was necessary to cross the broad estuary, where once the shipping of the world sailed into London on bumpy bottoms, to pick up the true seaside thread again at Southend.

It is officially called Southend-on-Sea, probably because at certain tides it is impossible to see the sea locally; and for the same reason this huge resort built for itself the most extensive pleasure pier in the world, over a mile long of automatic machines ("What the Butler Saw, insert One Penny") and the inevitable bulging breast symbol of a "Winter Garden" Theatre. By walking out on that Pier over what seemed to be interminable mudflats, although they were described in tourist handouts as extensive sands, it was possible to reach what Londoners once liked to call "the briny." Also there was that species of cold draft that similar brochures called "tonic air"; and, when the eye had tired of distant grey seascape, a marvellous view of the sprawled town with its "seven miles of attractive promenades," its necessarily heated open-air swimming pool (at least as large if not so sumptuous in appointments as that of a minor television star in Beverly Hills), its "beautiful parks and gardens," and, on each distant, misty side, its inevitable efforts at permanent residential respectability: Thorpe Bay towards the North Sea, Westcliff-on-Sea and Leigh-on-Sea farther up the mudflats towards the smoky curtain in the sky that was the rest of London.

Some wit even went so far as to coin a phrase for this area: "The Thames Riviera." Doubtless he knew the true Riviera in all its modern horror. But the local publicity men swiftly adopted the phrase for use in their advertisements, and probably believed that they were writing the truth.

Not far up this coast is Foulness, which has been nicely chosen as the site of London's new airport, England's most imaginative project since London was built on its original swamp.

This is Essex, a county that has been partly ruined by the outpourings of London, but does still contain much delectable countryside as well as the drab, romantic menace of the East London streets and decaying docks, about which more may well be said later. Meanwhile the climb must be started up the North Sea coast of England, first to Clacton-on-Sea, a large resort but one without definite character. All the usual strange and dated features are here, but not on the bawdy and grand scale of Brighton, Margate and Southend. It is better to continue to the ineffable Frinton, described in the guide books significantly not as a seaside town but as "a very select residential watering-place," the reference to water being obscure as the people who go there rarely drink water if they can help it but only wish, in a very small and harmless way, to assert their social superiority to those who visit less select resorts for their holidays. The guide books also claim, quite charmingly, that the ancient St. Mary's Church there was "one of the smallest in the country before enlargement."

Frinton is small, proud and not particularly pretty, but, even more than Bexhill, represented the summit of ambition for a particular type of Englishman in the first half of the 20th century: a place where he could feel quite at home among his social equals, the summit indeed of egalitarian ambition because here there were neither the raucous poor nor careless aristocrats to afflict the senses of propriety. Frinton was for a long time the seaside equivalent of Mrs. Gaskell's *Cranford,* but alas, a more permissive age has seen its gradual social decline. When the stockbrokers and their wives start paying big money to laugh at delightfully filthy books and plays then it is no use their trying to maintain a precarious apartheid of behavior and residential choice.

Felixstowe next is the first of the resorts upon that great bulge of the land which is half Suffolk and half Norfolk, and has nothing to distinguish it save an incredibly ugly modern church—and the beginning of that ominous adjective in the advertisement, "bracing." Here the air, straight across the steely wastes of the former German Ocean, redolent of herring, cod and dim, faraway naval battles that could never be fought to a satisfactory conclusion because of the fog, is brisk enough to make a man out of an Englishman often. The historian knows that some of Albion's most effective sons came from the region, people like Nelson, Constable and many founders of the great banks and insurance companies. The air of Felixstowe, Lowestoft,

Yarmouth and Cromer explains those urgent men as nothing else can. It literally goaded them to fame.

Yarmouth, self-entitled "Great," is one of the best buys here for a man who collects genuine antiques. It is very old, an historic English town with ruins everywhere (several of them from the last two wars when the port was continually hit by the nearby Germans) and is distinguished from all other resorts by the world's most concentrated (and not unlovely) tang of fish. This is because historically the Scottish fishing fleet came down each autumn for the herring and disgorged not only cranloads of silver on the quays but also hundreds of buxom women to perform the gutting and filleting before the kippers, red herrings and bloaters were tanned and smoked in the sheds. Also they stuffed others in barrels for the Continental trade.

Thus Great Yarmouth, inevitably combined with a more respectable satellite, rather grimly called Gorleston, has nearly everything that the specialist in English seaside resorts could desire. It has history— a 13th-century Tolhouse, a 14th-century ruined Greyfriars Cloister, a Nelson Monument, and the pathetic remains of those Rows that, before the bombardments, were even more interesting than their Brighton equivalents. It has the 19th-century tourist attractions, a six-mile Parade with hundreds of rooming houses resolutely facing the sea and, with equal bravura calling themselves hotel-this and hotel-that, as well as amusement arcades, pavilions for seaside concert parties and other leg-shows, annual sporting events, and probably as many saloons to the square mile as anywhere in England (partly for the Scottish fishermen who drink harder than anyone else in these islands, especially when they are avowed teetotallers with the blue badge of their pledge on serge lapels).

Yarmouth and Gorleston also have miles of not too unpleasant and quite yellow sands. If the visitor stir himself to play vigorous ball games on these he will not feel the worse for it afterwards, so that for the healthy the place can certainly be said to be in a sense healthful. (Weaklings should, however, beware, unless entirely suicidal in tendency.)

Farther north there is, at Cromer and particularly Sheringham, a quite different atmosphere, admittedly not less cold and gusty, but in the sociological sense. Inland lies one of the famous royal residences, Sandringham, particularly popular with the families of Edward VII and George V because it was inaccessible to the gapers. There they could live what they liked to imagine was a normal family life. Cromer, Sheringham and other little resorts on the coast were largely developed to accommodate courtiers and their servants in Edwardian times. They are inoffensive resorts today but with an indefinable atmosphere of cigar-smoke still, and whale-boned bodices, and optimistic sunshades, and of obscure scandals connected with ladies of quality and with baccarat.

It is, however, necessary to leap the broad Wash (one day, perhaps, to be dammed most profitably like the Zuider Zee in Holland) in order to reach the apogee of all these resorts, which is Skegness. The visitor who arrived there on a still, fine day would be most unlucky, as he would be quite unable to understand how the place had reached its present fame and fortune. It has indeed nothing particular to commend it save the usual English seaside features—until the wind begins to blow. Then it will be realized how utterly brilliant the English can be when placed finally with their backs to the metaphoric wall. One of their typical geniuses just sat down and thought, then came out with the publicity slogan "Skegness Is So Bracing." This was accompanied in due course by pictures, carefully drawn and colored, not photographed, of athletic people doing leapfrog on golden sands, and a new Lincolnshire industry was born, to be even more profitable than the fine local farming, cattle-raising, and making of mainly agricultural machinery.

A great man named Billy Butlin finally gilded this industry with his extraordinary enterprise. He came to Skegness on a typical, bracing day, took one look at the deserted Promenade and the holidaymakers as they huddled under umbrellas before the dim shop windows in the High Street, and had the culminating idea of the Holiday Camp.

This was the last, great product of seaside enterprise in England before the inevitable rush to the Continent began. Butlin designed his colorful Camps so that, for a single payment down, the wretched joy-seekers of England could be sure in all weathers of fun and games and comfort. He built high windbreaks, and waterproof roofs, and heated swimming pools underground with glass sides through which the lower parts of bodies could be freely seen. He imported entertainers, and chefs who knew how to provide chips with everything, and photographers who knew how to take bathing "beauties" from every angle; and then he organized cheer-leaders to arouse the inmates in the morning and put them through the regular paces of a carefully-planned day's program. It was all very sensible and caught on immediately, eventually to become a vast empire of such Camps all around Britain and even abroad. The idea was pursued by a similar man with a similar name, Pontin, and eventually burgeoned indeed in the great

Club Méditerranée of France. Butlin, who had bestowed the accolade on the English seaside idea, was suitably knighted by his Queen and became a millionaire—because he had taken pity on the English seaside holidaymaker and provided him at last with something positive to do during that awful annual fortnight.

If anyone really wants to know what it is like to be English today he should obtain the knowledge comparatively cheaply by taking a short holiday at a Butlin or Pontin Camp. After all, anthropologists go to Borneo without benefit of upholstery and bright lights.

Since the resort collector should by now be acclimatized there is no reason why he should not grit his teeth and proceed still farther north, which brings him to that very large and very idiosyncratic county called Yorkshire. It is a place of flat speech, great old-fashioned industries, and people who will not budge when placed in an awkward position; also of lovely purple moorlands and green dales wherein nice rivers chatter noisily over stones, the stone that is everywhere, dividing the fields with walls, creating the trim hamlets and smoky towns, and coming down in jagged cliffs to the vicious North Sea.

Flamborough Head is one such cliff, and it tries hard but not successfully to shelter one of the three main Yorkshire seaside resorts, which is called Bridlington. What more can one say, save that June at Bridlington for some reason or other knows an International Dance Festival, and July a Rally of Veteran Motorcycle Riders? (The noise in both cases is really very much the same.)

Far better to continue to Scarborough, which, surprisingly in this high latitude, comes second only to Brighton as a perfect great original among English seaside resorts. In some ways it is even better than Brighton, having a nobler situation on hills and cliffs overlooking the sea, and possessing a truly ancient castle and other historic relics that put poor "Prinny's" Pavilion rather pathetically in the shade. The architecture of the numerous terraces and square, crescents and "gardens" is, however, nothing like the real Regency thing in Brighton, although a fair enough mid-19th-century copy. It is in any case not extended far enough as are the lovely Brighton Regency vistas, because of the difficult and hilly lay of the Yorkshire land. But Scarborough is a fine large town, with extensive residential districts that never partake of the southern English suburban quality. Everyone at least tries to be "friends" up here, even though there have always been more true and wealthy aristocrats to the square yard in Yorkshire than in any other county of England.

The variety of Scarborough extends from concerts on the European scale, and art galleries of renown, to the bawdiest of fairground booths down by the old harbor, where also the holidaymaking worker from the mills of Leeds, Bradford and Huddersfield can cheaply visit King Richard III House (dating from 1350) and actually buy antiques therein (as these northern workers do). The ruined Castle on the Hill was built on the site of a Roman signal station, which was built on the site of a prehistoric "camp." Anne Brontë lies in St. Mary's Churchyard; and that great Victorian painter Lord Leighton was born in Brunswick Terrace; and St. Martin's Church has Burne-Jones windows and Rossetti panels. The British Tunny Club has its headquarters in this town; and the annual nine-day cricket festival is a ritual of the English not unlike that of the Catholics at Lourdes. It is something that must be visited before the English can be truly understood in their phlegm, their pretentiousness, and their simplicity. It is as different from, say, an American football match as a sewing party from a napalm raid.

The explorer might, however, require a few days off hereabouts from his almost too-fascinating journey. There can be too much of a good thing, and over-happiness can cloy. In that case a brief holiday could be taken at one or other of the Yorkshire resorts that, by a miracle, remain very much the same today as they have always been throughout the centuries, small clefts in the cliffs with fishing villages, such as Staithes and Robin Hood's Bay. The first is so selfconsciously quaint as to delight with that alone, because really there is nothing else to the place save memories of that Captain Cook who was born nearby and then worked in the village before absconding with some of his employer's money and running away to sea to present the world eventually with such discoveries as Hawaii and New Zealand, and then being murdered for his pains by the savages of those parts, a typically modern hero and man if ever there was one.

Robin Hood's Bay is both a great sweeping bay geographically and a village of steep narrow streets over which the old houses hang like gossips. For some reason or other these have never been pulled down in the name of progress and their continuing existence is one of the nicer wonders of our age.

The same applies to much of Whitby, although now the brief holiday is over and the main investigation continues. Whitby combines very ancient quaintness with a large fishermen's harbor and all the usual resort facilities. Yet the promenades and indoor amusements and sports events are still overshadowed here by true history. There are many Saxon relics, and 199 steps leading up to St. Mary's Church (which contains a unique "ship's cabin" roof) and the somewhat somber jet industry. For many centuries the locals have made articles of adornment from black lignite, and this became a very important industry indeed for the brief historical period in which Queen Victoria insisted upon plunging the whole nation into perpetual mourning for the husband she had probably harassed to death. Then everybody had to wear pendants, earrings, bracelets of Whitby jet. Many moderns will remember how their grandmothers were plastered with it and how their mothers completely hated the stuff.

At Runswick Bay, "beloved of artists," there can be seen gashes in the rugged cliffs whence the jet and also alum have been excavated; and the village is once again far too genuinely picturesque to be regarded as a seaside resort. The investigator would probably be more satisfied with such embryo Scarboroughs as Filey to the south, possessing all the landladies and seaside shelters and rude picture postcards that could be desired, or Redcar to the far north, Redcar with its "eight-mile stretch of firm sands"—quoting from tourist literature again. There is a sandbank affectionately known to generations of resolute holidaymakers as "The Stray," and a natural rock breakwater called "The Scars," and the town proudly plaques the wall of a Red Barnes House to commemorate the curious fact that there once lived Gertrude Bell, "Scholar, Traveller, Administrator, Peacemaker, and Friend of the Arabs." Also, of course, there are safe bathing, boating, sea-fishing, golf.

And here perhaps is the place for a brief digression on the subject of those rude picture postcards.

When all else has vanished there still remains art. The English seaside resort is not only in process of decay but may soon be a memory alone, save for ruins of stuccoed boarding houses and play pavilions here and there, ruins which the sands and tides will quickly and decently bury. What will remain (save, of course the present chapter of this book)?

It is possible that not only the historian and sociologist but also the connoisseur of art will in five hundred years time make a great deal of the outstanding aesthetic achievement of the English seaside at its prime, which was the dirty postcard.

Actually it was not dirty at all, being bright-colored and concerned largely with jokes about beer and big bottoms and improbable affairs between comparatively innocent crude people in cabbage-smelling rooming houses of the seafront. But it *was* considered as dirty and exceedingly daring at the time by those very childish people, and as such has a charm which may never fade but, indeed, glow brighter and brighter as the ages advance and fewer and fewer of the little treasures remain in connoisseur's cabinet for high financial appraisement and critical appreciation.

The brief story of these postcards is typical of all the sad, sad history of great art. A London hack artist named Donald McGill was of Scottish-Canadian descent. Some of his ancestors were stern elders of the church, and others gave their name to and were highly respectable in the councils of McGill University. He himself was born in 1875 at very respectable Blackheath, and brought up strictly in a family with social "ideas" that had lost the requisite money to promote them.

This fortunate youth was imbued at an early age with repressions and complexes and grudges against society. He then had the great good fortune to be an amiable failure in nearly all that he undertook. All he could really do well was draw, and this disability had immured him in the draftsman's office of a naval architect, where, in the occasional absences of the boss, he would doodle and sketch for his own amusement.

One day McGill was faced with the necessity of writing a message of solace to a nephew in hospital. He pondered awhile, and idly inscribed the words: "Hope you'll soon be out." Then started to draw on the back of a plain postcard. The picture showed a frozen pond with the notice "No Skating." Beneath the notice a man was struggling to extricate himself from a hole in the ice. (There is often a frozen pond on Blackheath.)

Someone persuaded McGill to send the card to a publisher and it, or another one, reached the hands of a man named Joseph Asher who had recently arrived almost penniless in England from Germany to establish a small business as publisher of greeting cards. Asher had observed on visits to windswept London resorts like Brighton and Margate that the holidaymakers there frequently had nothing better to do than buy cards with indistinct local views to send their friends. Just a few of these were well drawn and even funny, the work of quite famous artists like Phil May and Louis Wain.

Asher wrote to McGill. He said briefly that he might be willing to pay him just over a dollar for each humorous drawing submitted, cash by return and all rights surrendered. That was in 1905.

Thereafter McGill drew approximately six cards a week for years. During the First World War his publisher was interned, so McGill found another one, improbably named McCrumb, an American; and eventually the artist was turning out ten cards a week, and making at least £4 in English money or some $10 each seven days from this spare time work.

The artist worked continually through the 1920s, and some of his cards eventually sold as many as two million copies. Joseph Asher when he died left £40,000 "above the line." After the First War he had returned to the fray, a refugee then from Nazi Germany, and had set up the firm of D. Constance Ltd., recruiting McGill again. That firm eventually became very prosperous indeed, at Littlehampton in Sussex.

Asher was not only a clever publisher but also a kind man. When McGill became too old to dream the refugee set him up in a rent-free flat at Streatham in South London (with offices below and warehouse nextdoor). The artist was even given a nominal directorship; and pundits of the day such as George Orwell were encouraged to write about him. He became a small public figure, handsome and elegant, and finally attained the height of modern ambition, to appear on television programs.

During one of these the rude panel master Gilbert Harding said aggressively to McGill: "So you do those dirty postcards?" And the mild old man quite sublimely replied: "No, I am a Seaside Artist." (Discomfiture of stout party.)

In a newspaper article someone said of McGill: "He has made a fortune from comic postcards of fat women and henpecked husbands." And when the artist died in 1962 at the age of 87, ten years after his wife had succumbed to cancer in their poverty, *The Sunday Telegraph* said: "He was the most prolific postcard cartoonist and was reputed to have made a fortune."

Others revealed that McGill's cards had sold 170 million copies of 11,000 titles, and 350 million copies of 12,000 titles.

Soon after McGill's death his will was published. He had left, net, just £574 (about $1400).

McGill was therefore a true if not a great artist, the perfect mirror of an age and a distinct kind of society. He was bold and aggressive in method, equalled only by the American Currier and Ives syndicate in this respect; and the Disney style by comparison was quite sugary and insincere.

McGill drew a fat woman on the stage, with the Union Jack draped around her, and she is declaiming: "Many a battle has been fought under this grand old flag!"

A nurse in the maternity hospital opens the door to a young father. "Your wife's had triplets!" she says. "Well, I never did!" exclaims the young man. And the nurse replies: "Oh, go on, you must have done!"

An enormously fat woman on the beach, covered with scarlet bathing costume, is depicted with a child sitting on the sand under her protruding stomach, with the caption above, "I can't see my little Charlie!"

A fat woman sits in a bath and a plumber calls through the door: "Excuse me, Mum, but are you the lady with the rusty connection?"

A very corpulent female speaks to a workman. There is a handmark on the white door by her side. "Oh, Painter," she says, "I want you to touch up the place where my husband put his hand last night!"

Soon quite high prices were being paid at the auction sales for McGill original watercolors (he painted thus and half-tone blocks were made for the printing of the cards).

So they are of the past already, and, if still available on stands outside newsagents' shops at Brighton and Margate, Southend and Scarborough, Redcar and Blackpool, Morecambe and Torquay, are, like much of those resorts, in the relic class only. The people today send magnificent color cards of superb views in Switzerland, Italy, Spain, Greece, North Africa, and tomorrow will be sending them similarly from the center of the Gobi Desert and Indonesia.

But relics are highly significant and can be extremely valuable, not only to the historian but also to the investor.

Above Yorkshire there are bleak resorts of a kind in county Durham (Sunderland) and in Northumberland (Whitley Bay), but to maintain the high standard of his portfolio every collector should now cross the country to the true land of the "Wakes," which is Lancashire. The "Wakes" were the original church feasts or holidays, which came in the 19th century to mean a day off at the seaside for the workers in the cotton mills, and finally flowered as an entire week of salty roistering for each town at different times of the summer season.

Therefore the resorts of Lancashire, with two small exceptions, became quite different from all others in England, or at least much more so than all others in England. They became wholly of the earth and without any pretense at respectability. They were Coney Islands entirely, but essentially bottom-class English Coney Islands, without the rare American flavor but tangy with the sauce of the most primitive kind of Anglo-Saxons out for a good time: that sauce which the artist McGill rendered perfectly and pictorially in his crude drawings of fat women with exposed underclothing and alcoholics with red noses.

One of the Lancashire exceptions is Grange-over-Sands, situated where Morecambe Bay is a shallow wide inlet that completely retreats into its mother ocean at certain tides. The long flat waters and shoals and sandbanks and half-tone English skies have the same dim colors as the people who stay in the sedate boarding houses and wander among the trim gardens of this resort. It is an ancient, watercolor world, reminiscent of the illustrations in Edwardian magazines. Often the men have long, straggling moustaches, and the women can wear picture hats surmounted by bunches of artificial cherries wobbling. There is talk of service in India and bridge parties in Singapore and of that Lord Lonsdale, the local potentate once, who sported the yellow Rolls-Royce. Most of these people are just playing parts, but aren't we all?

The other exception is far down south near the cotton towns, and is called Lytham St. Annes. It consists of ugly red brick houses and white sand dunes and green lawns with a windmill. There is nothing to it but a kind of blessed peace for these parts. The South African practice of keeping the races out of each other's hair has been followed here with singular success. The roistering mill workers do not appear in Lytham St. Annes, which is almost wholly the preserve of the modern Lancashire upper classes, the managers and higher-paid technicians. If there were any local Kennedys left this would be Hyannis Port.

Running from north to south, the first of the big Lancashire seaside resorts is Morecambe. It has the advantage of a view to the Lake District mountains across the molten steel of the water, but nobody looks that way much. The great feature here is the "Illuminations." Miles of promenade and lamp-posts are strung with old-fashioned electric-light bulbs painted in colors, with set-pieces of the Disneyland variety here and there. Many of the crude people who come for their brief annual holidays—or who used to come, many of them now taking much longer annual breaks in more accessible and cheaper places such as Ibiza and Torremolinos—regard or regarded these "Illuminations" as an eighth wonder of the world.

Morecambe is, however, just a taster for enormous Blackpool, a place that in its day had no equal in all the world for triumphant success of sheer vulgarity. It was the unique fun city by the sea. And it was arranged so that the visitor need never, unless he was particularly inquisitive, ever see the sea. He could walk out along three piers with concert halls and ballrooms and amusement arcades, and scarcely be conscious that beneath him, somewhere, the grey swell ominously grumbled. He could arrive in the busy shopping center of the town and ask the way to the sea and be met only with blank stares. "Ee, luve, it's somewhere around but I never seen it meself."

The whole purpose of Blackpool was and is to take the annual savings of the visiting work people as quickly out of their pockets as possible and to give them such a good time in the process that they would always want to come back again. So the immense seven-mile Promenade was decked with gaudy color effigies of popular heroes, heroines and animals, and every available square yard became a shop or booth, offering food, drink, holiday hats, birth control and sex-stimulating devices, rude postcards, Goss-type commemorative china, souvenirs that were of no intrinsic or artistic value (save the genuine Goss perhaps, to be described in a moment), but, as trash, were suitable mementoes of a lovely holiday spent amid trash.

The redolent odors of fried fish and chip shops and vinegar and beery hiccoughs and cheap perfumery and good, honest sweat rise high from this town. At night the promenades and the shopping streets must be like a fairyland to people from inland towns like Oldham where the blackened mills rise balefully above the crowded tenements of crumbling brick. Next morning the same thoroughfares resemble an old whore caught with her makeup off, but no one goes out much in the mornings. The saloons are open early and it is best to take in a skinful as soon as possible, after which the world begins blearily to look wonderful again.

Once upon a time the Tower at Blackpool, a miniature of the Eiffel, was not only higher to these children than anything else constructed by man, but also the supreme phallic symbol below which the life of the imagination could for a short time become reality. Under the Tower was a complex that included a zoo, an aviary, a circus, a roof-garden, and a gaudy ballroom with a Wurlitzer. Indeed the town had five great ballrooms, one of which, the Empress, was the largest in Britain. Feet that had worn clogs for the rest of the year shuffled round to the beat of several famous dance bands, mainly in fox trots, slow waltzes, two-steps, rumbas. When swing arrived with the individual, more exhibitionist movements of a wealthier, younger generation of the 1950s, the great days were already over. What remained were elderly sentimentalists and those without the gumption to take the cheap flying trips to similar hells in Spain: also day excursion gangs of teenage rivals whose only object was briefly to beat up the place and, if possible, secure a few expensive puffs of pot.

The unique sound of singing groups such as the famous Beatles really came out of this strong, earthy place, but it was and is a brief phenomenon, pinned down in time only by the thoughts of a poet.

The fifteen "live" theatres and same number of cinemas in Blackpool, the Spanish Hall and Indian Lounge of the Winter Gardens, and the huge Olympia (an amusement park with every possible machine designed to disarray the lower garments of females) all emerged from a social order that has since been changed. When skirts have practically disappeared what is the point of long, revealing slides and haunted halls where every turn produces a cunning up-draft of deliberate, disconcerting air? When the telly at home brings all-America to everyone, what is the point of travelling miles to visit a theatre or cinema? Who is going to be impressed any longer by a Spanish Hall or by sickly northern municipal gardens or by a suitably named Grundy Art Gallery (in Queen Street) when everyone now can fly cheaply to Algiers, Athens and Granada?

Blackpool is a northern English idea that may occasionally be remembered as such, together with the indigenous postcards of Donald McGill and the rare china of W. H. Goss.

Goss was, like McGill, an artist who took a small interest of the people at a short, particular time in their history, and worked on it so well that he is likely to be remembered and collected profitably by the sapient.

The problem with the Blackpools was to get the money of the visitors as quickly and neatly as possible. It was found that the fools would buy cheap souvenirs, and liked to take home, for the mantelpiece and cabinets of the best, unused room, little objects that would remind them of the fun they had had and let neighbors know how widely and expensively they had travelled. Such objects were provided of wood and china and leather and would be embossed for each resort with words like "A Present from Brighton," or coats-of-arms with "Felixstowe" or "Morecambe" or "Margate" below.

Most of the articles were completely cheap and nasty, but one maker of such commemorative china turned out inevitably to be a small genius at the job. There is always one. From the gaudiest aesthetic manifestation comes at least one good man. W. H. Goss was an indigent potter of the Staffordshire "Five Towns," as forever set in amber by the novelist Arnold Bennett. This Goss made little pieces of souvenir china not only in vast numbers but also well. The body of his hard, cold paste was infinitely finer than that of his competitors (notably the Foley works and Willow Art and Grafton.). Then he displayed remarkable ingenuity in choice of subjects, ranging from splendid small busts of famous people to a remarkable life-size replica of Queen Victoria's baby shoe. (She was a diminutive baby because it is only four inches long and one and a half inches wide.) He made tiny Welsh hats and First War helmets, and jugs, and even vulgar chamber-pots, all with colorful applied transfers showing the armorial bearings of the municipalities concerned and often with interesting explanatory notes, not to mention his own clear mark, W. H. Goss with an eagle above.

These were sold originally for a few cents, then got into the poorer junk shops for about a quarter, after which they became a half-dollar, even a dollar—but, until recently, were still cheaper to buy as originals than in new, reproduction form. (An unholy number of these reproductions were so made.)

It is certain that genuine Goss will eventually be sought after by collectors and will be worth hundreds of dollars for the more important pieces.

So even Blackpool will not have lived in vain.

After Blackpool the other resorts of this coast are comparatively tame. Southport lives on Lord Street, a broad and tree-lined shopping thoroughfare that by some strange chance has never been vulgarized. Southport has all the features of the popular seaside place but does not belong properly to the genre. It is really too nice. It is necessary, for continuance of the true theme, to cross the brief water to the Isle of Man and great Douglas, not only the capital of the self-governing island state (which has its own Parliament, the House of Keys) but also a sandy, sea-swept Blackpool with knobs on, including wide streets, imposing terraces, a huge vaudeville theatre (the Coliseum), Douglas Head (a high bluff upon which entertainments are organized), a lighthouse, piers, promenades, horse-drawn trolly cars, and, at last, a climate that can occasionally, in the French way, be *douce*. Some of the warmish air currents that have created Ireland can arrive here and make the open-air life reasonably bearable.

The Isle of Man is quite beautiful and it is queer. The cats lack tails. The local coat-of-arms consists of three legs joined together at the tops with the excellent motto "Whichever way you throw me I will stand." The Tynwald, where laws are promulgated on a wild hill, is one of the earliest democratic institutions known to northern man, being at least a thousand years old. There is a Bishop of Sodor and Man and two High Court judges called Deemsters, and, annually, the world's most famous motorcycle races around the narrow roads and rugged lanes, always won formerly by British machines but finally one more demonstration place for the mechanical superiority of the Japanese.

After Lancashire the coast becomes Welsh for a long way down and that is not England anymore. Wales is to England rather like Mexico to California and Arizona, being essentially foreign although strongly influenced, and (unlike Mexico) actually governed by the larger neighbor. It is necessary for another seaside resort in England to come as far south as the Bristol Channel and Somerset again, that lovely Somerset of the still-young countryside which has the single redeeming feature, for the avid collector, of Weston-super-Mare.

The use of the Latin in the title was doubtless promoted in the first place by a certain dubiety about the actual presence of the true sea hereabouts, this Bristol Channel being a great inlet that is somewhat prone to ebb-tide mudflats. Yet Weston has its "golden" sands, that can be very pleasant when not whipped up by the strong western breeze into the unsuspecting eye; and it offers the holidaymaker a Winter Garden inevitably, and a Museum, and a "marine lake," and what the guide books describe as "unlimited resources for pleasure." But, after Blackpool and so much else that has been seen, this is admittedly not quite a connoisseur's piece as yet.

Nor are Minehead farther along to the west, and the north Devon resorts of Lynton and Ilfracombe. They are too quaint and small. Lynton is divided from its beach at Lynmouth by an incredibly steep cliff-hill, from which gorgeous views of jagged rock and sea can be obtained on the occasional fine day. At Ilfracombe the climate is even better and sub-tropical plants have been known to thrive. But it is a very long way from anywhere, even longer than North Africa these days, and must be regarded as the ceramist regards his odd piece of Victorian Minton ware, interesting but not from Chelsea or Bow.

The great peninsula of Devon-Cornwall is now arid ground for the specialist. It is by far the most popular English area among the English for their holidays at this time of writing, but for that very reason is not an area of vast, period "resorts."

North Devon and Cornwall as they come down to the Atlantic Ocean are superficially empty lands save for straggling hill farms and dim market towns. The famed Cornwall is indeed an unlovely ruin for much of its extent, as if there was once a great battle there and then there was no money for rebuilding and for decontamination of the various blasted heaths. But the small fishing villages have endured. It is necessary to leave the interior desolation and proceed down winding steep valleys amid rocks, till suddenly a cluster of old cottages and a stone jetty are venturesome enough to tickle the great raging sea with their toes, the sea of wrecks and smugglers, of black and blue moods, of high jagged cliffs and bloody rocks beneath the harvest moon.

This is beautiful but not the true seaside. Sometimes a brave effort has been made to create Cornish Blackpools and Brightons, but with such a conspicuous lack of success, even at Penzance and Newquay and that loose painter's lady, St. Ives, that today the English are still not ashamed to take a holiday there, at Polperro and Boscastle, Kynance Cove and Port Isaac, Mullion Cove and Tintagel. Sometimes the places with the lovely names—Bedruthan Steps, Mawgan Porth— have become considerable towns (Fowey, Looe) and in one case, Falmouth, they have congealed into a real port, salt-crusted with history. But they have always failed, largely because of the lack of good building land by the sea, to become worthy of the resort-connoisseur's respect.

Plymouth is not a seaside resort, but just a naval port which periodically spews out discontented people to fight Armadas and create Americas.

And the tour is now nearly complete. South Devon immediately after Cornwall has many small places that have tried hard with the aid of bandstands and promenades and municipal gardens to become greater than was intended for them by nature, and at least one town has actually over-succeeded in this respect. All have the characteristics of considerable natural beauty, clean sands, red cliffs, rivers that jump chuckling into the sea after threading a devious way through the interstices of the green, sleeping land above. Dartmouth is a small river resort from which embryo sailors have for hundreds of years ventured out for the first time into the eagerly-awaiting sea. Brixham is so self-conscious about its fishermen and its antiques that it has long since ceased to be entirely human. Paignton is a true Edwardian seaside resort but in miniature, and it is really no more than a suburb of that giant Torquay which is the Devon place that has over-succeeded in its ambitions.

Torquay, like modern Brighton and Bournemouth, has become more of a city than a resort. It is a fine place of permanent residence, and of hotels frequented by the kind of people who on no account build sand-castles. The only difference between Torquay and Miami or Monte Carlo is that Torquay, being English, is not so rich and accordingly does not accommodate so many gangsters. The collector will find little there of what he is seeking. And in the satellite towns and coves, Anstey's Cove, Babbacombe, Maidencombe, the ice-cream parlors and souvenir shops, the trips round the bay and the shrimping nets, there is undoubtedly the right atmosphere but not enough of it by half after the true glories of a Margate or Scarborough.

So it continues round the otherwise lovely coast. Little Dawlish has its moments, especially where the main railway line proceeds through the town at the sea's very edge, such an experience for the excursionists once that a very great writer indeed would be required to put their emotions into words. Exmouth tries equally hard with two miles of sea-front walks and other accommodating conveniences for the week-end frivolities of Exeter, the main town of Devon inland. Sidmouth is not so much a resort as an asylum for the aged, with villas everywhere and an occasionally mild if not unruffled climate that has always precluded serious development. The true English seaside resort is outstandingly a product of bad weather, and has evolved chiefly as a mean of mitigating the horrors of wind and rain.

Budleigh Salterton farther along, far from being representative of the English seaside, is a rare period piece in its own right. Once upon a time rich elderly aunts always lived there, together with statuesque seagulls who would alight on flagpoles and stand beautifully sentinel. One narrow road down to the sea had shops selling articles made of Shetland wool and strange felt hats and novels by forgotten writers such as Charles Garvice and Mary Roberts Rinehart.

Dorset, the next county, is nearly all like that, save for the first true resort on this littoral, which is Weymouth. This could perhaps be chosen as one of the most characteristic of the English seaside towns. It has a broad bay with sands and, when the sun shines, a plethora of shocking-pink bodies. A pier thrusts boldly out to sea, as if eternally testing the temperature of the water, and it is nobly graced by what is still called the "new" bandstand. The hotel and boarding-house buildings round the bay are often genuinely Georgian, severe, stuccoed and beautifully stuffy. Inside they have some of the earliest examples of true plumbing in the modern world. On the Esplanade there are statues of George II and Queen Victoria as well as a Jubilee clocktower. Visitors can drool over the Swannery or the stocks and Armada chest in the Guildhall, or visit the theatre in Alexandra Gardens. In the old days they would gaze at the Grand Fleet as assembled for their delectation in Weymouth Bay.

The rest of Dorset is pure Thomas Hardy and not for this chapter, save for the Jane Austen features of Lyme Regis, and the bracing air and somewhat meretricious appointments of curious Swanage, a resort undoubtedly but to be noted here for what John Mowlem did mainly. He and another local man named Burt went to London and became successful contractors. In the course of their business they acquired a lot of London and from time to time sent pieces of it proudly down to their birthplace. Thus Swanage city hall incorporates what was once the façade of Mercers Hall, Cheapside, and the Clock Tower was formerly the Wellington monument on London Bridge, while every now and then a genuine London lamp post of the 19th century will surprise the eye, often with the name of a London parish on it. A dog's paradise indeed.

Bournemouth, another Torquay, has long since forgotten its original purpose. It is a great city by the sea; and sometimes it is difficult to believe that it is by the sea. People can and do live there often without once exposing themselves to the raw affront of the windy waves. All the same there is a seaside resort here, as every fat man is said to contain a thin one, a resort that boasts a great stretch of safe sands, high cliffs, a six-mile "front," and those strange clefts in the cliffs called "chines" that, for the child, bestow an ineradicable memory of pine cones and possible sex maniacs among the dark, resinous trunks.

The Parish Church of Bournemouth improbably harbors the heart of Percy Bysshe Shelley, poet, and the more extensive remains of Mary his wife (author of *Frankenstein* and founder of the horror film industry).

Bournemouth has a monopoly of the coast for miles in both directions. Eastwards it becomes Boscombe, Southbourne, even old Christchurch, until suddenly the baleful influence wanes and a strange new world of the seaside develops, that ushered in by Milford-on-Sea and then Lymington, which are not so much resorts as overgrown villages with nice pubs and the promise always of the bright-cliffed Isle of Wight across the water.

The Isle of Wight is to the collector of seaside places like a cabinet of opaline, cameo, Burmese, Mary Gregory and vaseline glass to the specialist in fine Victoriana. It is a true island but also a miniature of the green, quaint England that is now fast dying away and will soon be only a literary memory like the New England of Nathaniel Hawthorne. First there is the port of old Yarmouth, fusty like an aspidistra, and then Cowes of the yachtsmen, with boat yards, and the birthplace of that Dr. Arnold who first gave Englishmen a public school education, and the spot whence the first settlers departed in

1633 for Maryland. A little inland on one side we have Osborne House where Queen Victoria for so many years sulked in the tent of her ineffable grief for a Prince Consort lost (in intervals of imposing upon nearly the entire world a special artistic style and culture forever to be known as Victorian); and a little inland on the other side we have another kind of prison called Parkhurst, where the British nowadays incarcerate the bolder spirits left among them. Ryde, farther along the coastal road, is pure resort, but with such a tangy Edwardian flavor that it is difficult sometimes to believe that there have been two world wars and Hiroshima since it was built. Then Ventnor, right round and facing the true sea, is nicely swept by rain and wind. Ghosts of a never to be recaptured childhood romp still upon those damp pale sands. The gritty feeling is in the shoes still, and the sound of the plaintive strings in a smug Winter Garden continues to evoke sad memories for an ageing man. (Another refuge from the elements was the Museum of the Literary and Scientific Institution in the High Street, open on weekdays *free.*)

The real English coast starts again at Southsea, one of the most truly nautical of all resorts because the ships for Portsmouth must continually loom and boom on the fog-wreathed horizon. The old town has a predilection for modest antique shops and the shingle beach for tar.

After which Sussex will be regained and once more the full glory of germinal Brighton awaits.

4

Pub

Alternating chapters of this book may be seen to deal with the dead and the alive aspects of the England under discussion. The country is partly a mausoleum and partly a still living and vigorous organism. The seaside resorts belong to England's past but the pubs very much to her present.

The pubs do actually comprise the true meeting place of the English, more than the churches and clubs and parliament houses. Every man must still work, but in his spare time he must talk, and in England he chiefly talks while standing up and drinking.

Pub, as said before, is short for public house and means a saloon, estaminet, beer hall or inn, but for the present purpose of sociological investigation and aesthetic amusement combined it must be extended to include bars in golf houses and ships and even the ubiquitous cocktail party in private residences.

Bring English people together for a specific purpose at a committee meeting or rally and they will rarely express themselves freely. Drinking alcohol, no matter how dilute, they and their icy souls slowly melt. They become increasingly like other people.

It has always been so, right back to the beginning of literary record. Chaucer in his *Canterbury Tales* describes how his motley company was gathered together at The Tabard Inn, Southwark. Langland in *Piers Plowman* puts a lot of contemporary people in a village alehouse and describes how they gradually become human. Pepys the diarist came to an inn where "The master of the house was a sober under-

Playing shove ha'penny and drinking draught beer in a pub of Pembridge, Herefordshire.

standing man, and I had good discourse with him about this country's matters as wool and corn and other things." That was 1668.

The early novelist Smollett perfectly described an 18th-century English pub:

> a little public-house on the side of the highway. . . . The kitchen, in which they assembled, was the only room for entertainment in the house, paved with red bricks, remarkably clean, furnished with three or four Windsor chairs, adorned with shining plates of pewter, and copper saucepans, nicely scoured, that even dazzled the eyes of the beholder; while a cheerful fire of sea-coal blazed in the chimney. Three of the travellers, who arrived on horseback . . . agreed to pass the time, until the weather should clear up, over a bowl of rumbo, which was accordingly prepared. . . . At a little distance, on his left hand, there was another group, consisting of the landlady, a decent widow, her two daughters . . . and a country lad who served both as waiter and ostler.

It was from the beginning and still is a democratic institution, the

An ancient English pub: note the upper windows filled in to defeat an 18th-century window tax.

one place where all classes in a class-ridden community could mix without fear of contagion. Thus the great Dr. Johnson to Boswell:

"There is no private house in which people can enjoy themselves so well as at a capital tavern. . . . You are sure you are welcome; and the more noise you make, the more trouble you give, the more good things you call for, the welcomer you are. No servants will attend you with the alacrity which waiters do, who are incited by the prospect· of an immediate reward in proportion as they please. No, sir, there is nothing which has yet been contrived by man, by which so much happiness is produced, as by a good tavern or inn."

Again:

"As soon as I enter the door of a tavern, I experience an oblivion of care, and a freedom from solicitude; when I am seated, I find the master courteous, and the servants obsequious to my call, anxious to know and ready to supply my wants: wine there exhilarates my spirits, and prompts me to free conversation, and an interchange of discourse with those whom I most love; I dogmatize, and am contradicted; and in this conflict of opinions and sentiments I find delight."

William Hazlitt, one of the best of writers in English (whose true heirs were Maugham and Hemingway) declared memorably how fine it was to enter some old town, walled and turreted just at the approach of night-fall, or to come to some straggling village, with the lights streaming through the surrounding gloom; and then after inquiring for the best entertainment that the place affords, to "take one's ease at one's inn!"

And the minor poet William Shenstone finally immortalized the matter when he wrote the oft-quoted verse:

> Whoe'er has travelled life's dull round,
> Where'er his stages may have been,
> May sigh to think how oft he found
> The warmest welcome—at an Inn.

Admittedly in the old days the inn was, for the quality, a place principally for food and lodging on journeys. For the common people it was always a meeting place, a home away from home, like saloons in hick towns to the Wild West pioneers (a custom brought from England to the wide plains and the Rocky Mountains) but two class-shattering wars were necessary completely to democratize the English pub, until the stage was reached when everyone, carpenter and financier, stockbroker and mechanic, clerk, and gentleman farmer, had what became known as his "local"—a tavern that he would religiously visit at least once a week if possible, if only on Sunday mornings while exercising the dog, buying the papers, and waiting for the roast beef.

These pubs vary from very ancient hostelries, often on sites going right back to the Romans, to large modern structures designed to catch motorists at crossroads and somewhat effeminately furnished by the smarter interior decorators. By a chance the favored local among really important people will be a small and stuffy tavern in a back street, or it may be little more than the bar attached to some great modern hotel.

But the procedure will be the same. The stockbroker or the artist or the policeman will arrive and push his way sheepishly through the broad backs around the old mahogany or oaken bar. He will call for

An English inn that was there before the first colonization of America.

a "pint of the best" or "a small bottle," or "a Worthington, please," maybe "a Scotch and soda" if he is truly bibulous, or "gins and tonics" if he is with a woman. Maybe this will be anticipated by friends already waiting, who will have greeted him with the ritual words "What will you have?" (Afterwards he must keep his eyes open for other friends who may arrive later, in which case it will be his duty to buy them a drink at once: and always he must be careful not to get in with too large a group, otherwise the necessity of returning all favors will inevitably end in chronic alcoholism.)

Very soon, however, it will be seen that the purpose of the gathering is really innocent. These people, especially in the south of England, do not visit the pub in order to obliterate their woes in drink. They do not undertake what a different class in some corners of the land, such as Barrow-in-Furness right up where Lancashire meets the Lake District, would proudly describe as "serious drinking."

They come primarily for a chat. It may be their purpose to find out from the local accountant what the latest tax impositions mean. They might want to discover exactly what the people at the corner house got for the property when they sold it the previous week. They will be after news of the latest Kennedy exploit and what their fellows think of it, or what are the chances of getting rid of their latest Prime Minister—and especially they will be interested in discussing cricket and football results and the behavior of their dogs.

There will be surprisingly little scandal, practically no religion, and of true philosophy absolutely none at all. If a man or a woman picks up a tankard of draft beer and says something about the inequality of human behavior and technical achievement then there will be a brief silence of the kind called pregnant, after which harmless chatter will break out decently to cover up the gaffe.

And the session rarely lasts long. The extraordinary licensing laws of England preclude that. Visits to pubs endure from midday to 2 P.M., or from 8 P.M. to 10:30 P.M. at the very longest.

Meanwhile modern doctoring of drinks and lowering of quality to preserve profits from the ever-encroaching bite of costs more or less ensure that few people get genuinely fuddled from their thin potations. Those who roister and reel are usually putting on a sympathetic act which has the warm indulgence of the others.

It is all arranged primarily to give neighbors a chance to have a carefully self-censored talk about current but not fundamental matters. It is the meeting-place of the clans and the modern Rütli-meadow kind of parliament of the people.

The feeling of the meeting is at once apparent, and each man and woman goes home with the news. There are no profound or embarrassing discussions. Someone says "I see they are increasing the charges for National Health spectacles," or "it looks as though we're going to be in the Common Market after all," and a few words from long-moustache here and bald-pate there, and perhaps even from mini-skirt on the high stool between them, gives the neighborhood man quite enough information to pass on to his wife when he reaches home: "There's a lot of feeling about this new charge for spectacles"; and: "People aren't half so keen now on getting into the Common Market."

Public opinion is being formed, in the pub.

What lovely names they have, the essence of the true, living England! And it is a fact that the affection of the people for any institution may be gauged in extent by the charm of the nomenclature involved. Nearly everywhere there is a "Bell," and the mind recalls at once the whitewashed village of Hurley in Berkshire and the perfect, pointing gables of the very ancient inn there. Or a coaching house at Stilton in Huntingdonshire—where the cheese does *not* come from—or historic houses with the same name in Gloucestershire particularly, at Tewkesbury, at Dursley, at Gloucester itself. But only once is there a "Rose Revived," this being a charming cottage inn on the young Thames at New Bridge, Oxfordshire. It was formerly a private house called the "Rose" or "Rose Cottage." Then the man who converted it into an inn decided that it should be called the "Rose Revived."

The inn sign itself survives as an interesting reminder of the illiteracy that, for thousands of years until recently, allowed most men to remain blissfully ignorant of the contents of the books. The people could not read or write and identified commercial establishments by the pictures or other devices that were dangled outside. The innkeepers mostly had beautiful painted signs—a wheatsheaf, a crown, a bell—because always-penurious artists were only too willing to do the work for the price of a few nights' lodging, meals, and drink. Today only the pubs, the pawnbrokers and the barbers announce their name by a sign, and the pubs are far ahead of the others aesthetically.

Hundreds of English inns are called the "Bush," either singly or in conjunction with another name, the "Bull and Bush" being an outstanding example. Those who live in wine-growing countries know how bunches of greenery from the vine plant will be hung over doorways. This became ivy in the old English days and eventually the

One of the loveliest of old inn signs, in wrought-iron right across the village street.

official vintner's sign. "Good wine needs no bush" was the universally understood saying once. Eventually pubs with the bush sign became known as taverns of the lower order.

The history behind these signs is often complex indeed. Many English inns are called the "Chequers." At Steyning in Sussex, not far from Brighton, there is a truly magnificent example of this curious sign, dangled over the street by a wonderful bracket of scrolled ironwork. And there is reason to believe that its origin is in the chequerboard used by Roman innkeepers for calculating how much money their guests owed them. A device exactly like the popular English inn sign of the "Chequers" may be seen at Pompeii. Similarly there are reminiscences of the Crusades in pub names such as the "Saracen's Head," the "Turk's Head," and the charming "Trip to Jerusalem." "La Belle Sauvage," on the other hand, comes from the very popular Red Indian princess Pocohontas who was brought to England by an early colonist of America.

No satisfactory explanation has yet been found of the pub name the "Leg and Seven Stars," nor of another cryptic sign, the "Case Is Altered." The "Goat and Compasses" is similarly strange, although it has been suggested that over the ages once-intelligible names have just become hopelessly corrupted by common usage. There is one good example of that in a sign showing a satyr and bacchanals (roistering rural drinkers). The name of the pub below it was corrupted in due course to the "Devil and Bag o'Nails."

If the visitor cannot understand why so many English hotels are called the "Talbot" he must be told, however unconvincingly, that a breed of sporting dogs had that name; and if he wants to know the reason for the name "The Old Fox with his Teeth Drawn" he should

English inn signs have a character all of their own: this, of the "Five Alls," is a collector's piece.

enter the pub in question and find out. It is a temperance inn, once called the "Fox."

The "Green Man," according to the antiquarians, goes right back to primeval lore and the Druids, men of the sheltering trees all of them as they fled into Wales from the German and Scandinavian conquerors of England. But a modern thinker would certainly not approve of that inn which is called the "Labour in Vain," and has, or had, a sign showing the abortive scrubbing of a negro by women. He might prefer the "Load of Mischief" with the picture of a man burdened and staggering under a monkey, a magpie and a woman. Another male philosopher, Thomas Hardy, calls an inn the "Quiet Woman," in his novel *The Return of the Native.* No doubt he had his shrewd finger on the masculine pulse.

The oak in one shape of another, and in many combinations of words (the "Royal Oak," the "Brave Old Oak") appears on the signs and in the names of many English inns, because Charles II sheltered in a tree of the kind at Boscobel when escaping from the battle of Worcester: also the ships of the Navy were largely fashioned from oak in those days and this wood was at the base of England's power and prosperity. A modern inn would have to be called the "Plastic Tray" to be similarly in touch with the economic facts of life.

The "Telegraph" and the "Comet" had nothing to do with science. They commemorated the names of famous stage coaches, of which the most ubiquitous sign is, of course, the "Coach and Horses." The "Volunteer Inn," found almost everywhere, dates the house neatly to the Napoleonic wars, when so many men were unwillingly pressed into military and naval service that to be an actual volunteer was indeed something special. Then public houses that have mid-19th-century names such as the "Engine Inn" and the "Locomotive," and the "Tram" and the "Canal" are invariably murky, poor and unpleasantly situated amid the squalor of industrial towns, representatives of an essentially ugly age.

The Guildhall Museum, small but one of the most interesting in London, contains many old inn signs, including a remarkable "Bull and Mouth." The effigy of a man's head below the great bull has the most monstrous mouth ever devised by artist. Very strangely a couplet below links this with the ancient Crete of the Minotaur (and the legendary drinking exploits of Milo).

Long since demolished, also, is the greatest inn sign of all, that once outside the "White Hart" at Scole in Norfolk. It went right across the road in a splendid archway or rococo wooden carving. But many magnificent signs still do span roadways, as that of the "Four Swans" at Waltham Cross, and the "George" at Stamford, and, perhaps best of all, the "Fox and Hounds" in the nice little village of Barley in Hertfordshire, where a carved hunt literally bridges the road in perfect silhouette, leading the wise drinker inevitably in.

For some reason or other the English have always regarded certain classes as "Jolly." These especially include "Jolly" weavers, cricketers, butchers and sailors. Other bucolic professions and crafts are represented by such as the "Hand and Shears," the "Gravediggers' Arms," the "Malt Shovel," the "Plough and Shuttle," and the "Beetle and Wedge." (A "beetle" was a large mallet of wood.)

The famous little "Beehive" at Grantham had an actual hive with living bees crooked in a tree outside the front door. Other inns with actuality signs include "Ploughs" with old ploughs hanging outside, and "Angler's Arms" with stuffed fishes in dangling cases, and "Horseshoes" with real horseshoes, and often an "Anchor Inn" with a real discarded anchor.

One of the most extraordinary aspects of the English as a people is that they appear outwardly phlegmatic but inside are natural poets nearly all of them. They writhe with interior sentiment, derived perhaps from their Germano-Celtic origins. The pub landlord is so often a red-faced beery individual, but he secretly delights in the name of his inn, the "Three Loggerheads," or the "Goat in Boots," or "The World Upside Down," or even the "Pink and Lily" or the "Blooming Fuschia." It is as if the world's being a dull and cruel place, why not some fantasy and fun on the way out?

In grim towns of the north, at five minutes to six in the evening, workmen will stand outside some dull tavern in the smoke-charged mist, "waiting for them to open." Inside afterwards strong beer will gradually send fumes to those simple heads and happiness will reign —until, of course, the inevitable return home with empty pockets to the waiting wife, who, even if she is an angel and utters not a word of reproach, will yet by her very mute acceptance of the situation turn the sullen roisterer into an actual brute. And that tavern will have been called, perhaps, the "Horn of Plenty" or the "Happy Philosopher."

All round the coast are wonderful little pubs with nautical names, the "Oyster Smack," the "Fish and Eels," the "Butt and Oyster." The seaside resorts as described in a previous chapter would have been quite unendurable for long generations if it had not been for the "Old Ship" inns and the innumerable drinking-places with fancy names along the promenades and up the tributary side streets. And the sleazier reaches, throughout dockland, of London's otherwise grim Thames river are continually redeemed by the presence of ancient small hostelries that come right down to the mud and sport such names as the "Grapes," the "China Packet" and that delectable "Prospect of Whitby," which has graduated in its time from a haunt of crude sailors to a fashionable meeting place for the gilded set.

The kind of pub formerly frequented by smugglers and wreckers in seafaring Devonshire of Drake.

In London itself there was a "Monster" (now demolished, alas), and (right in the heart of Mayfair suitably) a "Running Footman," and a "Devil" and a "Mermaid," and the famous "Cheshire Cheese" in Wine Office Court off Fleet Street, where Samuel Johnson and his 18th-century friends would once dispute, and in modern times the journalists and the lawyers still attempted to impose their ideas upon an unwilling world. And heaven only knows who the visitor might yet meet in the "Fitzroy" down Charlotte Street, named after the bastard of a king.

A most interesting holiday could be spent in England by a man who jumped from ancient inn to inn. It would be quite different from a holiday in any other country, and would be less depressing than the conventional tour of cathedrals, churches and museums. There are historic hotels in France, Germany and Italy, but not with the peculiar atmosphere of the English hostelry: so well-preserved and tactfully restored after the long years, not destroyed by innumerable rampaging wars as have been so many on the Continent, and always combining the functions of a night-place for strangers and a drinking-place for locals so uniquely. If France and Germany have some ancient hotels still they are not neighborhood clubs also. It is not possible to pass the night in a European tavern and at the same time communicate directly with the soul of a people.

By comparison with the cathedrals and churches and museums the English inns are organic, still-living growths in the community. In many ways they may annoy but they will never bore with deadness.

Perhaps the best formula for such a journey is to play it off the cuff. Travel direct to some main county town, such as Buckingham or Canterbury or Hereford, and book at the main hotel, which would really be an old and famous pub. Speak to the manager and local people in the bar and learn about other similar abiding-places in the county, which could then be visited in turn.

Thus that fine coaching inn at Georgian Buckingham, the "White Hart" in Market Street, would lead to many others nearby, such as the "King's Head" at Aylesbury, largely a Tudor-timbered building that has one of the finest 16th-century windows in the world, famed for its twenty lights and delicate traceries and moldings. The "Bell" and the "Bull's Head" are similarly historic in this market town. Buckinghamshire alone will be revealed to have some thirty important old inns at which the traveller can comfortably stay, and this is all within a very short distance of central London. Consider alone the "George" at West Wycombe, so perfectly Georgian in the front that it

*An English pub in Tudor black and white half-timbering and plaster
architecture.*

(with the rest of the village) has been preserved for the nation, but,
at the back through the narrow coaching arch suddenly, quite medieval
with half-timbering and with a hoary upper story bulging over what
was once the stable yard.

Canterbury is again easily accessible from London, and is a living
museum of historic interest, filled with hoary hotels and inns, among
which the little Falstaff, which has been there since 1403, is undoubtedly the leading showpiece. It is now a 17th-century building mainly,
which was erected on the site of a pilgrims' hostel.

The road to Canterbury, as readers of Dickens will remember, was
formerly one of the most frequented and important of coaching routes
(as are the roads to Buckingham and Hereford) and there at once
is another good idea: study those coaching routes and then follow
them by car, staying at what were formerly the main staging posts
on the way.

After that Canterbury route the Great North Road was most
thronged with horse-drawn coaches in the early 19th century. That

could be traversed right up to Scotland, with nights spent at some of
the most notable of all English inns. It will be necessary to leave the
great throughway at selected spots to find the ancient places, but
nearly always a small town will yield its prize. The Bath Road is
good similarly, and the Exeter Road, and the North-Western Road,
and the Norwich Road.

Herefordshire and Shropshire on the Welsh Marches are as free
from modern contamination as any region of England, and the stranger
will be delighted with the black-and-white half-timbering of the truly
historic inns thereabouts. The "Angel" at Ludlow is a magpie of
beauty with remarkable Georgian bay windows and much good talk
of cattle and sheep in the bars, but the yard at the back of the "Bull"
in the same town is straight from Chaucer, and Ludlow also has the
"Feathers," one of the most sensational of all hotel buildings. It is
not just black-and-white. It is wholly Elizabethan in the excessive
detail of its ornate, original decoration—nothing but elaborately carved
wood in stars with white backgrounds, windows with small, lozenge-
shaped panes, all surmounted by a series of sharp-pointed gables.
Inside the polished black and brown floorboards creak and the ceilings
above have almost unique plaster moldings.

Then Shrewsbury has not only the absolutely authentic "King's
Head" (which goes right back to the first Tudor period—with a sign
depicting King Henry VII, father of Henry VIII and exhibits two
stories of blackened beams and white plaster), but also the curious
"Dun Cow," which is very good for conversation in the bars and
snuggeries but has imitation beams painted on the outside plaster
like false eyelashes on a silly old woman.

Bridgnorth should be visited for the choice little "Swan"—choice
for architecture and history—and anywhere west of Hereford City
will be found village after village, amid green pastures, red plowland
and the constant dangle of hops, that exhibit what is scarcely believable in this callous age: old inns that are outwardly as they were
hundreds of years ago but inwardly as comfortable as any in the
world. There is the "Red Lion" at Weobley, the zebra masterpiece
of a village that is almost wholly black-and-white: much brass and
copper inside, such good ale, cider and local talk. Pembridge is a
similar village, and Leominster, and Presteigne. Hay-on-Wye, King-
ton, Knighton: they must all be seen if not always slept in. Hereford,
Ledbury, Ross-on-Wye have several ancient hostelries that are also
good hotels.

The scope is indeed tremendous from bottom to top of England

and several times across. At Higham in Norfolk is the "Dolphin," and it dates from Elizabethan times and was once a bishop's palace. At the other end of the architectural scale comes the little "Trout" at Godstow in Oxfordshire, just a cottage on the very edge of the Thames: but used to accommodating keen and monied fishermen as well as long generations of undergraduates. Then the "Peacock" at Rowlsey in Derbyshire not only exhibits the best kind of 17th-century

The "Golden Lion" at Ashburton in Devonshire, a glorious English pub.

rural architecture but also comfortably accommodates tourists who want to visit great Haddon Hall nearby, while the "Sondes Arms" in Rockingham, Northamptonshire, is just one of the humble stone buildings in that cozy village. It is as if the little houses just outcropped from the nice-toned sandy rock hereabouts: one of the statelier inns of the district is the "Talbot" at Oundle of the great public school. It is purely Elizabethan. Or at Towcester (pronounced, of course, "Toaster") is the "Pomfret Arms" that was formerly the "Saracen's Head." It dates from the Restoration period and is mentioned in *Pickwick.* (Slurk and Pott met there.) The atmosphere of the hotel is strangely aristocratic. Even the chairs in the bar are (or were once) like little thrones for their distinguished occupants.

A man could otherwise choose a tour of the loveliest villages in England, and after that Weobley in Herefordshire would surely speed at once to Castle Combe in Wiltshire. Until it was trodden over in our times by film-makers it had no peer for perfection of situation, in a rivered dell and of sedate small architecture. Being off the main roads it could for a long time preserve its rural life intact. Examples of both the larger and the smaller type of English inns are there.

Then it would be difficult to choose between the Cotswold villages. They are of lovely sandstone in nooks of rolling low hills where the lemon and the limegreen fields are divided by drystone walls and the straight lines of what were once Roman roads. The sandstone was fashioned into architectural beauty by a remarkable race of local craftsmen who were brought into prosperous being by the money of a wool trade long since lost now to Yorkshire and Australia. Even the gateposts are beautifully embellished, and there is nothing elsewhere like the mullioned windows of such hotels as the "Lygon Arms" at Broadway and the "King's Arms" at Chipping Campden, not to mention the "White Hart" at Moreton in the Marsh.

Another type of taste would inevitably lead to Grantchester near Cambridge and the "Red Lion" of Rupert Brooke notoriety (no, he was *not* one more Englishman who got caught up in Moscow). Cobham, Kent, is nice also, with one of the most perfect small inns, that "Leather Bottle" where so many literary men and characters have in their time tried to drown their sorrows. (Dickens was, indeed, an avid frequenter of inns. Hatfield in Hertfordshire is another very beautiful village, and the "Eight Bells" there was chosen by the novelist as a hideout for Bill Sykes; while the "King's Head," a noble hostelry at Chigwell [now suburbanized] was the "Maypole" in *Barnaby Rudge*. The "Great White Horse" at Ipswich is not only an excellent example of the Georgian best in old inns, but also features prominently in *Pickwick*. To this day will be seen the statue of the white horse over the superbly plain 18th-century entrance, which was described by this writer as "the stone statue of some rampacious animal, with flying mane and tail, distantly resembling an insane carthorse.")

In England the visitor is always best advised to seek an old inn for food, drink and accommodation (if not for actual sleep). London has some modern hotels, and there are two or three outside the capital, but the English today no longer possess the genius for hospitality that made their ancestors build these "Rose and Crowns," "Blue Boars," and "Cat and Fiddles." The large, new hotels are not only hideous with pseudo-American trimmings, but imperfectly managed by unfortunate, well-meaning people who are no longer permitted to train staff properly.

The guest who arrives in the middle of the evening will be told that dinner is over and often he will find, when he seeks his bill in the morning, that the cashier or receptionist has not yet arrived.

There is more chance in the old inns of finding adequate service still. A tradition lingers on: and in any case the outer shell and genuine interior of many of these places will compensate for the surly behavior and inefficiency of staff.

Perhaps above all the customs of the English inn as a place of accommodation rather than drinking are among the greatest charms of this country.

There is, for example, that almost unique institution, the lounge. Sometimes it occupies part of the lower floor of the hostelry near the front door, and then it quickly degenerates into one more bar. When it is distant from the front door or upstairs then it is far more interesting. It is a large room heated by a single, usually guttering fire, and furnished with many large, overstuffed chairs and sofas, that, in the most ideal examples of the type, are always covered with faded chintz, a motif that is continued in the drapes. Pictures are usually lithographic reproductions of hunting scenes.

The old English custom is for guests to assemble in the evening in this place and hold illustrated magazines in their laps. The pages of these are continually and rapidly turned but seldom read. Occasionally an eye will flicker round the room but will quickly turn backwards and inwards if unfortunately it encounters someone else's eye. Woollen cardigans and shawls protect ageing torsoes against the pervading damp cold until it suddenly becomes quite unendurable and then there is a general and early exodus to bed.

Rarely is a word spoken at these extraordinary sessions, and even overseas visitors are normally overawed into at least an hour's frozen silence. If by chance a human being arrives and talks then the temperature can fall so low that the vascular system of sensitive guests can suffer irremediable damage. Many a man can date his first stroke from an evening spent in the residents' lounge of an English hotel. Maybe an Australian has said something about money or a Californian about God. Worst of all a New England writer on holiday may have said something about sex. The resulting vibrations of disapproval in this dear old place will be almost impossible to resist.

Only one topic is really permissible and that, for some extraordinary, quite inexplicable reason, is the dog. A man or a woman may freely speak in quite a loud voice about even the amatory adventures of (preferably) their toy poodles or semi-naked boxers, and some polite interest will be shown by the assembled company. Certainly there will be no obvious disapproval.

The climax of this strange folk phenomenon was once observed at a hotel in Sussex that had been developed from a former private mansion of the nobility. The place also illustrated another feature of the English caravanserai, namely its increasing tendency to cater for specialists. All the people in that Sussex hotel were ardent dog lovers and had their pets with them. Each car that nosed up the long and odiferous driveway was welcomed by an assault of animals. The house exuded dogs, which rushed towards and barked and snarled at the newcomers, clawing at paintwork and slobbering over fenders. This could be intimidating and even dangerous, till the part-owner of the mansion came out, a large woman who slapped her outer thighs with a whip and shouted: "Dogs! Dogs! To heel!" At which the curs would, quite typically of their breed, subside like balloons from which the stoppers had been removed, and slink away.

(Interpellation by sensible editor of this manuscript: "Long live the cat!")

The large woman wore a faded suit of Lovat tweed, thick woollen stockings, and a shapeless felt hat with pheasant feathers stuck into the band.

The guests at that hotel were all dressed similarly and they obviously shared a common interest in dogs and tweeds, and in dogs and tweeds alone. They were mostly people of the former English ruling class who were now impoverished and living together out of necessity. The lounge that evening was palatial but frayed at the edges. There were about a dozen guests and about two dozen dogs. Every few minutes retired generals would rise creakily and fawn over Cairn terriers. Elderly spinsters looking after bedridden mothers who had discovered the secret of immortality would relate girlish stories of taking him (the Labrador) to the sea for a paddle, or her (the many-dugged Dachshund) to Brighton for afternoon tea.

There was a continual talk about diet, and heat, and worms.

The nice old bedrooms smelt faintly acrid and had suspicious stains on the eiderdowns.

There are specialist inns and hotels in England for fishermen, walkers, collectors of antiques, bridge players, even railway enthusiasts.

One of the last is, or was until recently, in Somerset. It is, or was, a grim, redbrick building that backed on to a main railway line. All night the expresses and the freighters would thunder by, and at the rear windows, in their night attire and dressing-gowns, the enthusiastic guests would stand and make copious notes of locomotive numbers and types. They would attempt to sleep it off during the day, in intervals of drinking pints of beer in the bar and arguing about the technical details of what had once been the most complicated and advanced transportation system of the world.

During that wonderful 19th-century era the new hotels of England were almost all built near to the railways; and it is still possible for a brave explorer to spend completely sleepless nights in these odd places. If he attempts to sleep he will, of course, be driven nearly off his head by thundering roars and deafening whistles and the chain-reaction explosions of continual shuntings.

The hotels for bridge players are, by comparison, quite frighteningly quiet. They are usually to be found in so-called watering places such as Harrogate and Tunbridge Wells and Cheltenham Spa. The guests assemble around the card tables as soon as they decently can, and for long there will be only the soft utterances of such words as "No bid" and "One spade" and "Three no trumps," and "Why did you not establish your diamonds?" Occasionally there will be a bitter altercation, but even that, in England, is conducted in a comparatively soft whisper.

The hotels for collectors of antiques exist in overgrown villages of the strip-development type which by a fluke have acquired several antique shops, more or less in a row. In this profession the snowball principle really does apply, and prosperity follows numbers. Half of the guests in the hotel will be genuine enthusiasts and the other half will be dealers who constantly travel in search of new sources for their stock-in-trade. The man who started it all in the village is normally a cabinetmaker or metal worker or potter, and in sheds at the rear of his establishment he employs many skilled men to make the antiques which the other dealers and the collectors seek.

There should, of course, be no recriminations about this. It must be remembered that the England of two hundred and more years ago was a very small place, infinitely smaller than even the miniature England of today. Since time and the depredations of Americans have completely denuded the country of its genuine old furniture and pots and pans and watery pictures it is a good rather than a bad thing that a whole industry should secretly have developed for their period replacement. Wherever there is a lot of antique shops there is usually a large-scale wholesale faker, providing in an ugly age the objects of beauty for which humanity has always had an unsatisfied hunger. This may indeed be the most vicious commentary on the present age, that for objects of beauty to be acceptable they must at least appear to be old.

High up on the Pennines in such counties as Derbyshire and Northumberland, and of course in that extraordinary Lake District, are the hotels for walkers, mainly old-fashioned individuals who dress as if for 19th-century voyages of exploration, and who delight to carry in their capacious pockets slim volumes of verses by such poets as Matthew Arnold and A. E. Housman, as well as ancient and battered volumes of the late Mr. Muirhead's *Blue Guides.* They are usually school teachers, librarians and journalists, and if ever the world is destroyed by nuclear warfare they will probably be the last survivors, as they have such strong boots and an infinite capacity for taking physical punishment.

The hotels for fishermen range from diminutive inns on the banks of the expensive ditches called trout streams to large establishments by the greater rivers and the ponds which the English call lakes. Basically the equipment is all the same, comprising glass cases of stuffed trout, grayling, pike, tweed hats with colorful artificial flies stuck in them, often ominously large brass scales in the muddy hall, and characteristic contortions everywhere as the fishermen engage in their chief form of healthful physical exercise, which consists of stretching the arms and hands wide apart to indicate the monstrous size of the one that got away.

Sometimes excellent fried fish will be served in these inns, from deep freezers and originally caught off the distant coast of Iceland, and just occasionally it will actually come from the local stream, if and when some village boys or poachers have been at work there with bent pins and garden worms.

The point about all these specialist inns and hotels is that the visitor can feel intimately at home in them only if he shares the interest of his fellow guests. He will discover what is a major feature of English social life, the parcelling off of most people into quite exclusive little cliques.

A most interesting holiday could indeed be spent in England by a man who knew absolutely nothing about and cared even less for dogs, fish, health-giving walks, faked antiques and the noisy remnants of railways. He would enjoy the wholly delightful sensation of existing during his stay in a complete social vacuum. There would be no need for him to talk to anybody and most certainly nobody would talk to him. He could play the part of the completely uncommitted visitor from another planet, or, even more than that, he would be the true invisible man.

One item of equipment he would need to bring with him, however, or he might never survive the experience and return again intact to his homeland. This must be some form of electric heating appliance of the bed blanket type with an elaborate range of plug adaptors. Without such an appliance he would probably freeze to death in one of the English bedrooms, which are rarely heated from a central source and in many cases are not heated at all. The Englishman throughout the ages has sedulously toughened himself for empire-building and fighting hopeless wars by spending his evenings crouching over a low fire of smoky coals and then rushing up to a bed chamber designed like an antique refrigerator for instant freezing of all exposed parts of the human anatomy. He undresses quicker than the people of any other race and throws himself into a large, soft bed and instantly pulls several old blankets and a fat eiderdown over his quivering body. This might be good for him. It has had its results throughout history—notably the red that once covered the world map and the very large Victorian families leading to the present-day English pre-occupation with sex as one of the more permissive sports—but it can often be quite fatal for the unwary stranger.

Always place the electric blanket in the bed, switched on, at some time before retiring to rest. And preferably undress while actually in that bed. The contact of bare feet with linoleum floors, and the exposure of bare shoulders to drafts from windows designed never to shut properly, can indeed shock the system most dangerously.

Some of the better-organized hotels do try to help. They provide gas fires which can be operated by the placing of a coin in a slot meter and the lighting of jets with an enormous and frightening explosion. Alas, the coins required are often unavailable because of the introduction of the new decimal currency, or the jets cannot be ignited because old-fashioned long wooden matches are temporarily lacking in the locality. Then the more sensitive visitors must lie awake all night wondering if they have turned off the tap the right way and they are not being slowly gassed.

It is thus a great and memorable adventure, this contact with the

English hotel or inn. The best are the very old because they have the charm of age, and the way to endure their undoubted discomforts and idiosyncracies is undoubtedly to spend most of the time in the bar.

The drinking habits of the English are as weird as anything they do. In the southern part of the country they are concerned mainly with spending as little money as possible; in the north they have been evolved for the opposite purpose.

The southern Englishman enters a bar nervously always and gets out again as quickly as he can after he has slaked his desire for alcohol and local gossip mixed. To assist himself in this endeavor he has throughout the ages initiated and passed draconian laws about the hours when drink can be sold. The foreigner must understand that this is the explanation of why the bars are rarely open in England when he wants a drink, and of why they start to close immediately he has started to enjoy himself. It will also partly explain to him why, in a crowded bar of London or Sussex or Kent the narrow backs will be almost ostentatiously turned towards him when he enters.

There may be a climatic reason for the social parsimony of the southern English. The weather can be muggy, compared with the north (as a result of the influence of the Gulf Stream drift), and this can induce such a feeling of personal well-being and complacence that charity is submerged. The soil is almost too rich and these parts have been free from real invasion for nearly a thousand years. Kindness and generosity are products mainly of harsh climates, poor natural resources and a difficult struggle for living.

There may also be a snob reason. Southern England has never ceased to be anxious to acquire the manners and customs of its aristocratic Norman conquerors. This is a costly business, so a man cannot afford to spend so much on drink as his less pretentious northern cousins.

Maybe it is just that the southern English, being the tough last to arrive in the country, are by nature mean, not only in the English but also in the American sense of the word.

The people in the north are completely different, as if they belong to another breed. When they enter a bar everyone turns round and shouts "What will you have?" The alcoholic hospitality is not only immediate. It is excessive. As for the licensing laws, they mean little and are openly flaunted.

The teetotaller should therefore spend most of his time in the south to be comfortable; and the man who likes good fellowship and the drowning of sorrows in drink should spend his English holiday largely in Yorkshire, Lancashire, Northumberland, Cumberland and Westmorland.

To enter the bar of an inn near London or the Channel coast is certainly better than to enter a lounge or bedroom in the same establishment. It is warmer and at least provides some interior heating after a time, even if there are no rocks for the Scotch and a double of the same is so sparse for over half a dollar that it scarcely covers the bottom of the glass.

But the people are not really friendly, no matter the brave efforts they often make to be so; and their attitude does seem to be: I must pretend to be sociable but not for long. Otherwise it would be too dreadfully embarrassing for all concerned, wouldn't it?

It is possible to walk in the street with a southern Englishman and to see a mutual acquaintance on the other side. The Englishman will turn his head and mutter: "That's old Jones. Remember the months we spent together in Vietnam?" Then walk on, rapidly, without so much as waving across to the former buddy.

"But why, why didn't you shout to him? Is something wrong?"

"Good heavens, no. But, well, people always feel embarrassed when they meet each other in this country. Most of us would much prefer not to be recognized. I suppose there's a kind of exquisite sensibility involved."

For the man with complexes and inhibitions and a dreadful, pervading shyness, southern England is therefore the place. You enter the bar of the "Red Lion" at something-or-other Sodbury and order a large beer in total silence and pay for it yourself and sip it gently and distastefully while listening hard to mutters that come round the tweedy backs on either side. These mutters mean nothing at all. It is a completely foreign language, certainly not English as taught at high school in San Diego. If you can take it perhaps you will order another large beer afterwards and clamber up to your bedroom with a reeling head to sleep instantly and sottishly with mouth open snoring. Two pints of English country beer are enough for that if you are not used to it. But you will never look back on the occasion as a really successful evening. You will have only the memory of a short, dangerous stay in the midst of a potentially hostile, very foreign and completely uncommunicative tribe.

On the other hand you will not have been forced to come out in the open as a human being and display yourself. There will have been absolutely no embarrassment—and it will all have been done at a minimum of financial cost.

No rudeness; no roistering; just good manners, unfriendliness and an absence of real life.

Of course there are exceptions. Many northern men have come south and in any case some isolated districts are as friendly as any in the world. But the foreigner will soon agree that, generally speaking, the south of England is not half so genuinely convivial as the north.

An extreme example of the northern difference is provided by a curious enclave of the land known as Furness. This occupies a promontory between the sandy estuaries of several Lake District rivers, but it belongs to industrial Lancashire rather than the pastoral and tourist-haunted Lake District. There is beautiful mountain and marine scenery and some remarkable historical remains. But the main town, Barrow-in-Furness, is still a perfect example of 19th-century industrial urbanism, a period piece that should be visited by all students of social history.

Far from everywhere, right at the end of the railroad, this clanging seaport contains several of the great engineering enterprises that temporarily made England's fortune after the Industrial Revolution, notably the shipbuilding yards and armaments works of Vickers-Armstrong, but also steel and iron foundries, timber yards, paper mills, flour mills, oil installations, paint, wire and clothing manufactories—and breweries.

The gentle rain falls and the old-fashioned electric lights in the streets could still be gaslights. The ghosts of trolly-cars bump past and men wear cloth caps. Clogs are not far away. Pubs on corner sites are still like Victorian gin palaces and always the dark, satanic mills are pointing to the Promised Land. There is a pervading odor of hops, soot and fish-and-chips.

Whether Barrow will survive much longer is an open question. The basic industries of the place, thanks to inefficiency and the bloodless revolution of the workers, can surely not compete forever with the modern installations of the south, let alone with the cheap importations from more vigorous industrial youngsters such as Australia and Japan. Barrow is not a western ghost town yet but may soon be.

Therefore it should be visited as a remarkable period piece, an isolated entity of Victorian industrialism. The raw and teeming population is not composed of Furness people but of immigrants from all parts of the north (and from the West Indies and Pakistan also) who came there during the last hundred years in order to earn higher wages than could be obtained in bitter country districts or under the enervating tropic sun.

The visitor is not advised to stay in Barrow itself. Two or three days of walking in the town will be sufficient to slake his sociological ardor. He will know enough. His best plan is to find accommodation in one of the quite well-appointed drinking inns that exist in semi-countrified suburbs of the place, such as Rampside.

The bars in such places do not open when they are allowed to by the laws of distant London. They open when people have stopped working, and during the long weekends they are open most of the time including complete nights. The stranger descends to the big drinking lounges and soon has several glasses on his table—they like to sit down for serious drinking in these parts, probably because the women participate equally with the men—all of which have been paid for at once by folk he has never met before in his life. If it is a Friday evening the session can be continued until the small hours of Saturday morning. And it can be renewed before and after Sunday dinner in the middle of that day.

Of course the stranger must take his turn in "shouting" drinks for the entire company from time to time, but there is absolutely no feeling of an eye for an eye and a tooth for a tooth here. It is assumed if a man does not pay his turn that he has no money; and immediate sympathy for him is expressed in the form of more drinks on his table.

Some of the old hands have their private pint mug and pour each new drink into whatever the contents, the resulting mixture being, towards the end, a potation too deep even for tears.

The chief of local police will be there, long after official closing time, and the church minister (if he is to be any sort of success in the district); and young men, the sons of small shopkeepers, after educational sessions at important universities in the south, will be drinking side by side with real characters such as deep sea pilots, garbage collectors and women who scrub the floors of the mills.

Sooner or later someone will start to sing and a choral session will continue, off and on, right through the alcoholic night, songs of the former peasantry in these parts, of the Deep South in America, of Hollywood, of Edwardian and First World War London, of the Jazz Age and the final era (at time of writing) of the Beatles and the Rolling Stones. It is the folk art of the modern people, whether in Zurich or Philadelphia, Sydney or Brooklyn (with, however, a basically American background, the ultimate cultural heritage of a shrunken world).

Yet the behavior of these simple people, apart from the singing, is essentially unmodern. It is wholly alcoholic and as such belongs to a former, nearly finished age. Whereas in London or Baltimore such a drinking session would inevitably end in far more dangerous sports than drunkenness, here there is comparatively little recourse to drugs and to sexual perversions. Of course such roisterers get sexy, but only in a bucolic, Bruegel way. Their prolonged beer and whisky sessions do not end in the ritual murder of a complete society. It is a "wholesome" and not a noxious thing ("wholesome" being the perfect Victorian word for this perfect 19th-century place).

Best of all are the local stories told and increasingly embellished during each succeeding bout of good fellowship.

Thus a crowd of them were driving home from the pub in a small van or truck. The driver was skilled as they all are with machines in the north, but reckless and well-fortified with strong alcohol. The road was typically narrow and twisting as it mounted and descended the local green hills known as "fells." Seen from the air that road would have looked like a snake in the throes of an epileptic fit. And in this particular part there were no stone walls, only small hedges of thorn.

They came down one hill at full tilt and the driver did not notice that the road abruptly curved to the right. He drove straight through the hedge, bumped across a ditch, and sped clumsily but surely over the rough tussock grass of a paddock. None of them realized what was happening till they were in the middle of a herd of cows, and then one of the brighter characters observed that it was a strange hour for cattle to be on the roads.

Thus they drove right across the field, and then they bumped across a ditch again, and once more burst through a hedge—to regain the road at the other side of the loop.

They scarcely noticed they were on the road again, and reached their homes and tumbled into their beds beside grumbling wives, quite oblivious of the feat they had performed. But one of them had a vague memory of the occurrence next day, and drove back along that road till he found the hole in the hedge and then the tire marks right across the wide field, and the hole in the hedge on the opposite side.

He was the man who took part in local car trials, and whose wife devised a system whereby he could find relief from the pangs of micturition without stopping the car at vital moments. This involved the use of an empty tire repair outfit tin with a sharp edged lid. He was using this when he had to swerve to avoid a flock of sheep, and the resulting closure of the lid, according to local gossip, was the cause of much sorrow not only to that wife but also to a considerable part of the female population in the district.

Yet in those crowded and bibulous sessions they were still talking quite learnedly, some of them, of Furness Abbey nearby, broken archways of red sandstone in a deep valley of the peninsula, the so-called "Glen of Deadly Nightshade," which was founded by Cistercians from Savigny in the year 1127, and of how Romney the painter lies buried in St. Mary's churchyard of Dalton, and of Cartmel with its medieval houses, and lonely Cartmel Fell Church of the three-decker pulpit and quaint epitaph to Betty Poole.

And if a man comes to write poetry in their midst, as he must, then they will listen to him.

5

Shakespeare

If there is one thing that the English have more of than any other people, it is poetry. Whether that is something to be proud of is an open question. People with poetry, to the majority of mankind, are queer. If not queers, they are rarely very nice, in the conventional sense of the term.

But undoubtedly it is poetry more than anything else that leads men into impossible positions from which they cannot retreat, to self-immolation, supreme achievement, and the stars.

The poetry in the English was never better exemplified than during the sequence of the film *The Bridge on the River Kwai* when the sick soldiers in the hospital rose from their beds and followed the tough little officer to the whistled strains of *Colonel Bogey* (an essentially obscene song in their version).

The poetry in England will be immediately apparent to the sensitive observer as he surveys the misty fields and hedgerows and the half-tone skies, as he comes across exquisite small churches amid great lowering warehouses, as he watches young people risking their lives on narrow roads in tatty old sports cars, as he reads the bizarre history of a people who enter world wars without any preparation whatsoever and start gigantic welfare states when they are virtually bankrupt.

The best of this country thus includes very prominently its tendency to make a rare song about everything, or its almost divine faculty for elevating the everyday into the transcendental. A motel in the States is just a motel, and brash at that. In England it is strangely beautiful or extremely and viciously ugly according to taste.

When the truck drivers continually wave one on as one passes them dangerously on the old-fashioned two-lane roads it is poetry of a kind; and the way the young people started to dress themselves and wear their hair after the virtual collapse of their industrial economy in the sixties was socially just a sad, sad song both to commemorate the brave days lost and to cock a snook at the imponderable future. The girls suddenly became the whores of a dream and the boys became Byrons, rear admirals and Western baddies all mixed up. The most popular film in the England of that time was *The Sound of Music,* because it represented impossible aspirations on a wide screen, and the second most popular was *Bonnie and Clyde,* because it showed mixed-up kids going down fighting and laughing at themselves in the process.

It might indeed be argued that the entire idea of the United States of America today is just one more product of the English poetical genius. All races have contributed to the American dream or nightmare but the underlying values of the great new society are as English as is the highly poetical language of the people; the frontier tradition, the concern for the underdog, the remorseless drive higher and higher.

The actual poetry of the English, as written in books and songs, exceeds in bulk and quality that produced by any other people. Only the ancient Greeks and the modern Americans had and have an output that can be remotely compared to that of the English. The actual written poetry of the French, Germans, Italians, Russians, Spanish and Japanese is a drop in the ocean of the English-speaking peoples (an ocean which began in ancient Greece).

The fact that the English in the second half of the 20th century seemed temporarily to have lost the art of writing and appreciating book poetry has nothing to do with the wider historical observation that is being made in this chapter. Orchards can be fruitless and fields can lie fallow for a season and it is often better so. Meanwhile any good bookcase continues to reveal what has been the greatest single achievement of the English, the supreme poetry that reached its greatest height in the work of one overbearing man, William Shakespeare.

The English have not been particularly good as artists, certainly not half so good as the Italians, French and Dutch. Constable and Turner attempted, not without influence upon the world, to make pictures from the illusive face of their country. Blake momentarily saw the face of his God in his less sane periods, and Hogarth was a jester whose social commentary can still be endured. Many minor people such as Crome and Bonington discovered how to perpetuate their pale native landscape in watercolors. In modern times such sculptors as Epstein and Moore followed the European and American methods of reproducing the essential ugliness of their age in plastic form but softened the impact with typically English poetic minds.

Similarly the only music from England that has definitely influenced mankind has been poetic folk-song. Elgar and Delius wrote big music in the European tradition but always with a lack of complete conviction and neither of them with a tenth of the fiery spirit and technical virtuosity of a Bach, Mozart or Beethoven. Nor did either of them express the spirit of the English people, particularly the people of the north, half so well as the cheap popular composers of folk ballads in Liverpool and London of the so-called Beatle era. The summit of English musical achievement has really been the nice but unsophisticated noises made by military and dance bands and by singers for the teenage market, with rhythm and sugary sentiment as the mainstays of the composition.

It is perhaps when art descends to craft that England has been most effective in its human contribution. The whole Industrial Revolution, from James Watt to Frank Whittle (the true pioneer of jet propulsion), is foremostly a tribute to English ingenuity allied to high poetic vision. And this came to especially fine fruition in what is now known as the communications industry, one of the great founders of which was that William Morris who, in his own words, found the domestic crafts of his nineteenth century age to be "sick unto death," and who stripped the worst wallpaper from the Victorian drawing-room. His method was to revive the purer designs of an earlier day. The patterns of his textiles and decorations, his needlework and jewellery had a lasting influence in America and in Europe, finally producing the strange revolution in taste known as Art Nouveau. And his printing and book illustration set a completely new standard for the books of all nations.

This was indeed a peculiarly English department, in which the only effective rival ever was Germany. From Caxton, through the obscure printers of the Shakespearian folios, to the early newspaper makers and the later publishers of London, the craft flourished and still flourishes. Even in the present international day a man who wishes to make books either studies what England is doing or comes to England. The original newspaper methods and advertisements were devised here. Watt's first steam engine, applied to printing, produced the original *Times,* great grandad of all self-respecting news conveyors.

An English inventor named Foster devised rollers for inking the type; one named Nicholson discovered how to do the actual printing with cylinders. Konig the German came afterwards. Applegarth started the real steam-printing. A Scot invented the stereotype.

The modern newspaper, for better or for worse, is an English invention, but, more than that, the tradition of reliability and sobriety which is behind all good journalists began and was chiefly cultivated in the English press (while many of the worst features of modern journalism have come from elsewhere). Similarly the craft of broadcasting in its most sober and reliable aspects is essentially an English development, thanks largely to the work of that great Reith who virtually created the B.B.C. as a public corporation without strings. The Italian Marconi had an Irish mother and an English workshop. David Hughes invented the first microphone and received the first wireless message on it. John Ambrose Fleming invented the radio tube or valve, and then the coherer (which led to Marconi's magnetic detector), and John Logie Baird (admittedly a Scotsman) invented in England the first practical system of television. England actually gave to the world its original television programs.

The newspaper, the modern book, advertising, power-printing, broadcasting, television—the cinema! Well, that last-named is surely an American invention at least. It is not. Lumière, of France, Jenkins of the United States, and Skladnowsky of Germany took out patents in 1894 and 1895 for systems of moving photography. Long before that others such as the Englishman Muybridge and the American-Frenchman LePrince had experimented with primitive systems, but the original patent of the true English father of the cinema, William Friese-Green, is clearly dated June 21, 1889. Edison invented his kinetoscope in 1891 and claimed that it was the original, but his claim was finally set aside in an action before the United States Supreme Court, which labelled the poor Englishman as the only inventor.

Friese-Green was an unfortunate man, who lived and died in poverty, because he had no money sense, only a dominating engrossment in his work. His key discoveries were the celluloid film and the sprockets at its side. He shut himself in his bare room one day and tried to create a clear film. He did not emerge from that room for a week, during which he burned half the floorboards to keep his pot of glue-like substance boiling. When he emerged the clear celluloid film was in his hand. He took his camera to Hyde Park Corner, October 1889, and produced the first true motion picture.

It was fitting that an Englishman should father this new craft, for modern photography had itself been largely developed in England. The first sound picture, although not the first practicable commercial system, was demonstrated by Cecil Hepworth in 1908 (Hepworth also being the maker of one of the first silent films in several distinct scenes).

At least that is how the poetic English look at it. They genuinely think that they were first in everything and that they are the most important people in the world still. It is a natural poet's way of selecting facts to support his secret aspirations.

But every Englishman and not a few foreigners know that there is absolutely no doubt at all about Shakespeare save a small underlying uncertainty that he ever existed.

The immense corpus of plays, and the great number of sonnets, and the one or two long poems do exist, and constant reading and analysis of them has, in many countries, been one of the chief factors turning youth against education. Consider such a marvellous knitting-together of English words as "Three April perfumes in three hot Junes burn'd/ Since first I saw you fresh, which yet are green/ Ah! yet doth beauty, like a dial-hand,/ Steal from his figure, and no pace perceived . . ." It is rhetoric of a grand order and is heady to read, yet to the unfortunate child must mean nothing at all save ineffable boredom. Shakespeare is "words, words, words," most of them double Dutch save to the most receptive and scholarly mind.

All the same he did occasionally say things that have continued to inspire mankind ever since: "Shall I compare thee to a Summer's day?" "When to the Sessions of sweet silent thought/ I summon up remembrance of things past." "Take, O take those lips away." "Golden lads and girls all must/ As chimney-sweepers come to dust." "O mistress mine, where are you roaming?" And: "Once more into the breach, dear friends, once more;/ Or close the wall up with our English dead."

These indelible lines, dug from the great and tiring mass of wonderful words as rubies are tumbled from the gashed side of a marvellous mountain, have sent men willingly to war and saddened long generations of philosophers. They have sustained lovers and invoked the homosexual's brackish tears.

Not only did the writer called William Shakespeare create the English language in its present form by revealing all its possibilities; he was the true father of the novel, the play and the film, not to mention their final apotheosis in the television soap opera. His plots still exhaust most of the possibilities of human nature. He is to other writers as is the sun to the moon; they are only his pale reflections.

Shakespeare's plays were re-born miraculously in his mind from a study of ignoble old ones. He took the Hollywood of his time and placed it on Parnassus. Simultaneously he fused the various parts of the old English languages into a rough, gleaming whole; and he created characters that went out and comforted the world because men recognized themselves in them. Hamlet, Falstaff, Othello, Lear, Macbeth, Henry V, Prospero, Caliban—they were the main types of human beings from Scotland to China and Russia to the deepest heart of the Brazilian forest. Shakespeare was, and is, a universal.

Yet he was produced by a people so often sneered at by others as a nation of shopkeepers.

We do not really know what he was himself. The biographical facts are so sparse as to be suspect always. It is possible for ingenious people to prove that he was a native of Stratford-on-Avon in Warwickshire, yes, but they have also been able to demonstrate with almost equal validity that he could have been the Earl of Southampton, Francis Bacon, Lord Verulam, or, indeed, a Russian.

But this is how the English like to think he was: His father was perhaps a prosperous wool-dealer, in the little country town of Stratford and was sued because of the mess he made in the street with his dunghill there. The boy got into local trouble for poaching or worse and ran away from the girl who had joined him in a shotgun marriage. In his will he left her only his second-best bed, but hers was the revenge because Anne Hathaway's cottage near Stratford is today a real money-spinner thanks to its attraction for visiting, matriarchal Americans.

He came to roistering London and held horses outside a theatre, then acted hack parts and did the Elizabethan equivalent of script-writing for as much money as he could get, which he saved carefully, and sent back to his native place for the eventual purchase of a fine gentleman's house there. He was not content until he obtained a share in the theatre where he worked, and he went on making so much money from this (but not from his plays and poetry as such) that he could retire at the age of about 46 to lead the life of a country squire, the ambition of all Englishmen from the Norman Conquest to Charlie Chaplin (whose similar target in Switzerland was an old country house in gracious grounds with black iron gates surmounted by gilded knobs).

The local Beadle or chief parish officer outside the cottage of Shakespeare's Anne Hathaway near Stratford on Avon in Warwickshire.

This final idyllic life of his ambition lasted only about five years, during which the supreme poet seems to have written only a few letters of expostulation about sales of corn and livestock to equally choleric neighbors; and then, at the early age of 52, he died. His grave is in Stratford churchyard, with a characteristically cryptic inscription about a curse upon anyone who disturbed his bones, but when the grave was opened by some curious folk in a more irreverent age it was found to contain nothing.

If a William Shakespeare did exist in Stratford he was an English-man all right, there is no doubt of that: one of those typical English-men that neighbors can never understand: the merchant and poet combined, the musket in one hand and Bible in the other. Englishman the hypocrite to his enemies, Englishman and godlike superman to his admirers.

Visit Stratford-upon-Avon with avid interest because it is a town that has been imagined rather than consciously built. The celebrated birthplace of Shakespeare is a modern invention largely designed like Reno and Las Vegas to catch the suckers. (How Shakespeare himself would have liked that phrase, and indeed all of the lovely American inventions that have brought the old language of England to vigorous life again in our time!) It consists of red-brick, restored buildings that are largely new on the forgotten foundations of the poet's humble town, and most of these just want money for souvenirs, food and drink and the kind of English hotel accommodation that has already been described in another chapter. The long-distance buses arrive at the "Birthplace" and disgorge their package tour hordes with cameras.

At least the American visitors have subconsciously discovered how to put the place in its place by the characteristic speed of their arrivals and departures. They come, switch on their Japanese ciné-cameras, switch them off, and almost instantly go. It is a marvel of the transatlantic hustle which still, in spite of all disappointments, is the greatest redeeming feature of the new people.

The sensitive visitor is best advised to seek an inn or small hotel in a country village near Stratford. The elm trees and sad hedges will be around and the rooks will be building their nests in the high boughs over against the squat Saxon church tower, from which solemn bells will toll the inevitable passing of the hours. In the sanded bar of the pub there will be raw beer and games of darts and shove ha'penny played by lineal descendants of Quince and Bottom, Bardolph, Pym and old Jack Falstaff himself.

It will be possible to walk down narrow lines to the rusting gates and collapsed walls of some great house where once a family lived that so aroused the young poacher's ire that forever after he lampooned them disgracefully in his immortal plays.

There is the great castle of Warwick the Kingmaker, one of the finest in the world, in the constituency represented later by that Anthony Eden who, at Suez, finally broke the English spirit about which the poet had sung so supremely well. "Let the four corners of the world come and we will shock them." Washington and Moscow said "Stop," and an England that Shakespeare would certainly not have recognized came abruptly to an end. This other Eden!

There is Leamington Spa with the nice bow-windows and stuccoed pilasters of its Regency architecture, but only the phantoms left of the Empire-builders who once retired here for the bridge-playing reward of their long dedication to an essentially other-worldly idea— the pacification and education of those who were not born with their advantages the whole world over.

There is that huge and squalid city Birmingham, part of which is Shakespeare country (with factories where the Forest of Arden formerly admitted the illicit love of Rosalind and Celia). It once supplied half the globe with guns, pots and pans, silver-plate, bicycles and articles to be sold to tourists in Mexico City and the isle of Capri as genuine local antiques. Now it is dying, dirtily, noisily, and may with any luck soon be verdure and forest groves again.

There is the hideous modern theatre at Stratford, like a Hitler bunker or a play factory of the grotesque mind, where half the modern film and television stars get their initial training in the art of acting a part wrongly, and where the fabulous dramas are presented in trappings that were certainly never intended by the genius himself.

There are swans on the river Avon but choking weeds also, and the thatch on the beamed cottages is filled with mice and fungus because the men who once knew how to renew it now prefer to work in nearby automobile factories and strike as often as possible because why shouldn't they?

Shakespeare and his legionary imitators established England's pattern of life for a long time to come. Artists are at once true mirrors of their age and distorting mirrors. The distortion provides the pattern for the future. The artist is a sentimental fool. He has no knowledge of real life. The picture he paints is idealistic and other-worldly, showing things as they are but also as he would like them to be. People stare at these pictures, or read these books, or watch these films, or listen to this music, and then begin to model themselves on the new, false pattern.

England was a Shakespearean land for a long time, and the best or the most interesting parts of it is still a place where men think they know their place or, at least theoretically, would be willing to kill for love or hate. Innumerable suburban tragedies are still set to the grand, tragi-comic pattern. The colonization of America, the conquest of India, the opening-up of Africa, the triumphant wars against France and Germany; they were all accomplished by men who were still playing parts on the Shakespearean stage, noble parts, villainous parts, but fustian all the same. And constantly justified to themselves and to the world in such rhetoric, Shakespeare-based, as no other language has ever known. Winston Churchill was the last Englishman to strut that way. When his country was on the verge of final defeat he ranted like Henry V before Agincourt; and there were still sufficient Englishmen left at that period to fulfill the minimum requirements of a shooting script.

Meanwhile, however, a great change had been taking place in the ideals of the people. Once again the artists or poets were responsible, those of the 18th century with their prim intellectualism and finally those of the 19th century with their all-time high in literary hypocrisy.

The Shakespearean age had its last fling with Churchill and the Battle of Britain but was already finished. England had acquired other ideals from its artists, those of the Cambridge laboratory and the Victorian diningroom-cum-parlor. These were increasingly to be influenced by the dollar philosophy of the American Northeast and Middle West and of its dream-child, Hollywood.

Therefore a visit to England today can be very disappointing if confined to the conventional runways. It is on the face of it now a dying, drab country, enlivened by the grotesque protests of the very young. The adults think only of getting by with the least possible effort, wanting to be regarded as better socially than they are but universally unwilling to do the necessary work to attain that ideal. Heroism is a back number, and marriage, and divorce; and even the deadening but sometimes exciting pruderies of the Victorian age are out-of-date.

This is of great importance to the English but does not mean much to the man who visits their country for pleasure. He has his own, even worse problems at home. He wants to be happy on holiday, and, if possible, inspired by what he sees so that when he goes back home he can make things better there.

What remains of the better, more inspiring England of Shakespeare should therefore be sought out carefully. Some of it might still be found in the Barrow-in-Furness that has already been described, or in the country inns here and there. And there is the Forest of Dean.

It is a curious, comparatively unexplored area that occupies some high ridges above the north bank of the river Severn, stretching from the Gloucestershire farmlands up to the black mountains and green valleys of Monmouthshire and Wales.

It is a region of primeval trees and of cottagers' glades and of sad ugly towns that once got that way thanks to the proximity of coal mines. These mines are now nearly all worked out. Most of the miners have long since departed for the better money and inferior life of the Midlands industrial areas. This is not a new thing. Once before, some 1700 years ago, the Romans similarly abandoned the area after briefly working it for iron. There is indeed something about this forest that rejects development as a healthy body rejects cancer. Like the rabbit it may well survive when all else has gone, the rabbit and the ageless fern.

There was a cottage at Pleasant Stile, Littledean, on the edge of the forest above one of the most beautiful scenes in the world. Far below this cottage to the south lay a prospect of descending farmlands and trees and then a great river in the shape of a lyre. It was the ancient Severn, named from Sabrina, sweet fluvial goddess, and its curious curving course at this point was conditioned by certain strange geological features of the land. Anyway, it was possible to stand outside the pink-washed cottage (with the hollyhocks and the fat, fruited trees) and stare down at this broad, silver snake so far away, at the beautiful shape of its eternal questionmark, and at the fringy cliffs of Awre on the left, and, everywhere around, what another poet described as the colored counties, the fields in patchwork and the lacing trees, the spires of churches and (at that time) the cottonwool smoke of trains, leading to the high Cotswolds, and, far left, to that magic hill called Bredon which cannot be mentioned without poetry at once flashing like a flame in the scholar mind.

But the forest lies behind the cottage and grassy rides thread it like waft lines in a carpet, leading the walker onwards as if upon some quest of Arthurian legend. Lo, and the trees break to reveal an embowered cottage with tall chimney smoking. A nymph in the garden glances like a deer and vanishes into the dark interior. A cur-dog lifts his mangy head and howls. An enormous man comes out, with arms like steel bands, and he advances threatening. It is the flaming tinman or worse. He says "Marnin, sir, nice day it be for the taties," and then holds some conversation about village and county cricket.

The forest walks of Dean continue almost interminably thus, till the Speech House is reached.

The building dates only from Carolinian times, somewhere between

1630 and 1685, and is a piece of Williamsburg dropped in this improbable place, but the site and its customs and traditions go back to the earliest inhabitants of this land. It is like the Rütli meadow in the heart of Switzerland. Democracy did not begin here. Democracy, the rule of the people by the people, is one more crazy idea that never really got started. The Swiss peasants of Rütli thought they were going to rule themselves but have always been the slaves of Austrians, French, international financiers and themselves. Consider how the great democratic society of the United States of America so soon became the prey of gangsters and the Tammany Hall system, then finally of the television shyster and the commercially guided poll.

Similarly the Court of Verderers and of Free Miners at historic Speech House in the Forest of Dean was never anymore than a sop to the people, bestowed regally by the true London rulers of the land. The local men would meet here and rule themselves, which meant making respectful recommendations to distant masters.

But the place, like all abodes of impossible dreams, has a certain romantic aura, not at all disturbed by the folksy trappings of the modern hostelry that now occupies the old building. It is possible to stay there very comfortably and daily to have the illusion of happiness during those interminable and soft-gliding walks down the forest rides. In Speech House Wood are the huge holly trees, and Spruce Drive is equally evocative of what the poets created in ancient England, impossible tasks self-set by perfect, gentle knights: ideal, ideal, ideal— and absolutely no reality whatsoever save the floods that yearly isolate the nearby city of Gloucester without so much as a hand being raised to prevent them, and the awful decrepitude that has overcome the once-great houses and estates of the region, the jewel-set Flaxley Abbey where the last aristocratic owner had to serve his one-time tenants as their milkman, or Westbury Court that once had the finest formal water-garden in existence, till the Welfare State and the weeds came.

All is lovely for the antiquarian and the poet; and for the sociologist it is a cobweb land of the sleeping princess, rich of soil, mild of climate, and awaiting the inevitable coming of the awakening prince and his more vigorous, less stupid people.

At Newland, where the forest suddenly falters at the western prospect of dark Wales, there is an oak tree with a girth of nearly 50 feet. It must have been there before Shakespeare or America were even thought of. The church is famed for its "Forester" slab and table-tomb.

Then at English Bicknor on the northern edge of the forest is part of Offa's Dyke, a great earthwork constructed by Offa, King of

Mercia, to protect England from the Welsh that England feared because it had wronged them. This was some 1200 years ago; and the Dyke originally extended 100 miles from the River Dee to the Severn at Beachley. It can be seen also at such sweetly named places as Mansell Gamage, Lyonshall and Bridge Sollers.

The remaining people of the Forest of Dean still live by strange, outmoded Shakespearean precepts of behavior. An old coal miner with bristling white moustache was regularly given a lift by car up the steep hill to his village and would always ask at the end how much he owed for the ride.

The Cotswolds opposite are equally Shakespeare country but the memories are buried deeper and more often overlaid by the meretriciousness of what modern man always does to nice places if he has the chance. Cross the great Severn plain and mount the escarpment to Broadway, once England's loveliest village which at a certain stage in her career became a tramp. She is superficially perfect, with such tinted and unified stone architecture of mullions and pointed eaves as not even a Disney at his slick drawing-board could possibly conceive. All this illicit love is conducted in the most perfect of taste, but illicit and commercial it is. Nearly every building of the large village accommodates a man or woman who came there from afar for business purposes and is just after the visitor's money.

The other main Cotswold showplaces are less obviously whores, but all live now by selling their charms (whereas they originally sprang from the stony land to accommodate successful wool growers and merchants and, for hundreds of years, were genuine emanations of the vigor in man). Perhaps the most impressive is Chipping Campden. The tall and dormered houses are miniature cathedrals all. One of them, Grevil's House, was the original home of the wool merchant whose progeny became kingmakers as well as Earls of Warwick. But Campden is strangely dark and even gruesome beside, for example, Bourton-on-the-Water, which spans the busy little river Windrush with many almost Venetian bridges. The sun shines often here and lemons the delicate fields around. There is always the sound of water and anglers at the inns. The architecture is once again so perfect as to be almost unendurable. It can move a soft man to easy tears and the hardest have been known to blink.

Winchcombe is not much of a place now save for the architecture and pubs such as the old Corner Cupboard Inn and the George with its pilgrims' gallery, but it was once the capital of a Saxon kingdom, and then the seat of a mitred abbot and capital of a shire. Hailes Abbey, nearby, for hundreds of years made money out of pious pilgrims who came to see its famous relic of the Holy Blood of Christ. Sudeley Castle, up the road, was the home of Catherine Parr, that remarkable woman who survived Henry VIII's bed, and it was reduced to its present ruinous state by the cannonballs of Oliver Cromwell. Spoonley Wood near the castle has the remains of a Roman villa, and Belas Knap, above it all, is a neolithic burial place where many skeletons have been found dating back to the days before England was so much as an idea.

Stow-on-the-Wold, Moreton-in-Marsh, Cleeve, and then the southern Cotswolds leading down to Stroud and Cirencester, they all present at least relics of the England that is still the most interesting and stimulating to know, a country of high if impossible ideals, and of unimaginable plagues and squalors, and of a singing poetry always in the very way of life whose fallow-period today is the true tragedy of a once-great people.

Stroud is ugly, but not the West of England broadcloth made in its dark tributary valleys, where the mills peep above trees quite coyly and keep their feet foursquare in the water whose power originally made them. A visitor should always hasten to buy these fine worsteds while they are still made. They are among the best industrial products of a fast-vanishing England. If Shakespeare came alive again he would recognize them, and it is certain that, whoever he was, he roamed hereabouts and found names and customs and ideas to fructify the basic ideal of what was once a nation.

6

London

There are three cities. The first is the West End, the second is the East End, and the third is Greater London or the suburban areas. Normally the tourist knows only the first, which, for the sake of convenience, can be taken to include the commercial City and some outlying places such as Greenwich and Hampton Court.

Thus the tourist is guided like an animal to Buckingham Palace, the Tower of London, Westminster Abbey and the Houses of Parliament, to several Wren churches and to the National Gallery and the Tate and the Victoria and Albert and British museums. He walks in Piccadilly and stares at the statue of Eros, and he shops in Bond Street and Regent Street and Oxford Street, and he listens to the subversive orators in Hyde Park.

These things have come to be done so automatically that they are almost meaningless and usually a disappointment. The tourist posters in the travel agencies of San Francisco and Melbourne are infinitely more attractive than the reality, thanks to the development of color photography and offset-litho printing.

The fact is that London cannot be regarded as a beautiful city architecturally. It possesses some masterpieces of architecture, usually hidden away or overshadowed by monstrosities, but as a whole, as a city, it is ineffably squalid and lacking in good architectural taste by comparison with Manhattan and Paris, even Rome, and especially Amsterdam. The styles are too mixed and there is overmuch cheap and nasty Victorian and Edwardian building, even in the grand places. Trafalgar Square with its Nelson Column, once the heart of an Empire, is a very good case in point. The column is all right, and the

open space, and the Landseer lions, but all is spoilt by the buildings
that surround the square, that squat National Gallery like a sooty cruet
dusted with salt, and then a series of inelegant commercial structures
encrusted with tasteless decorations, with bird lime and with the
hideous metallic skeletons of electric signs.

Most of central London is like downtown Brussels only unfortunately much bigger.

It was not always so. Before the Great Fire in 1666 the city was
more or less homogeneous. It must have appeared like a small town
in remote Herefordshire or Shropshire today, with half-timbered buildings mounting to fairy-tale roofs and here and there a Gothic or
Romanesque palace and church.

The Great Fire after the Plague was very like an act of God, or
at least a justification of the Malthusian law of population. Malthus
maintained that the natural order contained a built-in check against
over-population. When there were too many creatures of any kind
they were brutally cut down to size by disease, war or some great
physical disaster.

Before the Great Fire there had been the Plague in London and
England. This had checked the population in a very big way. And
if some deity like a cosmic sanitary inspector had been watching he
might well have started the Fire to destroy the germs afterwards.

The Fire started in Pudding Lane and ended at Pie Corner, a fact
that gave true Londoners much cause for satisfaction during long
generations afterwards. The grandmother of the present writer, a
Londoner, continually advised him of the strange coincidence, as if
it had possessed some transcendental meaning.

It started in a baker's shop of Pudding Lane, which till then had
been traditionally the street of food shops (probably right back to
Roman times) and altogether it destroyed 87 churches, including the
original St. Paul's Cathedral; also dozens of public buildings such as
the Royal Exchange, the Custom House and the Guildhall; and the
total number of houses burned to the ground was 13,200, occupying
some 400 streets.

It was at the time the largest fire ever known (statistics not being
available of Nero's similar godlike effort to purify Rome). Most of the
houses were made of wood coated with inflammable pitch, and they
nodded their heads together like old women in the narrow lanes; and
in the immediate Pudding Lane area were many warehouses filled
with oil, pitch and tar, wine and brandy, gunpowder, wool, and
wooden building materials. The blaze rapidly became so intense that

it actually crumbled the stones of buildings such as St. Paul's. The noise was quite deafening to a spectator such as the diarist Pepys, who, in intervals of burying his wine and the Admiralty papers in a pit dug by order of his friend Sir William Batten, could note how the fire over the city was in the shape of "an arch of above a mile long," making such a "horrid noise," "the crackling of houses at their ruin."

Evidently Pepys stayed up all night watching and helping, but in the morning he put his bags of gold and his plate into a cart and drove off to Sir William Rider's at Bethnal Green, now a squalid industrial district of the East End, then a place of fields and cows and fruit trees. Apparently there was little loss of life, because at that time the people were not organized to fight for their possessions. They just fled before the flames. They did not return with fire brigades to put them out. Two hundred thousand of them camped in Moorfields alone, then a bosky pleasant haunt, now a drab area of bricks and mortar.

The principal tragedy was in loss of houses, furnishings and stock-in-trade, but this was mitigated by loss of records. No taxes nor debts were paid in the ensuing year because all documents had been destroyed.

As for the new London that was rapidly built, the people were delighted with it. One of them wrote: "The new buildings are infinitely more beautiful, more commodious, more solid."

But this was a contemporary judgment and, as such, quite erroneous. Most of the rebuilding was done in a short four years of hectic, cheapjack activity. And it turned out to be the most curious mixture of mock-historical and modern trash that the world had ever known in one small place concentrated. It established what is basically the London that horrifies the architecturally sensitive today. The overriding style was meant to be that of ancient Greece and Rome and, of course, no style could be less English. To this day a tender observer feels uncomfortable when he comes across a fish market designed like a temple of Diana or a Christian church in the shape of a heathen place of sacrifice. It is a cold, rigid, pompous style, made for semi-Asiatic emperors and not for grey English skies, milky sunshine and an essentially unpretentious but rough people.

By a miracle one of the exponents of that style, Sir Christopher Wren, happened to be an architectural genius. His new St. Paul's Cathedral, and many small churches, also Chelsea and Greenwich Hospitals, rise above the folly of the style and are magnificent in their own right as expressions of his soaring mind. When Wren used

*Sir Christopher Wren's magnificent St. Paul's Cathedral in London, with
Scott's historic polar exploration ship "Discovery" in the foreground.*

brick he was particularly felicitous. It is a fact that the most attractive
English building is in the native brick, save where, as on the Cotswolds,
a local stone is the right medium.

Anyway, London became a dismally dull city aesthetically after
that tragic Fire—dull, but freed at last of the Plague germs which
its now-fried rats had for aeons carried.

Modern London—the central city part—was created by jerry builders after the Great Fire, but also by Sir Christopher Wren and his

architectural disciples, by John Nash, the Victorian and Edwardian jerry builders, and by German bombs during the Second World War.

The outstanding influences for good were those of Wren and Nash, the last-named being a Welshman from Cardigan, born in 1752, who served his architectural apprenticeship under Sir Robert Taylor, a good old follower of the by now quite debased Wren classical school. Nash himself inherited money and at first led the life of a country gentleman, but lost much of his fortune in speculations and was forced to

St. Paul's Cathedral, London, one of the few complete masterpieces of neo-classical English architecture.

come to London and practice his trade. By a chance, the fact of his "gentility" and "good connexions," he met the Prince Regent, that compulsive builder whose Brighton activities have already been described. Thus he obtained contracts more or less to remodel much of central London, his first important work being the transformation of the old Marylebone Park into the modern Regent's Park region. Here Nash adopted the Adam brothers' Edinburgh principle of uniting several houses or buildings with a single stucco façade. Plaster was his great weapon, and, imposed on mock-classical orders, it produced an effect which, by the sheer force of his energy and opportunities, is still quite wonderful in the mass.

Architecture, like human beings and ants, is always successful when sufficient of the same-minded are gathered together. The skyscrapers of New York, individually cheap and nasty often, are immensely successful and even beautiful in the mass. John Nash, with the Regency power and money behind him, could destroy whole areas of central London, and the monotonous stuccoed rows with which he replaced the old buildings were effective by sheer force of numbers. But at the door of Nash also lies the responsibility for so much of the drab ugliness of northern and western areas of central London that were designed in Victorian times by less talented disciples who were working for cheap, mass-production builders.

Again acting on princely instructions, Nash projected the Regent's Canal; and it was he who was eventually given the contract to drive a thoroughfare through London's most congested shopping area so that the Prince Regent would be able to proceed easily from Carlton House to the new park. The result, old Regent Street with its famous quadrant, embodying as it did the architect's favourite principle of the continuous façade, had an unfortunate career. It was actively disliked by most Victorian Englishmen because of its plainness and monotony. But the loss of it has been bitterly regretted ever since it was pulled down and replaced by the present uninteresting if inoffensive conglomerate of buildings, largely in the pastiche style of what might be described as post office classical. Only the majestic curve remains of Nash's grand idea.

In 1815 Nash was appointed architect, valuer and agent to the Board of Works and Forests. Commissions from the Prince Regent included the complete remodelling of old Buckingham House into what is now known as Buckingham Palace (still "Buck House" to the true Londoner). This building has since become an idea rather than a royal home. Scarcely anyone who walks up the superb—the chancefully superb—Mall to the broad place where tourists and pigeons gather to quiz the sentries and stare through the tall railings in a hopeless effort to get a glimpse of the godhead, scarcely a man or woman among these ever looks at Buckingham Palace with a critical architectural eye. Which is just as well. The building is an elongated box with pseudo-classical decorations, and succeeds only by its size and by the aura of power that still surrounds it.

During his work on the Palace Nash designed a triumphal arch for the main gates. Maybe "Prinny" did not like it. There were, however, so many objections that the object was removed to the north-eastern corner of Hyde Park and became the famous if fundamentally unimpressive Marble Arch. This stands where once the malefactors were left to dangle from Tyburn Tree, a stone's throw now from "Speakers' Corner," where modern enemies of society are allowed to talk their heads off without let or hindrance. England is justly proud of this curious institution and much of the world wonders at it. But it should be remembered that London has been the wealthiest city in the world and as such can, or could, afford luxuries.

The Haymarket Theatre, the Gallery of British Artists, Suffolk Street, the Church of St. Mary, Haggerston, the United Service Club, Pall Mall, and the east wing of Carlton House Terrace were among other buildings designed by the perspiring Nash. They wear well if strangely. Somehow they are not quite English. Yet they are as pleasing as anything in London, a sad commentary on the architectural genius of the English in the 19th and 20th centuries. The lampoonist put the matter succinctly when he jibed at Nash:

> Augustus at Rome was for building renown'd,
> For of marble he left what of brick he found;
> But is not our Nash, too, a very great master?
> He finds us all brick, and he leaves us all plaster.

The Brighton Pavilion represented the terrible summit of the Nash-Prinny collaboration; but, on the other hand, some of the Brighton terraces and squares and crescents by followers of Nash are superb, and we must forever thank this architect for his virtual creation not only of sweet St. James's Park in its present layout, but also of our modern concept of town-planning in the mass, of ruthlessly destroying then building up a city quarter again as an organic whole. The man died in 1835, after which came the deluge. Modern London is architecturally just a mess, and even the odd islands of surviving Nashdom here and there are strangely beautiful compared with the hideous rest.

What London could have been like if the aesthetic taste of the people had not faltered after that Great Fire is shown by two buildings, the lovely little Tudor palace of St. James, and the surviving half-timbered houses from the pre-Fire period in Holborn. These have been restored again and again but are still completely English and beautiful.

The best of London's West End is not architectural but in certain unique trappings of the place, such as the buses and the taxis, the tailors of Savile Row and the picture dealers and hatters and shirt-makers of St. James's, the huge acreage and comparative safety of the verdurous parks, above all the sense of being at what was once the center of the world. It is, like Paris, a place for the luxurious spending of money, but, unlike Paris, is not a place in which it can be equal fun to be a poor and struggling artist. It is a city of the Bisto kids, two slum children who in old advertisements for a gravy powder were depicted standing outside a restaurant and sniffing wistfully at the emerging odors. Really to enjoy it the visitor should bring a lot of money to spend. He cannot walk about and be happy in London without spending liberally. This is not because prices are higher than elsewhere. They have always been rather less than elsewhere. It is because the best of London is the quality goods and services offered.

There is a hatmaker in St. James's which still makes the most elegant men's hats in the world, and which has occupied the same drab little shop since 1759. To some visitors it will look as if absolutely nothing has been done to that shop since 1759. These insignificant premises and completely old-fashioned methods enjoy a world-wide export trade, but if a customer is not instantly known by name when he enters after an absence of years then he is entitled to feel aggrieved, and to take his custom rather ostentatiously elsewhere.

This is the city of international specialists, the snob shops of the world, auction rooms that obtain the highest prices for the most important treasures, arcades of windows where only Wedgwood is sold, or Russian icons, or new sporting guns, or cardinal pictures. There is, or there was for hundreds of years, a unique regard for handmade quality in central London.

Alas by the time these words are printed the compliment may be out of date. The trend of the age, even in central London, has been so vigorously away from the tradition of individual craftsmanship that what has been written here may be largely a memory already.

Many people come contemporaneously to London to look for what they have been led to believe is the new avant-garde contribution of the place to human pleasure and progress, namely the "hippy" clothing and other articles of adornment offered in King's Road, Chelsea, and Carnaby Street off Regent Street. Such seekers after cheap sensation are usually disappointed, finding these teenage fashions to be largely American in origin. The sartorial customs of Las Vegas and the Hollywood Strip have been adapted to English conditions and the youngsters did for a time strut around as if dressed up for an Edwardian charade. At a time of national disaster they assuaged their sorrow and bolstered up their pride by desecrating the finery of their strong ancestors, wearing Lily Langtry picture hats and scarcely no skirts, wearing the uniforms of Victorian admirals—yes, often the real uniforms, brought down from the mothballs of box-rooms—with marijuana cigarettes between the defective teeth.

It was a curious phase, to be succeeded by perhaps the most unimaginable of revolutions.

The London taxi is without compare, a true descendant of the hansom cab that clip-clopped through the gaslit fogs of Sherlock Holmes and the Edwardian stagedoor mashers. It still has the characteristic odor, compounding cigar smoke, petrol fumes and feminine scents, that to the returning Englishman from African jungle or Californian clearing is always an incitement to a weird joy which, indeed, passeth all understanding. It is still essentially a horse-drawn vehicle only with a motor engine, and there is nothing else like it in any other city known to man.

It all began with a Mr. Joseph Aloysius Hansom, who in Victorian days suddenly brought together several ideas, based on the original "hackney-coach," an unsatisfactory vehicle as described by a writer in the *Monthly Magazine,* 1825:

> Nothing in nature or art can be so abominable as those vehicles at this hour. We are quite satisfied that, except an Englishman, who will endure anything, no native of any climate under the sky would endure a London hackney-coach; that an Ashantee gentleman would scoff at it; and that an aboriginal of New South Wales would refuse to be inhumed within its shattered and infinite squalidness.

The time had come for one of the sudden leaps of civilization. The notion of the *cabriolet de place* was brought from Paris, and the day of the hired coach was over; but this startling vehicle—it ran fast on two wheels, and the driver perched on a queer seat between the body and the offside wheel—was not yet perfection. Passengers sat uncomfortably under strange, box-shaped hoods, which earned the name of "coffin-cab"; and at any moment an accident to horse or wheel or shaft might pitch everybody forward into the dung-beslimed and cobblestoned road.

To remedy these defects the "omnibus slice," "duobus" or "backdoor cab" was invented by a Mr. William Boulnois. It consisted of a box, upon two wheels, with room for two passengers facing each other inside, and a seat for the driver on top. Unfortunately the backdoor favored the old and dishonorable practice of "bilking," as is illustrated in the story of the sportive young peer who set out to prove for a wager how easy it was to swindle a cabby. He hailed one, and directed him to Kensington. Then he secretly left by the backdoor, to observe with glee the cabby's rage and consternation. But as the cabby was returning to town, the young peer unobtrusively took his seat again, called out, and asked what the driver was doing, leading him so far away from his destination. The poor cabby was unable to answer for astonishment, turned round, and once more travelled the Kensington road. But when he arrived there his fare was gone again. Convinced that he was the victim of supernatural forces, he whipped up his horse to get back home as soon as possible. At the last moment he could not resist one more peep into the cab, and there was his noble passenger again.

Thus Mr. Hansom's opportunity had arrived. His was a square vehicle, with wheels seven feet six inches high, taller than the body, that had a door at the front and driver's seat just above the door. He drove it from Hinckley in Leicestershire to London, greatly diverting the countryfolk, who gathered at crossroads to throw cabbage-stalks; but in the metropolis he sold his patent to a company for £10,000, then worth about $50,000.

Unfortunately Mr. Hansom, like most great innovators, was essentially a fool. He never received all his money, and the first cabs of his invention were failures on the road, being ruined by many faults of construction. Hansom just knew the penury and distress that comprise the inevitable price of immortal fame; and his invention was taken over by a Mr. John Chapman, secretary of the Safety Cabriolet and Two-Wheel Carriage Company. With great ingenuity Chapman corrected Hansom's mistakes. He placed the driver's seat at the back, but fixed a sliding-window in the body, to communicate between the cabby and the passenger; and he so constructed the framework of the front part of the cab that it rested on the ground when tilted forward. Fifty of the new cabs were placed on the streets and within a short time they earned a long-lived popularity.

Not that the invention of English coachbuilders was exhausted. The four-wheeler was an early competitor of the hansom, then the Clarence —more familiarly, the "growler"—and Lord Brougham's preference for these vehicles and his choice of a specially designed one eventually gave them his name. By contrast the hansom became the choice of youth and dashing disreputability.

There was never anything to equal the hansom at the height of its glory. Its exterior, said one delighted mid-Victorian, "is as glorious as the sun and as many-hued as the rainbow." Hansoms darted about the streets like fish, decorated in primary colors as startling as their proprietors could obtain, and picked out in the strangest devices: gorgons, porcupines, unicorns. Time blackened and sobered and at last demoded and antiquated them; but their music is in the lines of an English poet, and they are part of the endearing period furniture of the last true English novelists, Hardy, Wells, Bennett, Galsworthy. Their outline may still be faintly seen in the strange, unique London taxi of today, and in the race of men apart who drive them.

The year 1833 was eventful in England, where it signalized the passing of the Reform Act and the first Factory Act, to begin the breaking of the power of the aristocratic rulers, and the abolition of the slave trade—and the invention of the first motor bus.

The word "omnibus" has not today the splendid sound that it had then. It was coined, according to legend, by a French proprietor of horse-drawn diligences, who borrowed it from a little grocer in his town. This man of enterprise was named Omnes, and had painted over his shop the words "Omnes Omnibus." The coach proprietor borrowed the happy thought straightway, calling his passenger vehicle "l'Omni-bus"; and it was heard of in England and adopted by coachmen there.

Today the term "bus" means different kinds of vehicle in America and England. But the English usage is the more correct, applying to public vehicles that provide regular transport in city and suburban streets, and it really dates from 1833 when another great original man, called Walter Hancock (again from Stratford, that birthplace of genius) placed on the road an uncanny coach without horses that travelled at a rate of ten miles an hour as driven with a continual hiss and roar by a steam-engine.

Hitherto there had been omnibuses, yes, but they had all been pulled by horses, fine, flashing vehicles, bright with paint, patronized by ladies and gentlemen, and rarely approached by the common horde save in wonder. Fortunes were made by their proprietors. The finest horses in the land were chosen for their gaudy shafts and polished traces. What a gay scene it was at the "Angel," Islington, of a bright summer's morning, as Mr. Wilson's "Favourites" were lined up in readiness for their triumphant journey down the City Road to the Bank and onwards merrily across the river to Elephant and Castle!

Hancock's invention of the steam bus was to alter all that, but not immediately. His first two vehicles, curiously called "Era" and "Autopsy," did frighten the horses all right, but failed signally in driving them off the road. The "Era" ran a regular journey from Paddington to the Bank, carrying fourteen valiant passengers for sixpence apiece (expensive for those days) and consuming its eight to twelve pounds of coke and one hundred pounds of water to the mile. There were occasional breakdowns—indeed each one was an occasion for the local populace—but surely the march of invention was not to be stayed by little setbacks like these.

Yet the triumphant progress of "Era" and "Autopsy" was fated to end in temporary ignominy. Maybe it was the fares and the breakdowns; maybe it was just the essential conservatism of the English. Anyway, most Londoners used the steam buses once or twice for the novelty and then went back to the horse-drawn variety.

In vain the enterprising Hancock constructed another and brighter and better steam omnibus, and gave it the ambitious name of "Automaton." This was built to carry 22 passengers and travel at no less than 13 miles an hour. On one extraordinary occasion, with 20 pale observers aboard, it licked down Bow Road in the East End at 21 miles an hour! Even these impressive figures, however, had little effect upon an ignorant nation. A great agitation against the innovator was hatched by proprietors of horse-drawn omnibuses, who hired thugs to strew loose gravel in the path of the portly "Automaton," and otherwise hamper its puffing progress; and this agitation, taken to a venal Parliament, culminated in the Turnpike Act of 1840, which imposed a heavy toll upon "steam carriages."

Hancock took his despised vehicles with him into involuntary retirement, from which he emerged only once or twice to complain of his bad usage and to claim compensation. He had, alas for him, made the mistake of giving his fellowmen something that they had not possessed before. That is obviously the fatal mistake.

But his shade today would gaze down at London in pride indeed.

The central streets are each day almost completely jammed with large, red, mechanical omnibuses. The city is choked nearly to death with these vehicles, the most peculiar feature of which is that they stick together like crystals in mutual attraction, and by some miracle of disorganization are never really there when the foot passenger truly wants them. They are one of the great sights of London, and if not among the most sensible products of England are certainly unique.

After Hancock the horse omnibus had it all its own way till Edwardian times when the first petrol engines were gingerly affixed. Many great companies operated in central London and the vehicles were always representative nicely of the fairground school of popular art until they were nationalized and all became the scarlet same and, like prehistoric monsters, began to slide slowly towards the complete traffic jam of obsolescence.

Central London should thus be avoided by all visitors save those who can follow a map and explore it on foot. Such an exploration is possible, because the center is not very large. But the hard pavements can quickly discourage all save those who are very young and vigorous or who pay regularly for the attentions of a good pedicure.

Otherwise the frustration of taxis and buses in traffic jams, or queues for underground trains, is sure to spoil all the pleasure.

The man who can still walk and follow a map will enjoy the many theatres and concert halls and will find curiosities in London that are rare or completely absent elsewhere. He will linger on Westminster Bridge and still agree with "Daddy" Wordsworth that the prospect around him is at least touching "in its majesty," although he will certainly not agree that "Earth has not anything to show more fair," nor that he has never felt "a calm so deep." The only calm hereabouts nowadays is that experienced by the frequent suicide who leaps from this bridge into the murky Thames water, a single glassful of which, according to legend, is sufficient to poison an elephant.

All the same the sight of the broad and curving river and the brave Pugin pile of mock-Gothic and blackened stone that is the "mother of parliaments," and broad-beamed, very ancient and genuine Westminster Hall, and the barges chugging and the red buses roaring by in their interminable files of frustration, even the new buildings of the post-Kaiser and post-Hitler periods, is strangly stimulating and beautiful.

Why?

The Houses of Parliament are not only architecturally a reproduction: they are a reproduction of something that never was, being, like pre-Raphaelite paintings of the Victorian era, an attempt to pin down a contemporary romantic ideal of what was once the best: in this case the best of the so-called Gothic period. Yet, by heavens, the attempt comes off! It is tinsel, it is sham, and it is quietly and soberly beautiful and, in some strange way, a perfect expression of *parliamentarianism,* that noble concept of the 19th century which, like the concepts of

"Big Ben" clocktower and Pugin's "mother of parliaments" at West-minster, London, together with a red-coated old soldier or "Chelsea Pensioner."

hellenism and chivalry and Christianity and patriotism and even con-
jugal love are already just antiques.

It is one of the most moving buildings made by man, like the Taj
Mahal, and St. Peter's, and the Doge's Palace, and the equally brave,
equally false Capitol at Washington. It represents an idea in stone.

But also it is a masterpiece of architecture as such, the long shape
of it with the two terminal towers of unequal height—so that Big Ben
is not only a clock but also a sentinel standing guard over "democracy" and has his wife at the other end to carry on the good work if
he fails as he must—and above all the use along the enormously
protracted facade of slender Gothic mullions which at once guide the
eye upwards continually and diversify what would be an over-plain
front with the slender ridges of the Perpendicular.

It is a lovely building, most attractively situated, whatever its aesthetic and political falseness. And the strange Victorian architect
triumphed not only over the basic badness of his conception but also
over the fact that he had to erect the building between two of the
finest examples of genuine early architecture in all England, namely
Westminster Hall and Westminster Abbey.

Westminster Hall is now part of Pugin's masterpiece, acting as a
gigantic hallway leading into it, but was built as a banqueting hall
by William Rufus. The first Law Courts of King John were established there, and it was within those cold stone walls that their
enemies arraigned, tried and arranged the judicial murders of such
as Charles I, Sir Thomas More and Warren Hastings.

Westminster Abbey goes back to Edward the Confessor, and was
constantly remodelled by subsequent fond kings, till Christopher
Wren was finally given his job of rebuilding the western towers and
front, classically smearing the lovely English growth of the past.
Inside it is the same. Half the might of England lies buried or commemorated there, but the cold influence of the early 18th century
ruins nearly all with its essentially foreign pomposity.

In the old days there were these two cities, that of Westminster
and that of London. It is easy for a good walker to stroll along the
embankments of the Thames, passing various touching relics of
England's imperial past such as Cleopatra's Needle (so sooty and
unregarded yet going back to the Egypt of some 2500 years ago, and
brought to England most perilously by sea in the 19th century after
being presented to the British Government by an Egyptian crawler)
and soon he will be in the old City. It is almost wholly commercial
and ecclesiastical, that perfect combination for worldly success, and

possesses neither extensive residential population nor real organic life. But on quiet Sundays it is better even than an historic country town for peace and for interest. The great banks and insurance companies rise to the invalid sky above narrow, traffic-smoothed streets of Val de Travers and Trinidad tar. Old golden signs hang outside famous financial enterprises in Cornhill and Throgmorton Street. The Bank of England itself is like a low and lowering fortress of Portland stone; and, opposite, the Royal Exchange and Mansion House give at least the impression of what the center of a Roman city with its dominating forum must have looked like. The ghosts of those original civilizers

Part of London's original Roman wall, with modern American-English architecture in the background.

are still there for those who can feel them, and at least the superficial outline of their architecture—which disputes throughout the City with the ecclesiastic spawnings of great Wren for the privilege of making the many ultra-modern buildings look completely cheap and silly. These were given to London by property "developers" after Hitler had conveniently provided spaces with his bombs, and sometimes they are noble. More often they are just downtown copies of Manhattan

What is left of London's Roman wall again, silently rebuking the transient modern.

without the redeeming height, created so that typists can show their legs through innumerable windows to passers-by and so that window-cleaners can make deserved fortunes.

There is the pitifully-dwarfed "Monument" to the Great Fire, which in childhood it was such a holiday joy to ascend (admission 6 old pence in those days), and many superb "Halls" of the old City "companies" (or guilds of like-minded merchants and manufacturers) and the parent "Guildhall" itself with its excellent, dingy museum of

Part of the ancient Tower of London from the river Thames.

objects from the remote past found locally during excavations; and there are the Inns of Court in the so-called Temple region, where some of the Tudor architecture again shows what London might have been if only England to herself had been true.

The Tower of London finally protects the great city on the east

A "Beefeater," or "Yeoman of the Guard," explaining the Tower of London to visitors.

from marauders up the broadening river. William the Conqueror started to build it in 1078, probably on Romano-Celtic foundations. It consists today of that original White Tower and historic accretions. The visitor will remember many brave men and women and martyrs when he is shown the sombre Traitors' Gate. He will remember such as Walter Raleigh who finally rotted here and was bloodily executed not so far away as a reward for colonizing Virginia on behalf of his bad-tempered Queen and the queer Scotsman who succeeded her. He must indeed have considered at the end: "That's what you get for throwing down cloaks on puddles."

The collection of the Crown Jewels in the Tower will have a certain interest for those who wisely believe that diamonds are a girl's best friend; and the Armoury will provide some inspiration still for people who appreciate that the safety of a society is forever dependent upon well-wielded weapons by men-at-arms, soldiers such as are symbolically represented by the Tower "yeomen of the guard," those burly "Beefeaters" whose Tudor dress and tall pikes with tassels have always endeared them to children and other realists. (It is untrue, by the way, that they owe their girth to beef, which has long since ceased to be cheaply available or even palatable in a debased England. The name "Beefeater" is based on a typical solecism, the vulgar English pronunciation of the French term *beaufetier,* an "attendant at the sideboard," probably the original function of these decorative men.

(Indeed the "Beefeaters'" lot in original Tudor days was not without its fun. A chief duty of the Guard was to make the King's bed each night. During the process careful inspection had to be made for any dangerous weapon that might have been wickedly concealed in the bed linen. First a "Beefeater" had to tumble the mattress up and down. Then another had to run the clothes through his hands. Finally a "Beefeater" sprinkled the ready couch with holy and perhaps necessarily scented water. Every time the poor fellows touched the royal bedclothes, moreover, they had to make the sign of the cross and kiss the particular place. It was a continual process of bobbing up and down.)

And yet strangely enough Tower Bridge across the river will be even more impressive to some unprejudiced observers than is the truly ancient Tower itself. It is, like Pugin's Westminster masterpiece, one more demonstration of the fact that beauty will always prevail over authenticity and the historical beast. If a foreigner wants to draw symbols of London he will instinctively choose the Houses of Parliament and Tower Bridge, perhaps with the 18th-century St. Paul's dome in between, and all will recognize those symbols, even the aboriginals of New Guinea.

This magnificent bridge, one of the world's engineering and architectural wonders still, is essentially a 19th-century conception and product. But its massive machinery may endure when most of the less substantial products of our age are gone, especially if eventually it is sold to America, as it may well be.

The walker in London can penetrate to curiosities that are otherwise rarely attained. He can for example stroll into the East End from this point and know the second of the three great metropolises that come under the generic London name. This has traditionally been, from the earliest times, the abode of the true Cockney. It used to be, not so long ago, a place of raucous cries and whelk-stalls and laboring millions, interlaced with periodic foreign infusions of refugees from Continental oppressions, London's Brooklyn or Bronx. Every shop in a mile-long row would have a foreign name. There was an authentic Chinatown in Limehouse, but overbearingly the real Cockney Londoner was in charge, good-humored, hard-working, dirty and completely without those inhibitions that made the neutrality of the suburbs. He adored the royalty and West End aristocrats whom he so closely resembled in his mind; and he was the redeeming salt in the English dish.

All that changed with the Welfare State and the great colored immigration. On the one hand the East End was largely cleared of its slums and squalor and the people were given the wherewithal to become exactly like their suburban neighbors farther out, in clothes and habits of living. Most of them actually moved out to those suburban areas to become prissy commuters with two-car garages and annual holidays lasting a month in Spain. They were replaced in Bethnal Green, Bow, Hackney, Poplar and up and down the Mile End Road, also over the river up and down the Old Kent Road by refugees from Germany and eastern Europe and overwhelmingly by Negroes from the former West Indian and African colonies and by so many subtle Pakistanis that increasingly the street corners resembled those of Karachi rather than those of Cockaigne.

Thus a man who wants, on arriving from afar, at once to see England *and* as much as possible of her former far-flung empire, can do worse than visit London and spend some days at walking in the East End. It would be a liberal lesson in geography, ethnography and politics combined, although the visit should be made promptly before the scene changes: it is more than probable that one of these days a civil war will rage in these parts, at the end of which most of the colorful immigrants will be dead, unless those unfortunate people may by then have decided that they cannot stand the climate anymore and will most of them have wisely returned home.

One of the greatest and most typical of Londoners was the 18th-century artist William Hogarth. Perhaps he might eventually be regarded as the only great graphic artist produced by England. Whether

A "Pearly Prince" and "Princess," traditionally leaders of Cockney London across the tracks.

he was a true Londoner is another matter. There might be no such breed at all. Second-generation Londoners are not, of course, real natives of the city, and third and fourth generations of the breed have always very rarely survived. Families die out after fifty years in the foul air and amid the ghastly racket, as in New York also.

William Hogarth was born in the actual City of London, November 10, 1697, the son of a poor scholar and author. The child continually practiced drawing when his fellows were playing, and from the earliest age he had only the one ambition: to be a great and distinguished artist.

In order to provide him with a means of livelihood, the father apprenticed little William to an engraver of silver plate, and the boy became highly skilled at executing those cyphers and coats-of-arms, those acanthus leaves and bold curlicews that so nicely decorate old English silver. But young William wanted to achieve more than this. He would spend much of his spare time at wandering around the crowded narrow streets and studying the faces of the crude people there. It became a habit with him to jot down an impression on a finger-nail; and, when he returned home with all his nails thus covered, he would transfer the ideas to paper for eventual use in a picture.

Another employment of the apprentice Hogarth's was book design. His *Hudibras* of 1726, is well-known but not very good. Then he turned in his narrow sparetime to portrait painting, mainly in the form of small family "conversation pieces" as he called them. He did not charge high prices, and so he accumulated a large clientele. Two of his best portraits were those of Captain Coram and of Garrick as Richard III; but, the young man was already developing a fatal trait success-wise: this was a desire to tell the truth. His portraits today are accordingly unique as representations of men as they were at the time, but gradually became totally unsatisfying to those who sat for them and to his other contemporaries. As Hogarth developed this truthful style he increasingly lost the customers he had gained by his cheapness. At last no one could recognize himself in the absolutely faithful portrait that Hogarth painted of him, and this period of the artist's career was over.

His success (such as it was) and his true fame to this day came from the usual chanceful combination of circumstances. First, Hogarth had thoroughly learned the engraver's craft; second, he had become a self-trained observer of the tumescent London scene; third, he had fallen in love with the daughter of a famous man and, being rejected by the father as a suitor, had eloped with the girl.

This was the daughter of the fashionable painter Sir James Thornhill; and Hogarth, forced both to make some money and to prove himself in the father's eyes, had the idea of piecing together his multifarious artist's notes in a series of would-be popular engravings. This was the famous *Harlot's Progress* series, drawn by Hogarth and beautifully engraved by him as a mirror of his coarse age. It was, of course, successful as all pornography must be. Men like art but best of all they like what is to them at the time dirty art. Hogarth by chance had hit upon the infallible prescription for success and fame combined, so much so that the purseproud father was immediately quite reconciled to him as a son-in-law. Ever since the six prints of the *Harlot's Progress* were published in 1734 they have been universally popular, and the same applies to the eight prints of the *Rake's Progress* that followed them in 1735. Ten years later Hogarth published what a typical 19th-century writer described as "the least objectionable of these pictorial novels," the series known as *Marriage a la Mode,* and a reputation had been finally consolidated for every kind of taste.

Alas the artist had the usual inability to market his wares to the best personal advantage. Hogarth thought he could outwit the booksellers and the big picture dealers by soliciting subscriptions himself for the prints as they appeared. As a result he was banned by the trade and earned only some thousand dollars for all his best series. These were copied by forgers, dramatized in various forms, used as motifs on pottery and fan-mounts; and the artist profited nothing. He desperately flogged his Muse; and, with a prolificacy that has seldom been equalled in English art, he turned out picture after picture of his contemporary London society—and at the same time executed a large number of full-scale historical paintings. (Which, of course, he considered his best work. Nothing but envy and ignorance, he would say himself, prevented these major pictures from commanding as much admiration, and as high prices, as the most esteemed productions of foreign masters.)

Hogarth died October 26, 1764, at his house in Leicester Square, from what was probably an excess of spleen, brought on by a violent political quarrel he had had with the demagogue Wilkes.

Thus Hogarth was the typical Londoner and not only the greatest artist of that city. He suffered from the Londoner's inevitable illusion of grandeur and devoted his major energies to his worst work, being remembered for what he despised at the time, folksy, commercial, sex-stuff: the best record we have of what the people looked like and how they behaved then. His was pictorial satire at least as great as the literary satire of Petronius and Swift (and infinitely more just than that of Dickens and his illustrators). In his bold drawing and contemptuous rejection of artistic clichés Hogarth was, moreover, the first of the moderns but infinitely more accomplished than any of them became.

The third great London is the suburban area, but before this is visited the wisely foot-slogging tourist should take a look at some remarkable museums and historic objects which are scattered around the inner periphery of this city like currants in an otherwise stodgy bun. The Albert Memorial and the Albert Hall in Kensington Gore should be preserved carefully forever as examples of the very worst in Victorian taste, although certain modern buildings near them are nearly as bad while lacking the distinction of supreme ugliness. Nearby in Kensington Gardens will be found an example of the early best in London architecture, Kensington Palace of the rosy-red brick and sensible windows and white pilasters—and a most fascinating museum inside, which illustrates the long history of the metropolis perfectly.

Farther downwards in South Kensington are those enormous museums of the 19th century known as the Natural History, the Science and the Victoria and Albert. The last-named specializes in arts and crafts and the others in a plethora of dusty relics ranging from prehistoric monsters to fire engines.

Perhaps the most offbeat museum in London is the Wallace Collection in Manchester Square north of Oxford Street. It occupies lovely Hertford House and exhibits mainly French paintings, furniture and porcelains of the high late 17th- and the 18th-century periods. Some of the furniture is English of those periods and all is representative of heights never attained before or since in any country. It means nothing in an age of levelling down and of mass production and false art, but for that very reason it is one of the best things that the English can offer the truly inquiring stranger.

Another recherché experience is a ride up and down the river Thames as it threads London like a stitch of catgut through some great wound of the land. There are first the miles of squalid and decaying docks and warehouses, fringed by ineffable mud at low tides, then the dramatic voyage through the center from the Pool of London and Tower Bridge to Westminster, after which the stream noses through increasingly suburban regions until it displays reaches of great beauty and historical interest as at Hampton Court and Richmond. Then it becomes narrower and countrified and one of the most beautiful rivers in the world for those who like placidity and mist and great trees trailing, all diversified by weirs that rush and pubs that terrace the moving glass.

Of modern times the greatest inspiration for foreign artists in London has been the Thames, but not the country part with its natural beauty. It is the despoiled stretch between the docks and Chelsea that has fascinated the aesthetic eye from Canaletto onwards, the smoky warehouses and curious bridges, the chubby small ships that breast the turgid stream, the church towers isolate and the office buildings, above all, perhaps, the twisting vistas of an almost unearthly light and shade. There is nothing quite like this anywhere else. The Clyde in Glasgow can sometimes be similar but is more overwhelmingly an industrial ditch. Perhaps the continuous curvings of the Thames are responsible. As Hogarth himself said, beauty is a curve (hence the insistence on life classes at art schools).

Londoners themselves know with shame that they have always missed a great opportunity with the Thames. They should long ago have provided it with elegant buildings and embankments and gardens on both sides like Florence and Rome, or at least massed piles of modern buildings like New York. They should long ago have cleared away the derelict industrial structures of the south bank particularly and controlled the water flow with a barrage to eliminate the unsightly mud.

Maybe. Or perhaps the true charm of London and its river lies in the very absence of plan and improvement, in the muddle, the grime, the teeming life of the place, which is very like a wilderness of architecture and society as opposed to the regularity of a public park.

The parks of this city are again unique. Probably London has more of them than any other place. Certainly they are greener and more beautiful than those of Paris and the great American towns. Hyde Park is the most spectacular, with wide spaces of good grass and what remains of a magnificent forest of ancient trees, the oak, the ash, the elm, the plane and the hornbeam. It still resembles what it originally was, the great estate of a country house; and it has all the traditional features of such a property, the Serpentine lake (where the last of the true Englishmen like to break the ice before swimming on Christmas Day), and the broad ride for horses known as Rotten Row, with statues here and a bird sanctuary there, with lovers under the trees and twirling moustaches on the bandstand of Offenbach and Rogers and Hammerstein.

Then Hyde Park subtly changes when it becomes, to the westwards, that pleasance known as Kensington Gardens, more feminine, prettier, with some excellent baroque statuary and other stonework round the water that leads to the orangery of the Palace. There is the Peter Pan bronze as rabbit-rubbed by generations of small hands in innocent delight. James Barrie, who brought this authentic magic to the place, has naturally been reviled for it ever since, as if he was in some way even a worse pervert than the cultured revilers (whose own brand of permissiveness largely rotted an entire generation of little children). Even more touching is the Round Pond where grown men play with toy boats and around which they solemnly allow kites to pull away high above the trees, the hotels, and the monstrous traffic of animals gone mad. Elsewhere chairs are for hire and a game is frequently played by poor young writers and their doxies, which consists of sitting on the chairs as long as possible before the ticket man arrives, when there is a sudden wholesale departure; and down through rows of rhododendrons and the prime formal flowers beloved of Scottish gardeners walk the uniformed nannies with their prams, although the contents of the prams are seldom English in these days of disaster and even the nannies themselves more frequently come from Stockholm and Jamaica than from Seven Kings and Potters Bar as in the Galsworthy time.

Two remarkable parks ventilate the dead center of the West End. Green Park is small but delicious, falling away from Piccadilly as if in protest at the continuous traffic there, with the windows of the Ritz Hotel at one end and those of St. George's Hospital at the other. It is possible to leave the crowds and the noise and stroll downwards as through a shaven and treed meadow of delight till the quiet shadows that herald Buckingham Palace are characteristic of an entirely different area. As for St. James's Park, a little farther on across the Mall, it is indeed a little poem among parks. The atmosphere of it cannot be clearly defined. It is very small but the politicians stroll there as a relief from contiguous Whitehall. Thickets are haunted by the ghosts of homosexual scandals (where oft the tall guardsmen will clumsily lurk) and the famous pond can be peppered with the most exotic wildfowl. It is indeed possible to feel in this little sacred and profane place that the extremes of life have come beautifully together in what amounts to one beleaguered garden, a Churchill and a pelican in his pride, a memory of scandal and of heroism amid birds. How many Prime Ministers, strolling here self-consciously, must have envied the apparent freedom of lower forms of creation!

This is not only political, it is also traditionally clubmen country. The great men's clubs still exist around St. James's; and for some two hundred years, until recently, all this part was masculine. But today the buildings are mausoleums where once fortunes were lost at cards and newspapers guarded the replete occupants of leather armchairs after interminable luncheons. Some men still follow the old rituals but they are hollow and sentimental rituals now, as in a church. Life has moved on, to the discotheques and the ineffable coffee bars: and indeed the spirit of London's once-mighty clubland has departed with the wars and the revolution, to be found lingering on only in remote places such as Switzerland and Rhodesia and among the carefully collected oddities of California.

Symptomatic of this is the fact that modern Londoners no longer know how to pronounce their own place-names. They appreciate no more that the Mall is the "Mawl" and that nearby Pall Mall is "Pell Mell," nor that both words were derived from the Italianate ball game once played in nearby alleys with mallet and iron ring.

Regent's Park, far north of Oxford Street, has always suffered from being on the wrong side of the tracks. It has all the usual features, including a magnificent rose garden, and, weather rarely permitting, an open-air theatre, but primarily it houses for Londoners the great Zoo. This is a sacred place like Delphi in Greece. It must not be tampered with neither must it be mocked. No people have loved animals like the English, which is doubtless the reason why the poor creatures are so rigidly immured and so lovingly stared at here. An important part of every young Englishman's education is his regular visit to the Zoological Gardens in Regent's Park. Most of them carry away to the ends of their lives a far more vivid memory of monkey's bottoms than of the lovely white terraces of John Nash that circumscribe the vivid green.

London has many other parks. The enormous outer or suburban city is largely built around them. And one of the most remarkable is that great royal park of Richmond which has attracted several conurbations of brick-and-mortar to the west of the metropolis. It covers some 2250 acres of grass and gnarled old oak and other trees, with ponds, and waterfowl, and deer, and memories of regal events throughout the ages. It is possible to walk here and to have the sensation of living in a vanished age of London.

The true modern Londoners live hereabouts indeed, and in dozens of similar suburbs stretching far out into what was once countryside and to the sea at Southend and Brighton. It is a curious life, quite different from that of their ancestors, and not exactly paralleled elsewhere. American commuters go home from cities to distinct communities. The London suburbs are almost entirely dormitories built around municipal parks. And like all bedrooms they are essentially private places for sleeping and breeding and dying. Sometimes they were once real towns, like Richmond itself—a royal Tudor town that contained a principal palace of kings and that was a popular spa in the 18th century—but the interminable rows of little red-brick houses with carefully hidden gardens at the rear have in all cases killed what was once a local life and individuality.

Or it is not so much the dull, stupid and doll-like houses themselves that have murdered local life as the spirit of the people inhabiting them: a spirit which at all costs eschews display and emotion and anything that might give away social origins. The sole aim of London suburban man is respectability, or at least conformity. He is an ant who must be exactly as the others in his hill. When he produces individuals they leave the hill as soon as possible and become real men and women elsewhere. These suburbanites take enormous care not only to wear the same clothes as each other but also to think the same thoughts. If ever there is an enormity in their midst—and of course there frequently is—it is hidden carefully behind the thick drawn curtains of always first-floor bedrooms. What happens up there is nobody's business. Outside is all that counts, and there down the identically similar streets the duplicate and the triplicate men walk at the same times each day to the old-fashioned trains that convey them up to "Town," where they work at an occupation known as "business," consisting of trying by phone and letter to get things done in a world that naturally prefers to play and in our time has been given the full opportunity to do so. Their chief compensation is that they very rarely come in contact with real life.

The suburbs of London represent, like the great religions and the various hobbies and sports of man, an escape from reality. It is comforting, comfortable, safe and quite unendurable to a sensitive or ambitious person, the suburban life: and the fact that the local mental hospitals are increasingly filled with gibbering patients is, of course, one of its epitaphs. Another may be written in nuclear smoke when these quite defenseless areas are finally bombed.

A visitor is not recommended to linger hereabouts lest he lose himself in a maze of sameness and begin finally to doubt his reason. But a very brave man could find some rewards provided he mentally held his nose and left behind him a trail which he could follow back to reality afterwards.

Thus great Richmond Park itself, not only has the quaint old town of its name, with a splendid vista down to the twisty, treed Thames from its terraces (through gardens where a single naked statue still evokes giggles from the local life prisoners) but also has on its other side the Kingston where no fewer than seven Saxon monarchs were crowned. Near the Market Place is, reputedly, the original Coronation Stone; and it is interesting to see how no one ever looks at it, the principal preoccupation hereabouts being car parking.

History follows the Thames out here, clinging to it as if in desperation and to avoid being engulfed by the hundreds of thousands of little houses and the millions of even smaller men. Thus Hampton Court Palace comes next, a roseate Tudor pile with pleached walkways and the memories of peacocks strutting, which still justifies boldly the good taste and solid building of that Thomas Wolsey, son of an Ipswich butcher, who became the wealthiest and most powerful man in England under Henry VIII, a cardinal, a millionaire and a cad, until he slipped up over the matter of the king's divorce from Catherine and was reduced to the most abject penury and miserable end.

Lower Halliford should always be visited after Hampton, because there can still be seen here at least the outlines of what was once the loveliest of Thames-side villages, sufficiently lovely to hold and inspire such excellent writers in the English language as Thomas Love Peacock and George Meredith.

Then once-sweet Chertsey farther on not only recalls a poet, Abraham Cowley but also that Blanche Heriot, who, hearing that her lover was to be executed at curfew time, hung on to the clapper of the curfew bell till the time had passed and a reprieve had arrived.

Egham still sticks his head up proudly in this sea of suburbia because it fringes Windsor Great Park and contains Runnymede and that Air Force Memorial on Cooper's Hill which records the names of 20,456 men who in World War II temporarily rose above themselves and saved their country.

Windsor Great Park leads to the proudest castle in England. This is the heart of the matter, here and down at Runnymede by the river where King John signed Magna Carta in 1215, a document which enacted that no man should be punished without fair trial, that ancient liberties should be preserved, and that no demands should be made by an overlord to his vassal—no *unusual* demands—without sanction of the King's council. The trial business was good, and has remained good ever since, but otherwise Magna Carta meant practically nothing, as does Windsor Castle today and all its brave panoply of flags. The true power in the land resides elsewhere and the liberties of the people have become, as ever, just licenses for their inevitable exploiters, representatives and hired servants.

The actual historic City of London has in these days a population of only a few thousand resident people, far less than it had in Roman times. The vast suburbs of outer London house many millions. They go on, or so it seems to the lost foreign motorist, forever, and basically they are all the same, with identical cheap and nasty shops, and with the values only of respectability at all costs and that curious love-hate relationship with animals that produces innumerable riding schools for young girls (but *not* for young boys) and canary cages and zoos. The only true virtue of them is that from time to time a piece of grit chancefully enters the stupid oyster and produces a pearl, the rebel men and women who, thinking desperately for themselves, are cast out to become leaders outside and internationally famous. But these can never remain at home and be themselves. There are absolutely no indigenous schools of thought or art, or major disasters or great loves or world-shaking revolutions in the London suburbs. There are not even, for these millions of people, good local bookshops or art galleries or antique dealers or brothels with brocaded beds.

They have not ruined their world and they have created so many pretty gardens and well-behaved children, but they have done absolutely nothing else, and to have lived with them is a memory of purgatory.

Consider how the red brick and false oak beams and reproduction lanterns over the prim and cheaply-laminate frontdoors continues deeply south, through all the sullied county of once-lovely Surrey. It creeps like a virus without antidote into the former pristine woods and across what were, during aeons of time, clean chalk downs and heather-tufted commonlands between sandstone rifts with inevitable pine trees. Many beautiful villages remain, such as Abinger Hammer and Stoke d'Abernon (where the church contains the oldest English monumental brass, commemorating Sir John d'Abernon, dated 1277), and it is still possible to stand on a hilltop and survey an agricultural Weald of trees and plenty. But close inspection reveals the human disease everywhere, in the form of the similar, mass-produced houses, the creeping roads and pavements, the municipal control. It is now necessary to probe very deeply into the woods to discover what used to be the true beauty of the land, as into that enclave known as the Fold country: and no one in his right senses would any longer give specific directions as to how that area could easily be found, lest it like the other beauties of Surrey might vanish tomorrow.

Certain oddities should be observed. The new cathedral of Guildford is a perfect example of English architecture at its 20th-century summit, and, as such, incredibly ugly. Woking is not only the pure matrix of all modern London suburbs but has the inevitable reagent set deep within it: an Islamic mosque, built as long ago as 1889 and containing a copy of the Koran presented by, of all people, Queen Victoria. There is also a prototype crematorium here. Farnham has a 12th-century castle and the birthplace of William Cobbett, the radical author of *Rural Rides;* Weybridge has what was once one of the world's most important armaments factories as well as specialized residences for top-ranking corporation executives; Epsom has the Downs where the original Derby horserace is run; but Sutton and Cheam have wholly overrun the traces of that enormous Nonsuch Palace which in Tudor times was perhaps the finest in the world; and it is rarely remembered in quite horrible Croydon that the Archbishops of Canterbury for centuries occupied an almost royal residence there (latterly a school conducted by Sisters of the Church).

The malady now extends its cancerous tentacles into Kent. A typical center, Bromley, is completely identical with what has been described already, save that the writer H. G. Wells was born there (in a house suitably demolished now). Wells was one of the few children of these parts who tried to reproduce their atmosphere in literary form. He and perhaps George Gissing and certainly James Thomson (*The City of Dreadful Night*) were the true poets of modern London until John Betjeman appeared, John Betjeman who once and for all pinned down the triviality, emptiness and wry humor of life in these assembly-line streets.

From Sidcup and Orpington to Beckenham and Bexleyheath there is nothing but sameness superficially. It is a triumph of the mediocrity which has been the principal undoing of modern man. Beneath the surface there are just occasionally those oddities. Chislehurst has, amid its excessive drabness, quite a clutch of these for the observant, ranging from primeval caves to the grave in St. Nicholas's churchyard of that William Willett who invented "summer time." On the common at Chislehurst is not only a cockpit but also a granite cross to commemorate the death in Zululand, 1879, of the son of Louis Napoleon. And the ineffable Louis himself had, of course, come to this London suburb of all places after the cataclysmic débacle of Sedan.

The public school founded by Edward Alleyn in 1619 at nearby Dulwich has had a consistently strange influence upon modern literature, producing not only a great prose poet in the American thriller writer Raymond Chandler but also a similar English romantic in the quite unique P. G. Wodehouse. And Dulwich itself is not a suburb but partly a village which has its own organic life.

Northeast of the Thames lie the archetypal suburbs of Essex. They are the drabbest of all but also the truest. The working population of London originally crept out east, and the real land of Cockaigne is still this way. The suburbs in other directions were developed later to suit those who wanted to pretend they were not Cockneys. But the endless yellow-brick conurbations of Essex, from Romford and Ilford to Southend on the so-called sea, and from Walthamstow up via the Woodfords and Epping to Harlow and then very near to Cambridge, have at least the salt of the original working-class population and of vast successions of foreign emigrés to give them a certain savor. The inhabitants are mainly little men now who still metaphorically wear bowler hats and carry rolled umbrellas and commute each day to the commercial City, together with their ex-typist women and their inevitably white-faced children, but they are little men who can still joke when overwhelmed by disasters and who at least thought they saved the world for so-called "democracy" when the continuous bombs of the Second War fell.

There is Leyton, so squalid, situated in the ultimate depths of sameness and dirt, yet built on the site of a Roman settlement, with the "High Stone" of those conquerors still proudly displayed. Etloe House, once the residence of that great Cardinal Wiseman who won their rights for English Roman Catholics in the nineteenth century, afterwards became a home for mentally-defective girls. Wanstead Flats, an illimitable stretch of tufted grasses in the soggy autumn evenings, and Wanstead Park are sad haunts of local lovers and/ or sex maniacs; while Walthamstow, not far away, once produced George Gascoigne the Elizabethan poet ("Sing lullaby, as women do . . . Full many a wanton babe have I/ Which must be still'd with lullaby") and William Morris the inventor of modern English wallpaper and socialism.

Epping Forest is now a great tract of England's original Robin Hood-type woodland completely surrounded by the suburban disease. It enables the young of the area to see what their world could have been and to be usefully depressed or stimulated by the thought. Perhaps it is understandable that Churchill had his parliamentary constituency here, deep amid the bricks of the Woodfords but always with the wild trees on the fringe. He was supported and given his power during the most difficult days by the sponge-trousered, vicunajacketed men of these parts.

Dickens found Chigwell, not far away, to be the "greatest place in the world." Like most Cockneys at some time or other, he had probably got drunk there. And William Penn learnt at the local Grammar

School how to found one of the most important of the new American states.

Chingford, a typical dull suburb of the area, has a former royal manor intriguingly called Pimp Hall, and was a favorite night-stop for the first Queen Elizabeth when she went hunting in the forest.

Brentwood is a prissy place where only nice people live now (in intervals of working and whoring in central London) but St. Thomas Becket, bold, ambitious and worldly prelate who was of course canonized for his sins, had a chapel there, and the Protestant martyr William Hunter was burned at a local stake. The White Hart Hotel dates from the thirteenth century.

There is finally the northern and northwestern direction out of London, but by now even the most energetic inquirer will surely have had enough. He could, of course, go to Hampstead and Highgate and meditate for hours on the long succession of important Englishmen who have latterly lived hereabouts, important for their outstanding part in the country's ghastly decline and fall. Then in Wembley, Hendon and Finchley he would know only rows of similar dolls' houses and cut-price shops, inhabited and patronized by a race on the verge of self-extinction; and only occasionally would there be evidence of anything else. Even history has left few marks in this human wilderness, save perhaps at Enfield, strangely productive of writers and guns, and at Harrow-on-the-Hill, where the great school of the suburbs failed to tame Churchill and there are memories, quite strangely, of many other outrageous men (such as Byron). It becomes wholly unbearable when the line is extended to Northwood, Rickmansworth, and such places as Amersham, and that Great Missenden where London is finally the stupid tail feathers of its doomed ostrich.

7

Country House

In former days England was a country of a few houses, perhaps developed from old castles or manors, situated in great rural estates on the Roman plan, and of innumerable hovels in which the servant-people lived. This system endured for so long without revolution—as least two thousand years—that it could not have been wholly without compensation for the servant-people. And of course it was productive of nearly all that made England notable among nations and a conqueror of half the world.

In our time the servant-people have at last arisen and the centuries-old system has been smashed. But many of the former estates of the small ruling class remain. Their owners have faltered and lost all power but not all enterprise. Unable to lord it over their fellows any longer they have at least continued to make money—by turning their residences into popular showplaces and conducting the revolutionaries around the scenes of former grandeur in businesslike tours for a small down payment each time. They have developed self-service tearooms in the orangeries and picture postcard shops in the erstwhile halls of armored knights. They have planted zoos in the parks and organized antique dealers' fairs in what were once the gilded drawing-rooms.

These great houses thus provide one of the best and most entertaining means of knowing at least the shell of what England was at the time of its greatness; and a tour of them is recommended to all who want an excuse for moving about the country rapidly from one part to another.

The first residences of the nobility were uncomfortable stone castles,

The ancient Roman bath below the Abbey in lovely old Bath, Somerset.

and it is understandable that only one or two of these have survived
as places for semi-gracious living. Most are just ruins of the type
called picturesque, which means that artists were once able to make
a pittance out of depicting them. Stokesay Castle near Craven Arms
in Shropshire is one early building that has survived as a residence
and is open to the public. There are a moat and drawbridge and much

Bodiam, the perfect Norman castle in Sussex.

medieval tracery, with interesting additions that show how the place gradually became the next kind of private dwelling in England, a manor house. It is altogether one of the most curious historical conglomerations of buildings in the world. The magpie timbered gatehouse with sharp-pointed gables dates only from 1620, but the massive hall, constructed like all Norman buildings in the form of a church, goes back to about 1240; and another separate feature of the edifice, a real castle-like tower, belongs to around 1291.

The manor house succeeded the castle. It completely controlled the surrounding country and inhabitants, and was sometimes known as the Hall and sometimes as this-or-that Court, because the bailiff or representative of the lord would receive rents there and decide disputes. It performed the same functions in the old days as a city hall does today only with a more personal touch. This might have meant that a villein got whipped in front of his family and friends, but it also meant that the lord was in close contact with those whom he ruled, unlike our modern bureaucrats.

One of the few manor houses in England which is still in existence

Dunster in Somerset, a show village, with its castle held by the Luttrell family for hundreds of years.

as it originally was may be seen at Boothby Pagnall in Lincolnshire. It is a very small and insignificant building, dating from 1180, and shows exactly how these first true private houses of the great were constructed: with spaces for the animals, the hay, the implements and the servants on the ground floor, and the lord's or bailiff's living quarters upstairs (reached by an outside stone staircase).

Yet the most beautiful of all English houses is among the oldest— Compton Wynyates in Warwickshire. It goes back to about 1450 and is still inhabited and open to the public. There is a trick here, because the original small manor or castle was lavishly expanded in Tudor times. There are many towers, arranged as if in a fairy tale, with oriel and mullion windows and tall chimney stacks, and the pile is built of such a rosy Tudor brick that it looks like a proud old flower amid the darkling trees and the meadowed green (with yews all clipped in fantastic shapes by topiarists still and such gardens as recall a *Midsummer's Night Dream*).

The high pointed gables of Compton Wynyates contain plaster and timber work, and the entire house is really of Shakespeare's period when Englishmen were not only the poets they have always been but actually translated their romanticism into bricks and mortar (and wooden ships and faraway battles and a socio-economic system that has seldom been equalled since for practical effectiveness).

Next the wise observer would want to wander into the true Tudor period, which was when Italian influence started to daub the parapets and window frames with terra-cotta, and domestic building began to soar high in towers and double stories. Accordingly Layer Marney Hall should be visited in Essex. The remarkable gatehouse was erected in 1525. It is not beautiful but it shows how grandeur was beginning to eat at the brains of leading men. Similar in Surrey is large Sutton Place, dating from about 1530 and very Italianate (but not open to the public at the time of writing).

It was at Haddon Hall in Derbyshire that the Tudor court became a country house in the modern sense of the term. Haddon, built between 1567 and 1584, is rectangular, crenellated, and residential. The gardens rise above it in terraces with balustrades like those of Roman villas. The windows are tall and wide, with twelve large panes to each

One of the earliest types of English country houses, going back to Tudor times or earlier.

mullioned recess. Above rises the Peak; and the Vernon family who built the house were known as "Kings of the Peak." They literally owned the bodies and souls of everyone and everything in a considerable area around the house.

Once they had a beautiful daughter, Dorothy Vernon. She fell in love with Sir John Manners, a relative of another ruling family of Derbyshire who lived at a similar house, Chatsworth. (Still occupied by them, now Dukes of Devonshire, one of whose daughters was married to Harold Macmillan, the British Prime Minister who fell.)

Compton Wynyates, gem of all English Tudor houses.

Dorothy's father knew that he would not have a son, and he did not want his little kingdom to fall into the hands of the Manners at his death, so he told the girl that she could not marry Sir John.

The young people thereupon plotted an elopement, to take place at the time of a Christmas fancy dress ball at Haddon Hall. Sir John borrowed the tattered clothes of an old pedlar and wore them at the ball, masked. But he had a rival, named Gruson, who overheard the plot and, in an excess of jealous rage, found what he thought was Manners in the pedlar's clothes waiting outside the house at the end of the dance and stabbed him to death. Actually the lovers had got away some time before and had returned his clothes to the pedlar. Gruson was apprehended for killing this innocent old man, and the event caused so much excitement that Vernon swallowed his pride— after all, his daughter was damaged goods now—and rode over to Chatsworth to give the couple his blessing. Thus Haddon Hall and its great lands became in due course a Manners possession and helped that family become one of the most important in England.

Chatsworth itself belongs in its present form to a later period. There are still some pure examples of the true Tudor style to be seen, such as Hengrave Hall in Suffolk, which goes back as far as 1525–38, with a west front entrance archway of extraordinary splendor. The entrance is flanked by two bulging towers that are incorporated in the building and that rise to cupolas with much fretful stonework. Above the arch of the huge door is a heavily decorated and curving bay of windows, which culminate in crenellations and triple-pointed eaves with crowns. This building should always be visited because it is absolutely typical of its period, and was probably designed to the same plan as Henry VII's great palace at Sheen. Only pictures now survive of this. Like Nonsuch, Sheen is a memory beneath the suburban blight.

Now it is necessary to go up to Cheshire and Little Moreton Hall near Congleton to see the most perfect Elizabethan house of the half-timbered or Welsh type. It will be quite different from anything else in the overseas observer's experience, an overdone mass of blackened timbers and white plasterwork in between, the sort of house a zebra would build if he had the chance. Like the best of baroque it succeeds in impressing by the very excess of its decorative impact, and is thus wholly unEnglish in the modern sense of the term English. It comes from the heart of some Black Forest of the mind, or it is Oriental or even Melanesian. It bulges in all directions and floors run uphill and walls lean at precarious angles, but the original beams have become ironlike with age and are so wedged together that they never come apart.

And it can be seen that the stone and brick Elizabethan architecture of the south was really an attempt to translate this beam and plaster ornateness into masonic terms.

Elizabethan architecture was like the clothes of the people and the plays of Shakespeare: an expression of exuberance which the English rarely attained again. And it would probably be agreed by a quite impartial cosmic historian that the very best of England was actually manifested in this period. There were miseries, of course, but there

Burton Agnes Hall, Yorkshire, one of the best preserved of original Elizabethan mansions.

always are those in every period: the man who cannot get the third car he wants has an even more acute sense of deprivation than the man who possesses no means of private transport at all. Poverty is not an absolute but a relative thing. To starve is not necessarily more painful than to overeat.

There was, however, little starvation in Elizabethan England, but an enormous sense of achievement, and such high spirits everywhere that houses like Hengrave, and Moreton Old Hall, could be built as a matter of course to remain forever unequalled by architectural man.

Another superb 16th-century house is Burghley in Northamptonshire. It has the characteristic towered entrance as an integral part of the building, whose multifarious windows so nicely slit the local stone. The sky line is so fussy with towers and points and chimneys and crenellations that it made the prigs of the 18th century quite sick to observe it: and that brave Celia Fiennes, whose published *Rides through England on a Side Saddle* took place about 1700, was similarly shocked by the richness and above all the sexual freedom of the decorations within. She spoke of the art displays in Burghley: "Very fine paint in pictures, but they were all without Garments, or very little, that was the only fault, ye immodesty of ye Pictures, Especially in My Lords appartment."

About this time England reinvented the lavatory, a Roman refinement of living lost in the dark ages afterwards. The resounding pioneer was Sir John Harington, godson of Queen Elizabeth. In his book *The Metamorphoses of Ajax* he gave the plans of a water closet he had erected and which was subsequently installed in the royal palace at Richmond. Alas, it was too nice for the English, who continued to use more primitive methods until near the end of the 19th century, when Harington's principles were incorporated in the first ball and flush privies of London and New York.

The 17th century saw the rise of the architect. Hitherto buildings had been erected by their owners or by contractors, according to the principle of copying what had been done before: rather like many suburban henhouses to this day. One of the first great English houses erected according to the plans of professionals was Hatfield in Hertfordshire, seat then and ever since of the Earls of Salisbury, those Cecils who first earned money and power by giving Queen Elizabeth and her dangerous Court the sort of legal advice that they liked. A Robert Lyminge drew up part of the plans, which were completed by Thomas Wilson and Simon Basil. The immense pile cost only some $25,000 to build, and is a lovely home to this day (open to paying visitors certain hours of the week). The interior is craggy with elaborately-carved wood; and the great staircase, in particular, has few domestic equals.

The pioneer architects brought ideas from Italy and France mainly and wedded these to the ornate Elizabethan style of building. The great house of Knole, outside Sevenoaks in Kent and the seat of one more English ruling family, the Sackvilles, became typical of what was eventually designated the Jacobean style, a matter of over-tall chimneys and elaborate decoration inside and out, especially Italian plasterwork on ceilings, around cornices, and, combined with the first imported marble, over very rococo fireplaces. An entirely new style of furniture was designed for Knole to accord with the decorations, plushy and overstuffed and with tassels hanging. The ruling English were rich or displayed their wealth at this period as rarely again. It was not until they got with other peoples to California that they could renew the experiences, and then their "Xanadus" were never much more than corny.

Altogether one of the nicest of the surviving Jacobean houses is

Blickling Hall in Norfolk. It is approached by a wide carriageway
with lawns on each side and then separate wings of servants' cottages,
whose rows of tall chimneys lead the eye towards the central, towered
pile. More austere is Audley End in Essex, somewhat grim above its
pond, whereas Kirby Hall in Northamptonshire was possibly designed
in part by Inigo Jones.

Jones was the first of the great English artist-architects for those
who like the classical style. From his study of the Italian works of
Palladio he did more than anyone else to make the big houses and
public buildings of England look like second-class versions of Roman
forums and temples. Kirby Hall shows this bastard, imported style
to perfection; and really it has remained with the English ever since,
giving their land a forbidding Graeco-Roman character often and
making even Edwardian post offices look unnecessarily awful.

Inigo was born poor in 1573, and, after that advantage, had the misfortune to be sent round Europe by the Earl of Pembroke to educate
himself as an architect. He returned to London and became a stage
designer—some of his drawings for costumes and scenery can be seen
at Chatsworth House—then visited Italy again and became completely
enamoured of classical principles in architecture. His connections with
the English nobility must have been intimate because, without birth
or money, he was appointed in 1615 "Surveyor-General of the Works,"
which meant chief architect to the King and Government. He began
the Banqueting House in Whitehall and the Queen's House at Greenwich, but the King lost his head and his architect was foolish enough
to participate on the royalist side in the Civil War. He never recovered
from this political mistake and so left behind him very few completed
buildings. But he trained many young men, notably his nephew by
marriage John Webb, and Hugh May, and perhaps William Wynne;
and out of his ideas came Christopher Wren and the whole age of
18th-century "reason."

Wilton House near Salisbury in Wiltshire should always be visited
because it was designed by Webb and probably the splendid interior
was Inigo Jones's own work. He was much more successful inside
than out. Whereas the outside architecture of Inigo Jones was cold
and formal and pastiche and foreign his inside decorations were so
superbly Italianate as to yield masterpieces of gilt and white plaster
and painted baroque. The double cube room at Wilton is like the
interior of the abbey church of Einsiedeln in Switzerland, a cake made
for a wedding, but what a wedding!

The great Christopher Wren did not build large country houses, but his pupils constructed many, of which the most typical early example is Eltham Lodge in Kent. Here arrives what is generally known as the "Queen Anne" style, and by a curious chance it has turned out to be the most felicitous in English building. Whereas Wren's Pallidianism, derived from the pioneer work of Inigo Jones and from Wren's own visits to the continent, found its outlet in London churches mainly, the pupils of Wren applied the same ideas to quite small, mainly brick houses and the results are all Williamsburg today. Eltham Lodge consolidated the style forever: a squarish building of modern height in brick with many white-rimmed windows of the sash variety set with white-edged multifarious panes, and a roof rising on all sides above guttering with white teeth to a flat top suddenly but pierced by dormer windows: then finally a mock-temple front with white pilasters and a doctor's front door with brass knocker and an enormous pediment above these imitation flat pillars to break the front elevation of the roof.

It might be noted perhaps that the classical Palladian style in England repulses chiefly when it is executed in stone but looks not so bad in red brick and is almost perfect in the pure "Queen Anne" style of Hugh May as derived from his master Wren. Ramsbury Manor in Wiltshire is a similar prototype of our very best domestic building (American and English) and was probably designed by another Wren follower, the Dutchman William Wynne (or Winde).

The source of the red-brick and white-windowed style is generally given as Wren after Jones and Palladio, but all who know Holland well may prefer to recognise it as a natural transplant from Delft and The Hague as brought over by the entourage of William of Orange.

Other splendid "Queen Anne" or "Wren" houses in England, most of them small, are Mompessom House in Salisbury Close, several buildings in Chichester, Groombridge Place in Kent, Belton House in Lincolnshire, and The Moot in Wiltshire.

The outstanding architect of really large country houses in England was Sir John Vanbrugh, and, like so many successful English, he was essentially an amateur. He moved like an earlier Oscar Wilde in the world of high fashion and became a successful writer of light dramatic comedies. No one knows how or why he became an architect, but he was suddenly responsible for Castle Howard and for Blenheim Palace.

These are still among the very largest houses in the world. To come upon Castle Howard by chance in Yorkshire is like seeing a vision of ancient Rome in the middle of a farm, but a vision truly American in its sheer size. But for those giant dimensions it would be a monstrosity, a house built by a megalomaniac for a megalomaniac: and the strict Italian design is wholly defeated by the grim stone used (all the English Palladians forgetting that the mode was meant to be stuccoed and pink-washed and pantiled under vivid blue skies amid a mess of oleanders with cypresses inditing sharp points of shade everywhere).

Castle Howard chiefly betrays its theatrical origins. The whole place was designed for lordly effect—it had been commissioned by the third Earl of Carlisle—and Vanbrugh did have a nice stage producer's mind. If only he had piled his stones on top of each other in a truly English and not pseudo-Latin fashion! As it is we marvel at the distant spectacle of the place and shudder at the idea of having to live in it. Most of all, perhaps, we admire the superb wooded park as watered by its tarnish lakes and feminized by svelte lawns and brave gardens. There are avenues of lime and beech; and within the Palladian halls of the house are many masterpieces of English furniture, porcelain and silver, as well as some good foreign paintings. (But a visitor would wisely stay at the "Talbot" Trust House in nearby Malton, built, like other houses of the town, in a much lovelier style than the Castle.)

Blenheim Palace at Woodstock in Oxfordshire is not only geographically at the heart of England. It is perhaps the most important of all English buildings. The original Woodstock Palace there was a favorite residence of English kings from Ethelred II to Charles I. "Fair Rosamund's Well" in the huge grounds marks the traditional site of "Rosamund's Bower," where once his sweet mistress was regularly visited by that great Henry Plantagenet who gave England its best laws and wielded his Angevin rule from the Cheviots to the Pyrenees.

So John Churchill knew what he was doing when he chose the site for the estate and great house to be given to him by a grateful nation. He was a soldier of fortune from a family of hunting and shooting squires who proved, in the war against Louis XIV, that an Englishman could out-general the greatest in history. He beat the French and their continental allies hands down in a series of pitched battles—Blenheim, Ramillies, Oudenarde and Malplaquet—which, as demonstrations of strategy and tactics, could stand comparison with the best of Alexander, Caesar and Charlemagne.

Meanwhile his marriage to Queen Anne's favorite woman, Sarah Jennings, had brought him another kind of worldly success, so eventually Churchill became the first Duke of Marlborough with a small fortune granted for the purpose of building Blenheim Palace. It was

Castle Howard, Sir John Vanbrugh's Palladian masterpiece in Yorkshire.

in the Palace eventually that Winston Spencer Churchill was born. Meanwhile the Marlboroughs had allied themselves with the Spencers, perhaps the greatest and most consistently talented of all English families: and there was the extraordinary spectacle, over two centuries later, of another Churchill's saving his country again and with equal brilliance and an even more important personality.

Sir John Vanbrugh was the curious choice once more, for this great work of creating Blenheim; and it must be admitted that the ultimate result proved to be less unfelicitous than Castle Howard. From a distance the Italian origin of the pile is not so evident. It appears like a large school or hospital—which doubtless it will eventually become—and it even looks habitable. It is closer up that the grandiose mockery of the place begins. The main entrance is suddenly revealed as an enormous Roman and pillared portico, of the kind that led the way into ancient forums and that, in a later age, appeared with a flourish at the snouts of railway stations, bourses and fish markets. It is scarcely possible in this delicate English countryside, and one can only conclude that Vanbrugh was thinking of Drury Lane Theatre when he gave his architectural instructions thus: unless, of course, it was all a result of the continual ear-splitting rows he had with Sarah during the building. The first Duchess of Marlborough was perhaps the most splendid termagant the world has ever known. Eventually she quarrelled even with her placid old Queen. But she and John Churchill were always known as "happily" married, and probably they were. Certainly they made a supremely successful team.

Vanbrugh's great triumph at Blenheim was so to arrange the large central block in relation to its flanking courtyards that the impression of size given was even greater than the actual dimensions of the place. Thus he can be said to have created the most ostentatious house known to modern man, quite an achievement in such a cheap age as ours, and, thanks to the magnificent, historic site, and the later wonderful landscape gardens of "Capability" Brown, one that gives enduring if often amused pleasure. The detail work can be crass and vulgar—and yet suddenly most attractive, as, for example, the perfect bridge that goes from nowhere to nowhere over the still and reflecting lake that Brown made. In these grounds are statues leading to the high Column of Victory, and temples, and fountains, and a rose garden of dreams. There is even an artificial waterfall; and the small but battlemented High Lodge not only gives superb views of the estate and countryside but also recalls the tragic death there of the second Earl of Rochester. (A brave soldier, a cowardly roisterer, a drunk for five years continously, a scholar and pervert and one of the most sexually licentious men of all time, yet a beautiful little poet and one who came to his end repentant and mouthing an unnatural religion.)

Nicholas Hawksmoor was an architect who followed the styles of both Wren and Vanbrugh. His house to see is Easton Neston in Northamptonshire. It is another place of high and pilastered façades. After which came one more Dutchman, William Talman. He helped Wren to "improve" Hampton Court and then worked for a long time with the first Duke of Devonshire to transform Chatsworth in Derbyshire from a nice Elizabethan into an ostentatious Palladian house. The important west front there is undeniably noble with its height and solidity, but more a tribute to the lasting Romanization of England than anything else. Fortunately the new design allowed of wonderful great rooms within, which must be lastingly admired for their Jacobean woodwork. Note also the early parquetry at a time when floors generally were just covered with rush mats. Carpets were arriving about now from the East but were draped across tables (as in parts of Holland and Germany to this day). Marbles also were coming from Ireland and Italy, and were used at Chatsworth for fireplace surrounds.

A virtuoso of carving at this time was Grinling Gibbons. The choir in St. Paul's Cathedral, London, displays his typical work (with the trademark always of the peas in a pod) and a country house which particularly utilized his skills was Petworth in Sussex. The great house here is built beautifully in more of a French than an English Palladian style. It is not too high and the windows are long and sensible and there is not too much classical nonsense. Inside the Carved Room of Grinling Gibbons is a marvel of delicate tracery in carved woods: flowers, swags, musical instruments, cherubs, urns. Also in Petworth, a nice town, can be seen the New Grove of Grove Street, a 17th-century house where Gibbons lived while doing the work at the Duke of Somerset's mansion. This little house has a rookery and a secret chamber.

Tapestries from the Gobelin manufactory in France began to arrive towards the end of the 17th century and were used for wall coverings. Also a man named Marquet across the Channel had developed a method of inlaying furniture with woods of different colors, which became a favorite fashion in England of the period—particularly the sober English "seaweed" style of "marquetry."

But the most important item of furniture in these houses long remained the bed, an enormous, elaborate structure at the heart of the place like the resort of a great queen bee in a hive. And of course breeding was a principal occupation of an essentially dynastic class, and remained so until the 20th-century discovery of birth control and the sterile infidelities of such country house weekends as were to be depicted so amusingly by writers like the young Aldous Huxley. At first the beds were large planks on which malodorous straw mattresses were placed. They became, in Tudor times, almost country houses in themselves, huge and bulbous four posters. These pillars became slender in the next century and supported what were known as testers, dusty canopies which in some cases (notably at Knole) were made of gold and silver cloth (costing as much as $25,000).

The great master bed became a truly awful object after a major death in the family. It was completely re-draped in black and furnished with sable linens also. The walls of the bed chamber were darkly hung, and the widow or widower was expected to endure this rich sadness for months after the interment.

But there were compensations. The essayist Addison writes in *The Spectator* about the menservants who were favorites of titled women:

"I remember the time when some of our well-bred County Women kept their *Valet de Chambre,* because, forsooth, a man was much more handy about them than one of their own Sex. I myself have seen one of these male *Abigails* tripping about the Room with a looking glass in his hand, and combing his Lady's Hair a whole morning together."

Also they had black servants long before the 20th-century West Indian immigration. There is extant a Georgian advertisement for one who had run away: "A Negro Maid, aged about 16 yrs., much pitted with Small Pox, speaks English well, having a piece of her left ear bit off by a dog; she hath on a strip'd stuff waistcoat and Petticoat."

Perhaps the most curious English architect of the 18th century was William Kent, and his greatest house was—and still is—that Holkham Hall in Norfolk which he designed in its present form for a remarkable Earl of Leicester who is known to all good economists as Coke of Holkham the agricultural improver. Kent had come under the influence of Richard Boyle, Earl of Burlington, who patronized the arts and encouraged a tasteful development of the ineffable Palladian style. He thus made austere English use of the classical orders; and Holkham is not too bad, being built of white brick and decorated only with thin pediments and cornices. Inside the place is wholly magnificent. The entrance hall is a marvel in marble, rising above stairs to a half-domed ceiling, coffered over fluted pillars. There is nothing quite like it elsewhere, and Kent should always live for this masterpiece alone.

More than that, the lofty salons of Holkham are embellished with the furniture that Kent specially designed for them: a breed of furniture unique to the man and never to be seen again, truly architectural furniture, gilded wood chairs and desks and consoles and étagères built like Palladio designed his Tuscan houses.

The Adam brothers of Edinburgh, who designed some of the finest houses of the Georgian period, were more than architects. They were remarkably clever and erudite men who ranged over many fields of interest, finally giving their name to a distinctive style in decoration at least, classical again but much more purely so than the earlier *pastiche* of Jones and Wren and Vanbrugh and Kent. Those had gone to the Romans but the Adams really went back to the Greeks. And Robert Adam embellished, in the Yorkshire house called Nostell Priory, one of the few country residences in the classical style that is also quite beautiful. He added the north wing but that was enough. Similarly he made of Kedleston in Derbyshire a great architectural beauty both

Lansdowne Crescent, Bath, among the best pieces of building in all England.

inside and out: then took the medieval walls of Syon House near Isleworth, London, and filled them with Doric richness.

The Adams were the final purists of the Graeco-Roman genre, but, while they were working, others continued along the previous, less pure lines, such as Robert Morris, architect of the White Lodge in Richmond Park (soon to be associated with Pitt, Sheridan, Scott, Nelson and Queen Victoria, and eventual birthplace of the Duke of Windsor), and that Henry Holland whose Carlton House in London became magnificent in spite of itself, set a new fashion in the kind of furniture to be called "Regency," and changed history in other ways.

The reaction to all this nonsense was bound to set in and, of course, was almost worse than the classical nonsense itself. It consisted of going back to what was mistakenly thought to be the original "Gothic" style of English architecture. A majority of the English country houses of the 19th century were constructed in this horrid mode, vaguely related to the fine Perpendicular church architecture of medieval times,

*Carlton House Terrace, one of London's masterpieces of Regency archi-
tecture.*

but fussed up with frills and decorations that never existed then, and
used for purposes that the original ecclesiastical builders would never
have conceived possible.

But it was not all a simple method of primitivism or going right
back. It was also part of the change in the mind of western man
towards the end of the 18th century that made him gradually become
"romantic" instead of "classical." Rousseau wrote down the new idea
in readable prose. Life had been rigid and rectangular. It should preferably be curved and infinitely adaptable.

The first sign of the rot in the country house world was the landscape gardening of "Capability" Brown. He not only started a new
and extremely lucrative profession, the specialist laying out or remodelling of large gardens for the rich. He completely changed the
private landscape of England. His idea was that formal, Italianate
gardens were unsuited to the landscape and climate. He was right.
The native genius of the English is for a charming disarray under
half-tone skies. Nature does not obey rectangular rules but straggles
everywhere.

Lancelot Brown got his nickname "Capability" because he was a genius at the organization of disorder. Thanks to that genius he left behind a vast amount of beauty. He eliminated detail and straight lines and formal beds in gardens and estates. He tried to bring the country-side right up to the front windows of the house. Vistas were to be of a natural, English landscape with rolling hills and carelessly-placed woods: and all things artificial and necessary for living were to be hidden, particularly kitchens. A great part of "Capability's" time was spent on eliminating all hints of stomachs from the view. At Uppark in Sussex the servants could reach the kitchens only by an underground passage. At Harleyford the kitchens were put in a pit. At all costs the landscape must appear untouched by man. As a result the English garden became like a woman with her hair down and still is. Informality and a desire to fit in with the lines of nature are the motives behind English gardening save in the smaller municipal parks.

This might or might not have been a laudable development. It could of course be argued that all man's progress has been at the expense of nature, unless it is recognized that man is part of nature himself and the formal devices of his brain represent the new "natural" order.

But the fact is that England had in some two hundred years built most of her grand country houses in what the architects mistakenly thought was a Graeco-Roman style, severely formal; and of course the gardens had been laid out in that Italianate design also. Then "Capability" Brown, and, later, a similar great landscaper called Humphrey Repton, swept away the formal gardens and replaced them with what amounted to controlled wildernesses. It was all wrong. The classical buildings were out of place in the English countryside, but even more out of place were informal English gardens around classical buildings. No wonder the 19th-century aristocracy, completely mixed-up kids after all this, suddenly went in for their hideous if wildly "romantic" so-called Gothic as a natural extension of "Capability" Brown's ideas.

It took a writer of genius first to erect an actual neo-Gothic building. This was Horace Walpole's Strawberry Hill at Twickenham. It was a mixture of nearly everything that 18th-century man thought was medieval. Not an inch of stony space was left without some kind of pseudo-ecclesiastical, mock-early English and Perpendicular decoration. Later on Sir Walter Scott encouraged the idea in his poems and novels and in his extraordinary battlemented house of Abbotsford. Then the Pugins came from the French Revolution to work with Nash and eventually, as described in a previous chapter, to make at least one masterpiece out of the method, the Houses of Parliament at Westminster. It is a fact that every artistic style, no matter how outrageous or wrong, has at least one outstanding achievement of lasting beauty and importance.

The most famous architect of the neo-Gothic in his time was James Wyatt (1746–1813). His greatest houses were Ashridge and Fonthill. The first is a porcupine of spires, like a nightmare of some Plantagenet churchman set down in the gracious countryside as an eventual home for Prime Ministers. Fonthill, fortunately, is only a memory. It was erected on the orders of William Beckford, the scholarly, crack-brained heir to England's largest single fortune at the time (1780, when Beckford was 21; and the fortune had suitably come from West Indian plantations). The eventual Gothic Abbey, as designed by Wyatt and his nephew, was almost as large as the fortune. An enormous 260 feet high tower rose from the huge, church-like building into the mild Wiltshire air not far away from Bath. Inside it was like an early cathedral only more so. The central ceiling of the great hall was 78 feet high. It was encrusted with mock-Gothic detail, and so was every other part of the house including the kitchen cupboards.

Mad young Beckford was wildly impatient to have the building completed. Five hundred men worked day and night on it, using flares at night. As a result much of the work was skimped, and in particular, the builders forgot to provide the dizzy central tower with proper supporting arches. Beckford spent nearly a million dollars on the construction and on dubious antiques to fill the rooms to overflowing; and, characteristically, when all was finished, he instantly grew tired of the folly and sold it at a loss, retiring to Bath with a depleted income and a disease from which he eventually died. Meanwhile he learned of the builders' mistake and informed the new owner, who replied with typical English cheerfulness that the house should last his time. It did not. The tower collapsed in a gale one night and the building was destroyed. No one had the heart to clear up the mess; and some of the ruins can still be seen near Fonthill Gifford in the huge park that had been specially "landscaped" in the Brown style for Beckford. The millionaire deserves to be remembered less for this "folly" than for the often excellent books he wrote, available in American reprints even today.

Wyatt's nephew, who subsequently became Sir Jeffry Wyattville, a very English transformation, should chiefly be remembered for the work he did at Windsor Castle. He transformed that immense Norman pile into the splendid building that it is today. Sir Charles Barry, who

Windsor, the home of England's kings and queens for centuries.

worked with Pugin on Westminster, created another neo-Gothic masterpiece in Toddington Manor about 1830. Suddenly in sober Gloucestershire this fair building of pimpled towers and spikes and delicate perpendicular lines is seen among the cows. It is, for some strange reason, wholly acceptable. After that came the deluge of true Victorian over-building. An architect named Waterhouse erected Eaton Hall in

Cheshire, one of the largest of all houses but also one of the worst; and thereafter it was not until Lutyens and his essentially "Queen Anne" revivals that the English country house could be safely described again. The Lutyens period was brief but nice and was succeeded by a complete blank. No more large houses will be built in England until another people occupies that debased land.

It is, however, a sad commentary on western civilization that the country house as described is still to be regarded not only as among the very best products of England but also nearly unique in the world. There is not the same variety in French chateaux; and Italian villas and the superb Dutch town houses tend to be all of a kind.

Perhaps it is the English climate, which makes shelter so important, but the houses of this country are perhaps the most important features of it. The suburbs that have been condemned in a previous chapter are huge masses of boxlike houses which dominate the landscape completely, much more than any other feature of life in the land. A visitor from another planet would surely say: "This world is inhabited chiefly by inanimate creatures made of a bricklike substance, with smoke occasionally coming out of their peaked heads"; and he would probably think that the men inside and around them were no more than insects who preyed upon the larger creatures.

Pick, for example, a dozen great works of English fiction, and it will be found that in at least ten the authors describe the habitations of their characters first and leave the characters themselves to emerge almost anyhow and much later. In any case there will be a house somewhere in the book, not just an inanimate lump of a building but one that is very much a character in itself. Sometimes there will be a house that is the true genius, evil or good, of the story.

Thus a favorite Surtees deals with many matters other than *Hillingdon Hall*, but it has its name, and surely enough it begins: "Hillingdon Hall was one of those nice old-fashioned, patchy, upstairs and downstairs sort of houses that either return to their primitive smallness or are swept away for stately mansions with well-arranged suites of company rooms, leaving perhaps the entrance or a room or two to disfigure the rest and show what the edifice originally was." And so it continues, all about Hillingdon Hall, to the end of the chapter.

Neither *Wuthering Heights* nor *The Tenant of Wildfell Hall* has a first sentence descriptive of the house that is to play such an important part in the story; but the Brontes are perhaps the most house-conscious of all novelists. Anne described Wildfell Hall with typical care:

> . . . a superannuated mansion of the Elizabethan era, built of dark grey stone—venerable and picturesque to look at but doubtless cold and gloomy enough to inhabit, with its thick stone mullions and little latticed panes, its time-eaten air-holes and its too-lonely, too-unsheltered situation—only shielded from the war of wind and weather by a group of Scotch firs, themselves half-blighted with storms, and looking as stern and lonely as the Hall itself.

Oliver Twist was scarcely a homedweller in the English sense, but the first sentence of his history describes the habitation that formed him: "Among the other public buildings in a certain town, which for many reasons it will be prudent to refrain from mentioning, and to which I will assign no fictional name, there is one anciently common to all towns, great or small, to wit, a workhouse; and in this workhouse I was born." And *Barnaby Rudge* begins: "In the year 1775 there stood upon the borders of Epping Forest, at a distance of about twelve miles from London . . . a house of public entertainment called the Maypole . . . an old building with more gable-ends than a lazy man would care to count."

Most of Dickens's workhouses are still to be seen in England and most belong to the ugliest period of 19th-century neo-Gothic, but already have a crude period charm. The pubs, on the contrary, are quite charming nearly all the time: and the above-mentioned "King's Head" at Chigwell is typical of the best still.

The novels of George Eliot (old horse-face) contain many famous houses, from *The Mill on the Floss,* which begins with a chapter describing Dorlcote Mill and its environs, to *Felix Holt the Radical,* the opening sentences of which are obviously designed to fix in the reader's mind Transome Court in Loamshire, "a large mansion built in the style of Queen Anne's time."

Thackeray's Castlewood Hall, and the other Castlewood in Virginia (which at that time was just transported England); Mrs. Mayfield's farm in *The Course of True Love Never Did Run Smooth;* R. D. Blackmore's Nowelhurst Hall (the New Forest home of Cradock Nowell); Hardy's *Under the Greenwood Tree* dwelling, "a small low cottage with a thatched pyramidal roof, and having dormer windows breaking up into eaves, a single chimney standing in the very midst"—all are houses that are at least minor characters in English fiction.

Galsworthy's *Forsyte Saga* is, of course, a series of novels almost entirely about property, the Englishman's principal preoccupation at all times when he is not thinking about sex; and the house at Robin Hill may be regarded as one of the outstanding characters in the series. Possibly Arnold Bennett was a much more important novelist than Galsworthy; and his magnificent *Old Wives' Tale* suitably begins and ends with a house—the drapery store with apartment attached of the Baines' in St. Luke's Square, Bursley—while the ghastly new house at Bleakridge is in many ways the genius of the *Clayhanger* trilogy.

One of the best writers of English prose in the first half of the 20th century was C. E. Montagu, and his finest novel is *Rough Justice,* which begins with a description of a house, The Chantry. Meanwhile the young Aldous Huxley made his money almost entirely out of descriptions of country house parties where the characters aired their knowledge in intervals of getting in and out of each other's beds. And P. G. Wodehouse eventually gave an immortal American gloss to the subject with his novels about Blandings, the funniest of all fictional pigstyes: although perhaps the great houses in the bleak conversational fictions of Ivy Compton-Burnett are the last word in satirical demolishment. *A House and Its Head* is the perfect example.

Another English novelist lastingly to represent her age is Nancy Mitford, and her Alconleigh is

. . . a large, ugly, north-facing, Georgian house, built with only one intention, that of sheltering, when the weather was too bad to be out of doors, a succession of bucolic squires, their enormous families, their dogs, their horses, their father's relict, and their unmarried sisters.

Uncle Matthew, the aristocratic dictator of this grim but amusing place, was so typically English in his eccentricities:

My Uncle Matthew had four magnificent bloodhounds, with which he used to hunt his children. Two of us would go off with a good start to lay the trail, and Uncle Matthew and the rest would follow the hounds on horseback. It was great fun. Once he came to my home and hunted Linda and me over Shenley Common. This caused the most tremendous stir locally, the Kentish week-enders on their way to church being appalled by the sight of four great hounds in full cry after two little girls.

At the same time these country houses of England gave rise to what was for long the most popular school of detective fiction. Thousands of books were written that began with a rural mansion and the death violently there one weekend usually of the most unpleasant member of a family or party. Thereafter the game was for the reader to spot the murderer among the characters forced by the police to remain indoors until they had completed their business. Agatha Christie was the most popular writer in this *genre*. She would begin characteristically: "Enderby Hall was a vast Victorian house built in the Gothic style." And she would go on, very much like the great Ivy Compton-Burnett, to give the world the impression that in these latter days the typical English mansion of the English upper classes was solely a place where people hated each other.

Consider alone how the novelists actually named their books after houses: *Bleak House, Northanger Abbey, Orley Farm, The House with the Green Shutters, The Other House, Bramley Parsonage, Nightmare Abbey, Crotchet Castle, Melincourt, Castle Dangerous, Mansfield Park, Danesbury House*—and of course Virginia Woolf made her name with *To the Lighthouse*.

In reality the country houses of England have become in our time just places where the inhabitants try to survive. At one end of the scale is the enormous Woburn Abbey of the Duke of Bedford, who inherited the estate and a crippling tax bill when he was a young, remote member of the family who had been making his own hard living as a farmer in South Africa. He immediately applied to the running of the place those principles he had learned in the school of colonial self-sufficiency. He did not mind but encouraged the sneers and laughs of his peers. They were good for publicity. He turned Woburn into a kind of Coney Island of the shires and made it a favorite vacation haunt of the very people who had toppled his ancestors. Similarly the Marquess of Bath imported dangerous wild animals into the beautiful parklands of Longleat and gave the English one more glorious zoo.

A certain Elizabethan priory was turned into an antiques business by its desperate owners, or rather an antiques business and a hotel combined. Those who took the bait and stayed there were apt to find price tickets on everything they encountered, from the bedside table to the toothglasses in the bathroom. It was only a very strong man who could spend a night there without buying something.

Then there was the remarkable de Quincey of Herefordshire, descendant from a long line of wealthy local squires (and of that original drug addict Thomas de Quincey, author of *Confessions of an English Opium-Eater*). He saved the family bacon by developing on the lovely farm of The Vern not only an outstandingly fine strain of

Hereford cattle but also prize-winning species of fox terriers, goldfish, Hackneys and humming-birds. With the proceeds he could buy Guardis when they were still cheap as well as beautiful investments in porcelains and he could pad around in slippers and behave like the dilettante that is every Englishman's real ambition.

Others preferred to do it the hard way and married American or Jewish heiresses. The most remarkable, perhaps, were the Astors, one branch of which made Cliveden House in Buckinghamshire temporarily as powerful a political center as the Kennedy hideout in New England. This was the home of the "Cliveden Set," which, for quite

Longleat, ancestral home of the Marquess of Bath in Wiltshire, with gardens designed by "Capability" Brown, now pleasure grounds for the people.

a time made and controlled and broke the leading politicians of the country. The Palladian-style mansion was designed by Sir Charles Berry in 1851 and was wholly *pastiche.* It was in a cottage on the grounds that the Profumo scandal festered and England's ruling class finally died. (Although the girls who did the dirty work lived on most lucratively to tell the tale).

Many of the great houses remain in being as headquarters for cranky religious organizations, American universities in England, as hospitals, nursing homes, and holiday rest places for officials of na-tionalized industries and trade unionists. Where the peacocks once strutted and Maud was implored to come into the garden by her importunate swain the heavy men now discuss wage structures in broad North Country dialects. Or lunatics caper where once such a philosopher as Bertrand Russell could make his apelike passes at a high-thinking Ottoline Morrell.

Far cleaner are the small estates maintained bravely by blue-blooded descendants of the original robber barons who themselves drive the tractors on their farms and renew a strength that might yet be useful to England again.

At the lower end of the scale is the great house in Somerset where an old woman wheeling a baby carriage filled with vegetables was asked if the place could be inspected. She said that it could and herself conducted the tour, at the end of which she gratefully accepted a tip. Then she was asked by someone with an instinct: "You are not by chance Lady So-and-So yourself?" To which she replied that she was and she must now hurry off to the village to sell the vegetables.

Lowest of all was a noble pile so filled with cobwebs that it looked like the frozen house in *Dr. Zhivago.* It was inhabited by a surly man, unshaven among the tatters of his French chairs and allowing his several dogs to urinate on the remains of an Aubusson carpet. He suddenly bared his hairy chest and revealed several red circles amid the brushwork. "Ringworm," he said. "I caught it from the Short-horns. Can't afford the vet."

8

Wheels

The English made little mark upon the outside world until they learnt how to carry their goods in ships across the seas. But after that the tiny vessels of this island race made many perilous voyages and wherever they went had a profound effect not only upon the native inhabitants of faraway, strange places but also upon themselves. To-day's map of the world is the memorial roll of their captains, Baffin, Frobisher, Drake, Hudson, Hawkins, Davis, Dampier, Cook and so many more. These men returned to England with tales and gold and other diseases.

It is necessary to visit Devonshire and Cornwall to learn about this phenomenon, because most of the voyagers came from those counties. Maybe it was the blood of the Phoenicians in them. A lot of these sailors from the Levant had left their offspring in Cornwall and Devon after digging for tin there in order to make swords and other useful domestic articles. But in any case these counties would have headed the ocean race for the simple reason that they stuck out in that direction and had the natural harbors.

The staple industries of early England were mainly concerned to feed home bellies and clothe the backs of Englishmen. Then those captains brought back their tales and their gold. There were peoples in other parts of the world who had no cloth at all, no knowledge of metallurgy, no firearms, no unifying Christian religion. There was high adventure to be had among them, and a mighty profit. Why not send out more and better-organized merchant fleets?

Thus came the great "companies" of traders which first opened the world's major export markets.

There were the Muscovy Company, which brought the first western amenities to Russia and the lands of the Baltic; the Levant Company, which braved the Mediterranean pirates, made terms with the Turks, even established itself in Constantinople; the East India Company, which oiled the Orient; the Hudson's Bay Company, which made the first money from the frozen north of America; and many minor others. The English were not the only people to produce brave navigators and good travelling salesmen at that period. But they were always the most interested in just making money. They sought power not for the hell of it, nor even for the glory, but just for the cash consequences. Shakespeare put it all into the nutshell of *The Merchant of Venice.* Antonio and his fellow sea traders were essentially Englishmen with English ideas.

Neither North America, Australia, New Zealand, South Africa nor several of the rest were discovered in the first place by the English. But these wholly mercenary people invariably remained where others failed to stay. They did not want to oppress and dominate or impose their culture. The Dutch were nearest to them in ideals and methods but far more brutal and less tactful. The English always came with a sword for self-protection, but their principal weapons were ledgers and goods for sale, backed up by Bibles. They never destroyed whole native civilizations and strutted about in gleaming armor, twirling fierce moustachios, as did the cruel Spanish in South America. Either they cultivated empty lands like Australia or they organized old lands like India for better business. Their methods in those days were almost exactly the same as the colonizing habits of Americans in the second half of the 20th century in such countries as Switzerland and England. Occasionally they had their Vietnams also, but they extricated themselves as quickly as possible from these similar grave blunders.

The first English merchant-adventurers strove for their own monetary advantage but in the process they manured the whole world nicely with their consumer-goods. And it should be remembered that in the English language the term "goods," to signify articles of trade, comes from the same root as the word "good," which means the opposite of "bad." "Our chief desire," wrote Richard Hakluyt in the 16th century, "is to find out ample vent of our woollen cloth, the natural commodity of this realm." It is perfectly true, though strange to relate, that not lust of conquest but desire to trade created the enormous British Empire. And one of the reasons why the British Empire so quickly disintegrated in the 20th century was that it had ceased to become profitable.

The method of sea-fighting by "broadside" was invented by the English, but far more important was the invention of the woollen blanket, by a merchant named Thomas Blanket, of Bristol.

Their descendants eventually became totally ashamed of those original adventurers. They could see them only as frequent pirates and slave-dealers. But these ungrateful, narrow-minded children forgot that the merchants were making their world at least materially better, and did actually subscribe the money in due course for a Navy that cleared the seas of piracy and slave-dealing.

The Royal Navy was developed not for the purpose of conquering other nations but to keep the unpleasant Dutch out of the Thames and act as a police force for English traders on the seven seas. It was not so much the land strategy of the Duke of Wellington that defeated the all-conquering, rampaging Napoleon as the ships of the Royal Navy which successfully blockaded all the overseas trading activities of the French. Thus the infuriated scream of the grand Emperor that the English were no better than a nation of shopkeepers. They were. The English had always been more interested in providing men with goods at a suitable profit than in assembling men in masses and leading them to their doom. The English might well have been one of the dispersed tribes of Israel. The only real revolution ever to afflict them was of course an Industrial Revolution.

The steam engine as such was invented by Edward Somerset, second Marquis of Worcester. It is described in a book he wrote in 1663 entitled *An Admirable and Most Forcible Way to Drive Up Steam*. It was, however, necessary to wait a hundred years until a clever Scotsman could be found to do the actual work. He was James Watt, who in 1769 made a machine that used the steam from boiling water to operate a piston and a wheel. The modern age was born in that year. Other British inventors had preceded Watt, but he was the first to perfect the steam engine as a commercial proposition. It was used only for mining operations until 1785, when it was applied to the machinery of a cotton factory. The Revolution had begun.

How fortunate it was that the steam engine began in England and not in a country where it might have been used not for making cotton goods but for making war! A different people might have tried to make a military weapon out of it at once—indeed, a certain ignoble European inventor constructed a steam wagon for military purposes only a short time after Watt's beginning—whereas the English naturally thought of the money side alone.

The sea merchants had opened up markets all over the world for English textiles, but these were hand-made still and could not be produced quickly enough for the demand. It was a most distressing situation. Nothing is worse than inability to supply good customers. Swiss watch manufacturers have suffered nervous breakdowns in such circumstances. So the English were really put to it. They got to work on that steam engine—and other machinery.

The most typical of the inventors was Richard Arkwright. His career demonstrated once and for all the virtues of poverty and the folly in modern methods of giving children everything and shielding the little dears from the realities of life at all costs. Arkwright was born in extreme poverty, the youngest of thirteen children. He had no education, and his first job was with a travelling barber. It was said of him: "He manifested a strong bent for experiments in mechanics, which he is stated to have followed with so much devotedness as to have neglected his business and injured his circumstances. His natural disposition was ardent, enterprising and stubbornly persevering; his mind was as coarse as it was bold and active, and his manners were rough and unpleasing."

Arkwright set himself the task of inventing an improved cotton-spinning machine. By adopting an arrangement of rollers that moved with different velocities, he succeeded in perfecting his "spinning-frame." He took out his first patent in 1769, that remarkable year of Watt and the steam engine, and, entering into partnership with another man, became a manufacturer on a large scale. In 1771 he established the first power-driven cotton mill. He became High Sheriff of his county and was knighted by the King. A contemporary wrote of him: "The most marked traits in the character of Arkwright were his wonderful ardour, energy and perseverance. He commonly laboured in his multifarious concerns from five o'clock in the morning till nine at night; and when considerably more than fifty years of age, feeling that the defects of his education placed him under great difficulty and inconvenience in managing his correspondence, and in the general management of his business, he encroached upon his sleep, in order to gain an hour each day to learn English grammar, and another hour to improve his hand-writing. Arkwright was a severe economist of time; and that he might not waste a moment, he generally travelled with four horses, and at a very rapid speed."

Arkwright invented the spinning-frame, Hargreaves the jenny, Crompton the mule, and Cartwright the power-loom. These were machines for making cloth that had formerly been spun and woven laboriously and slowly by hand. Attached by belts to the new steam engines, they at once increased the output of the cotton industry by 200 percent. The same principles were applied to the woollen and linen industries with similar results. It was discovered that chlorine could be used for bleaching, to take a few days over the process instead of a year. Calicoes were printed by steam-driven cylinders instead of by hand. Mackintosh invented the process of waterproofing. The sky darkened over central and northern England as new industrial chimneys poured out their sooty smoke; it blushed with pride as the furnaces forged the necessary iron.

Indeed much new fuel was needed for the boilers and metal for the machines, and it was necessary to discover processes for producing both quickly. Coal mining had been a matter of scratching the surface of the earth by hand. Iron had been smelted laboriously by charcoal in the depths of forests.

So the English invented most of the processes now at the root of metallurgy and mining. The methods of sinking a shaft, of pumping out water, of providing ventilation, of hoisting the coal to the surface, were suddenly original English methods. Sir Humphry Davy was not only the great electrical and chemical pioneer; he also invented the miner's safety lamp. It was discovered in England (and Scotland) how to smelt iron by coal instead of burnt wood. The first cast steel was made in Sheffield. Meanwhile the Yorkshireman Joseph Bramah constructed the first machine tool, perhaps the most important single device of modern industry—a device that produces machines from machines. (Bramah also invented the first patent lock, as well as a machine for printing bank notes—the father of inflation—a hydrostatic press, and a liquid pump.)

James Nasmyth invented the steam hammer, so that iron and steel could be molded easily into any shape; and Whitworth, about the same time, devised a machine for taking measurements to one-millionth part of an inch, to ensure perfect engineering accuracy.

The goods could now be produced, but existing methods of transport were far too slow for distributing them. Men still travelled oafishly on roads of mud, and in cumbersome vehicles drawn by poor horses in relays. They were at the complete mercy of wind and tide when they took to the rivers, the new canals, or the sea.

In 1767 the first rails of cast iron were laid down in England. Subsequently it was discovered how to make flanged wheels that would not run off the rails, and to construct the rails of hard steel in the safe shape that soon became universal. But rails and wagons on them were not much use unless steam power could be harnessed to the wagons instead of slow horses. The peculiar English were far more interested in this problem than in the issues of the contemporaneous French Revolution, or, indeed, in the loss of the American colonies; and it was in the year 1804, when Napoleon crowned himself as Emperor, that a Cornishman named Trevithick invented the first steam propelled carriage that could travel quicker than any horse-drawn vehicle.

The man who devised the proper steam locomotive and railway system, George Stephenson, was born near Newcastle, and first employed in a coal mine. Once again this original had the advantage of initial poverty and no formal education. He taught himself to read at the age of seventeen. In that brave European year, 1804, he was working as brakesman at a colliery, and had control of a stationary steam-engine. He thought of adapting this machine to the purposes of transport, and at last constructed an engine that would draw coal trucks at the rate of four miles an hour. In 1825 Stephenson completed the first railway line in the world, between Stockton and Darlington. Europe was still in the Middle Ages, but Stephenson's locomotive could draw a train of 38 carriages, laden with goods and passengers, at a rate of twelve miles an hour.

The invention greatly alarmed some people at first. An old man later recalled that he had been waiting with other passengers for the arrival of Stephenson's "Rocket" at the station: "When the train drew up at the platform, the engine-driver suddenly let off steam and blew the engine whistle. The effect upon those nearest to the engine was like throwing off a bombshell, for they rushed back, helter-skelter, away from the engine, and two or three were knocked down."

When the London and North-Western Railway first came to Crewe it found a lonely farmhouse on the summit of a hill with pasture and cornfields all around. Soon Crewe became the greatest railway center in the world. Thousands of rails intermingled there, and workshops covered hundreds of acres. This was the prototype for similar transportation systems in all lands. The railway was found to be the main artery of development and prosperity. It was the first practicable land means of carrying heavy goods across long distances, cheaply and at high speed. The North American continent did not become viable until the great railroads were laid across it. There was iron ore in the distant mountains of Sweden, but it was useless until a railway was constructed across the mountains to the coast. Switzerland did not become the world's wealthiest little country until the lines of steel were threaded around the peaks and lakes. To this day the principal urban conurbations of man are noisily built alongside the railways; and a successful individual's proudest and wisest boast is to have been born on the wrong side of the tracks, which means the side where the money is made.

The settlement of remote parts of South America would have been impossible without the brave railways, often fantastic feats of English and Scottish engineering largely financed with the savings of hard-working Englishmen; and of course the hordes of immigrants swept across the United States and Canada and Australia and New Zealand and South Africa in the wake of the liberating steel road.

A financier named Hudson was largely responsible for the remarkable spread of the finest railways across every part of England. No country acquired such a perfect system, and the tragedy of the phenomenon was that its very perfection tended to make the English so self-satisfied that they did not think it necessary in due course to develop similar motorways. Another tragedy was that Hudson himself came to a sticky end and that the English allowed their railways eventually to molder for lack of up-to-date development.

The railway became a prime weapon in war, but was essentially a peaceful device in itself, built to help and not to hinder mankind. English railway engineers of the 19th century would hardly have pushed this thought to its logical conclusion by maintaining that they had worked with the direct object of reducing barriers between peoples. They would admit that they had labored for wages and self-satisfaction alone. But there was certainly the contingent phenomenon that the railways opened up the world and made such achievements as America possible.

Thus a method had been found of distributing the products of the Industrial Revolution by land. What about the sea?

Foremostly the English are a seafaring race, for the simple reason that the sea is the only way they can get anywhere. No place in their little island is more than a few hundred miles from the sea, and until the coming of the airplane no boy could get away from his parents unless he had the courage to go aboard a ship.

This is not a book about Scotland but about England, but when William Symington tried out the first-ever steamship in a Scottish loch, 1787, not only was Robert Burns present but also the entire English nation in spirit. The invention would never have taken place without English parts and capital and encouragement; and Scotland in 1787 was virtually an English possession. It was in 1802 that Symington successfully tried out his second ship, the *Charlotte Dundas,* and not until 1807 that America's Fulton launched his *Clermont,* a craft modelled on the plans of Symington and equipped with the machinery of Watt.

Thereafter England thrust steamship lines across the oceans of the world, and contributed most of the ideas that eventually made the most splendid of passenger liners, the *Queen Mary* and *Queen Elizabeth.* There was a period when England had more shipping on the seas of the world than all other nations together. The first ship of iron was built in Britain, the screw-propeller, and the turbine. Could it be wondered that her architecture became so ugly when she had these other, more important things on her mind? Her marine surveyors produced charts for all the oceans. Buoys, lighthouses and lightships, to reduce the perils of the sea, were first introduced by the British. The International Code of Signals was initiated by Captain Frederick Marryat in 1817. The first unsinkable lifeboat was invented by William Wouldhave in 1789, did service until 1830, and never lost a hand in that time, while it saved hundreds of lives. Marine insurance was devised to cover financial losses at sea, and the London institution of Lloyd's became a common word to all languages. The timing of the world was first adjusted to the "mean time" at Greenwich, and weather forecasting for shipping was an English invention.

John Smeaton was the son of a Leeds lawyer, and was intended for the same profession, but showed a strong inclination for mechanical pursuits. In 1753, after a course of foreign travel, he submitted plans for rebuilding Eddystone Lighthouse, which had been burned down; and his proposals were accepted. Hitherto lighthouses had been constructed of wood, in the shape of towers. Smeaton used stone, and modelled his building like a tree, broad at the base, narrow at the center, broadening a little again at the top. The result was the soundest and best lighthouse the world had seen up to that time. During the work of construction, moreover, Smeaton discovered a novel method of binding the stone blocks, the first Portland cement (without which no modern city could stand up for a moment). This man also invented the mechanical bellows that are still a principal instrument in iron smelting.

Samuel Plimsoll was a native of Bristol, and, poor man, also a member of the British Parliament. He said he was shocked at the negligence of some shipowners, who loaded their vessels to the water-line regardless of the safety of their men. Actually he was inspired by the opportunity to make his name as a politician. And he made an immortal one. After much endeavor, Plimsoll was responsible for an Act of Parliament, the Merchant Shipping Act of 1876, that made it illegal to load ships above a certain mark. All British ships and the best of other nations thereafter bore this sensible sign, even more sensible than humanitarian, because men can be quite cheaply replaced but not expensive ships.

The whole science of navigation, marine and aerial, is largely built upon English methods and devices. Hadley had invented the sextant as long ago as 1731, and it was at the same period that Harrison gave the world its marine chronometer. (A country could sometimes be grateful because he got £20,000 for it, equal to perhaps $100,000 in those days.) Lord Kelvin improved the mariner's compass as we know it today, and he devised the automatic sounding machine to replace lead and line. The same scientist's measuring instruments and mathematical tables are to be found in every chart room. Barometers used at sea are based on the improvements of Sir Harry Englefield.

One of the most important discoveries of modern times has been refrigeration. The first shipment of frozen meat came right round the world from New Zealand to Britain in 1882, thanks to an English invention. Sheep were frozen on board the sailing ship *Dunedin,* and, after four months' delay, travelled to London. They arrived as fresh as when packed. Today the world has an everlasting larder thanks to this initial enterprise.

Then England faltered. It might have been the three wars, the South African, the Kaiser's, and Hitler's. It could also have been the vast emigrations from this country, which fructified so much of America, Canada, Australia, New Zealand, South Africa. More likely it was ideas, the new "liberating" ideas of intellectuals such as Shaw, Wells, Lawrence, Huxley, Russell. These ran contrary to the Victorian "virtues." The pursuit of the happiness and well-being of the greatest number gave England a Welfare State but did not encourage men like Arkwright any longer. In fact the morality went in the opposite direction, and a man who laid too many bricks in an hour was regarded by his fellows as a felon.

As a result England increasingly lagged behind in mechanical invention and achievement. Her ships were beaten by those of America, Germany and Japan. A flash of the old genius appeared momentarily in the English invention of the hovercraft, but this was not developed commercially as it once would have been.

What remains of one of the original Roman roads in England.

Macadam and Telford were roadmakers of genius who discovered many of the methods still used. Kirkpatrick Macmillan made the pioneer bicycle; and the wire-spoked wheel was the product of an English mind—also the chain drive. English and Scottish enterprise are inextricably mixed up here: the pneumatic tire was a joint discovery of the two peoples. And an Englishman should have invented the automobile.

That he did not is a first indication of what was happening to the country at the end of the 19th century. Already when the first motor-cars hissed and banged their way down the narrow roads there were un-English protests. Nothing would ever come of these ungainly monsters and they were not really wanted. The wonderful railways were surely best. The politicians listened to this voice of an already decadent people and tried to restrict the growth of the new invention by law. A man had to walk with a red flag in front of the first motor-cars that rolled in England.

So Daimler-Benz and the French companies got their initial lead, an advantage which they never really lost; and meanwhile, over in the States, such men as Ford and Chevrolet were given exactly the right circumstances in which to develop mass production of auto-mobiles and eventually to establish an industry which, in sheer size and ingenuity, made the Industrial Revolution and railway achieve-ments of little England look like the work of primitive apes.

In their final phase the English could excel in only two depart-ments, very high quality products and miniatures, and this was par-ticularly exemplified by the way they entered the automobile age. At first they grudgingly accepted the Daimler patents and used them, and some fine isolated engineers made good early cars such as that Daimler and the Wolseley and Sunbeam and Riley and Lanchester. But it was as if they and the people did not have their real heart in it. A little boy at that period was much more interested in "The Flying Scotsman" railway locomotive still.

But in one case at least an English automobile manufacturer set a standard that has never been equalled since, in England or elsewhere. This was F. H. Royce, son of a miller, born in a cottage, again self-educated. He delivered newspapers at the age of ten for a few pence a week, and he worked as a message boy. Then he determined to make himself an electrical engineer, and studied through the usual weary nights after work. Eventually he became such an engineer, and he invented a very reliable electric crane.

The Rolls-Royce car was a remarkable achievement, the result of collaboration between the engineering skill and strong character of Royce and the stylish ideas of a young sporting aristocrat named Rolls, one of the first of the great English motor racing aces. Royce told his workmen that every part must be made by hand and as much care lavished on the most insignificant part as on the whole. He went round the factory with a little hammer and he smashed everything that he thought was imperfectly made. His gods were power, smooth-ness, silence and money and he spent as much time on perfecting the muffler as on any other feature of the car. He sent out commands to his agents that cars must not be sold to people who might use them roughly, and that they must be bought back and destroyed if they were not properly maintained. He did not affix fenders, because he said that Rolls-Royce owners should not need them.

Meanwhile the languid but steely Rolls set about winning all available road races with the great prototypes, and the car was driven through mountain snows and desert sandstorms. With the outbreak of the 1914–1918 war it was ready to bear guns and armor and to survive the mud and blood and tears triumphantly. Afterwards it became increasingly the millionaires' plaything and world status symbol and eventually without compare as an automobile, but, alas, long after the deaths of its original makers, no longer the mechanical piece of perfection that it was in the pioneer days. Instead the genius of the marque was transferred to the air.

The British Daimler paced the Rolls for some time but eventually was beaten into a name alone, affixed to the cars of another excellent make, a lifetime behind the achievements of its German cousin the Mercedes. The true British automobile became a miniature as developed by William Morris and Herbert Austin, mainly perhaps because the people had not bothered to develop a modern road system. England's first motorway was not built until the great American roads and the German autobahns were becoming ancient monuments. English surfaces were always good, but until long after the second war even the main highways were narrow and winding. They became jammed with traffic; and oil had to be imported when it could have been extracted from the North Sea or made from coal; so the manufacturers could not develop big modern engines and the kind of spacious family cars that were already speeding in the Grand Tourismo class across Europe and America.

It has been said that Rolls-Royce took to the air. This is so, in that the jet engines particularly of this marque, based on one final English invention, enabled the greatest American aircraft manufacturers to beat the world with them. (The work of Frank Whittle, a most typical Englishman, was almost wholly responsible for the world development of the jet propulsion principle.) Then Rolls-Royce suddenly crashed, having agreed to make superb engines for American aircraft at too low a price. Pride had once more gone before a fall.

The invention of practical flying machines was not English; and, no matter how the island people tried to master the ultimate method of transport, they could not, at least in the commercial sense, do so well as other nations. America beat them hands down, and even the Germans and French and Dutch eventually overtook them in the world's markets.

England could have led the air race (as she won so many of the early actual races). The original De Havilland "Moth" was the most successfully ubiquitous of all light aircraft and an intrepid record-breaker. The first amphibious machine that could alight on land or water was invented by Thomas Sopwith, and the original flying-boat was English. Handley-Page's 1918 model was the largest aircraft ever till then, and the same pioneer developed the slotted wing. World speed records were consistently broken by Englishmen in English planes between the wars, and during the second war the decisive battle was that when the English Hurricane and Spitfire fighters went up and shot down sufficient of the German invading bombers to convince Hitler that he could not invade Britain and take over the enormous industrial potential of that country. (With that potential he could easily have defeated America and Russia.)

After that war Rolls-Royce found it necessary to sell its secrets under license to American manufacturers in order to keep in business and gradually the English aircraft industry fell behind, eventually being forced to buy its principal passenger and military aircraft from Boeing, Douglas and other foreign firms.

Yet the visitor will always find much to delight him in the fast-moldering English transport system. When he arrives at Southampton Docks or London Airport he may have to carry his own bags and suffer interminable delays because of the frequent strikes which are a characteristic system of this dying economy. But the quiet Customs officers in their smart uniforms will give him the impression at once that he is in touch with one of the most civilized and also one of the funniest of lands. And, once on the extremely crowded roads, he will feel that the age of the stage coach and the hansom cab is not yet completely over.

Small and often extremely aged cars jostle for position with excellent long-distance buses, the construction of which has always been a highly successful English specialty. The drivers of these cars often look as if they have horses' reins and not steering wheels in their hands, so importantly do they sit and with such extreme care do they proceed upon their journeys. The standard of driving in this country is probably the highest in the world, if judged by considerations of safety and politeness. And meanwhile race tracks can be visited in England and elsewhere where youngsters still win international speed championships.

It is an amusing country, extremely old-fashioned by cosmopolitan standards, but still contains some of the stuff that gave humanity the modern industrial age, if it is considered that the best of America and Germany and Japan, right up to the 1970s, still could not beat young Englishmen (and Scots and Australians and New Zealanders) on the international motor racing tracks.

9

Balls

Of course the wonderful English did not invent games as such but they were definitely responsible for the modern concept known as "sport." Stone Age man probably played with the bones of his victims. The ancient Greeks made a religion out of running and jumping for prizes. For hundreds of years after that life became too grim for such nonsense, but all the time strange little games continued to be played in odd pockets of the world, notably *boules* in France, a grown-up kind of marbles on gravel under the shade of plane trees by castle walls, and the Basque *pelota,* granddad of tennis (which was developed by early kings of France as a means of showing off their legs to their boyfriends). Shakespeare once again went to the heart of this matter when he made young Henry V say:

> We are glad the Dauphin is so pleasant with us;
> His present and your pains we thank you for:
> When we have match'd our rackets to these balls,
> We will, in France, by God's grace, play a set
> Shall strike his father's crown into the hazard. . . .

Golf might have originated in Scotland or in Holland or in Greece. Soccer football similarly has a universal origin. Croquet is mean enough to be a French invention and even cricket is not necessarily English, although the game as played today could belong to no other country. And the various indoor sports, ranging from the chess which began some 1500 years ago in the Orient, to the bridge which in its present gnomic form started on Harold S. Vanderbilt's cruising yacht in the good year 1925, owe little to the English as innovators.

But the spirit is another matter; and it is not too much to say that the whole idea behind modern games is an English idea.

It emerged originally from the medieval tournament and the concept of chivalry based on the remarkable Christian ethic. Those wild barons and muscular knights were tamed by the priestly inheritors of Jesus Christ's turn-the-other-cheek doctrine into at least picking up their opponent's sword and returning it to him occasionally. A "very perfect gentle knight" was an individual who could fight as toughly as any but who had discovered he could humiliate his opponent even more completely by magnanimously giving him a second chance. He wanted him to know that he could beat him if necessary with one hand tied behind his back and without resorting to ultimate acts such as kicking below the belt. Anyone who was conquered by such a knight was really licked, not only physically but also psychologically. It must have been completely horrible and it was the real English contribution to western civilization. In fact it *was* western civilization.

But it lay concealed in the English psyche for quite a long time after the flower of medieval chivalry was finally trampled into the mud of the Wars of the Roses. Occasionally it popped up in Elizabethan times with such phenomena as Philip Sidney's handing his cup of water to another dying man on the field of the battle of Zutphen and exclaiming: "Thy need is greater than mine." It probably lost England her American colonies in the 18th century, when the redcoats so often refused to deploy their full strength against the simple colonists. It would not have been sporting!

And it came right out in the open again about the middle of the 19th century when England was so powerful and had so much money that she could afford to develop special boarding schools for her elite.

It is essentially the idea that you are sufficiently strong to be able to concede several points and still win. It is, as a corollary, the notion that a game is a game but sport is something above just winning and losing. It is winning or losing so that you are always demonstrably the moral superior of your opponent. Consider these facts.

In November 1914, at Ypres, General French needed a reliable officer to carry important dispatches across an area exposed to enemy fire. His aide-de-camp mentioned an officer's name. The General hesitated. "Is he completely reliable?" he asked. "The man I want must be a super man. What do you know about him?" The aide thought for a moment. "Well," he said, "he's played Rugby football for South Africa against England." Whereupon the General's eyes brightened. "A rugger man, eh? Call him in."

Perhaps soccer football is the most popular of all English games. But it is little more than a century old in its present form. The rules of what is known as Association football were drawn up at a meeting held at Cambridge about 1849. Prior to that men in all lands had kicked balls or stones as an occasional amusement; they had even organized themselves into teams. But this had been haphazard and unsatisfactory. Rules were required—a proper *sporting* code whereby you could win without ostentatiously appearing to do so. Once these rules were provided the game became a national sport. It appealed particularly to the common people because it could be learned easily and no great skill was required. It made a fine spectacle and was the first of the big spectator sports which eventually became the only valid excuse for the invention of television. And the rules were devised so that the team which won was the best team not only physically but also morally.

By the end of the 19th century soccer football had thousands of players and millions of supporters in Britain, but had not caught on very well in other lands, save in the United States and Canada where the rules were changed and the game became bloodily real. But thereafter it slowly spread abroad in its English form. Eventually it became the principal sparetime occupation of not only Latin Americans but also of eastern European communists. And they began to win.

Sometimes England still triumphs in international competitions, but on the whole she has ceased to be preeminent at the game. This is because she continues to play it as a sport according to what she would describe as decent rules; and the most successful foreigners are those who play it as a business, quite viciously and with grim determination. It was all right for Englishmen to observe the medieval laws of chivalry when the other side also obeyed them, but not so good when Argentinians, Hungarians or Muscovites were the determined—and often state-aided—opponents. The big-hearted man could no longer say "Hard luck, old chap. I suppose I had to win but we were playing according to the rules and I did concede you a goal." Such talk would just not have been understood by his very foreign opponents.

There was, however, one branch of English football which, by a stroke of genius, enabled the players at once to have their sporting cake and to eat it. This was Rugby, first played at the great prototype public school of that name. The origin is particularly interesting. In

Association football.

1823 a boy of that school, the immortal William Webb Ellis, suddenly took it into his head to catch the ball during a game and to run with it. This was against the most fundamental of the rules of football. But it broke the English ice in a very subtle way. It brought the game nearer to the rules of life; and ever since Rugby football has nurtured the small band of Englishman who can be really relied upon in an emergency, the big husky fellows who will break necks if necessary to win.

It was said of Rugby football in the early days that "one great principle actuated the players—that it was immaterial if, in kicking for the ball, they kicked their opponents' shins." An old Rugby man has related how he once saw a player rush through all opposition and "finish his triumphal progress by kicking a halfback clean off his legs." Only Rugby in England could produce the story of the player with a visiting Australian team who appeared at breakfast with a deep gash on his face. When asked how he had suffered this injury he replied that the previous evening, confronted by a plate glass window in a shopping thoroughfare, he had been suddenly moved to leap through

Rugby football.

it, just to see whether such a feat was possible. (And the man was a teetotaller.)

The first official rules of Rugby football, drawn up by the Rugby Union in 1871, ended some of the more sensational methods of incapacitating an opposing player, but the game has remained quite incorrigible by English sporting standards, and as such has flourished greatly in such realistic lands as France and New Zealand, Australia and South Africa. The very best teams are those of the overseas British lands to which the most vigorous and freeminded individuals of the race emigrated in the 19th and first half of the 20th centuries. The New Zealanders, gaily called "All Blacks" long before color became a popular talking-point, were eventually to be quite unbeatable. The author of this book once sat down to breakfast with them in Wellington. The enormous young men were served with large beef steaks, on which were placed great dollops of spinach and poached eggs. And when one Rugby football team came to England from South Africa it was observed that an average player was 6 ft. 3½ in. tall, another weighed 220 pounds, and the average weight of the forwards was 203 pounds, while every man was a fast sprinter.

To achieve real fame in South Africa, remarked a distinguished visitor, it was necessary either to serve a long term of imprisonment for a political offense and then to write a successful book about it, or else to excel as a Rugby footballer. An Englishman became headmaster of a great school in Australia. He was told about one boy who was always getting into trouble. "Has he no good feature at all?" asked the new headmaster. "He certainly plays a fine game of Rugby football, the lazy young devil," was the reply. "Lazy and plays a good game of football!" exclaimed the head. "You are speaking of incompatibles. We'll have that boy at the top of the school in no time." And the prediction was fulfilled.

Eton, the most important of the English public schools, has its own peculiar sport known as the Wall Game. It is played under a wall that is distinguished by a white stone, which was originally inserted to commemorate a fight between two of the boys in 1805. This fight had resulted in the death of the vanquished. The story is grim, but lends point to the legendary remark of the Duke of Wellington that the battle of Waterloo was won on the playing fields of Eton. And it is not for nothing that nearly all British governments for a long, long time have been dominated by men who went to this essentially sanguinary school, a place where games are played according to realistic rules.

Moreover ordinary football in England has at the time of the country's decline subtly become a less and less "sporting" game. The players who were originally given only thirty to forty dollars a week as professionals were eventually tempted with big cash inducements to play to win; and meanwhile their methods were changed by increasingly hostile and ill-behaved crowds of spectators, who, sick of silliness, started to throw bottles and to tear off the seats from trains on the way home.

Yet the English conception of "sport" as opposed to winning at all costs is a very deep-rooted idea. It is expressed outstandingly in the extraordinary game of cricket.

Cricket is in a sense the national religion of the English, and it would not be at all surprising to discover that it goes back to the Druids. When a modern English writer wants to go all ga-ga and express his love for his native land in timeless prose he invariably writes an account of a village cricket match. It is proudly remembered that the regicide Oliver Cromwell played at least this game. Cricket was introduced to a wondering outside world in 1676 first, when, it is recorded, a ship of the Royal Navy called at Antioch, and some of the ship's company rode up to Aleppo, where they "did in a fine valley pitch a princely tent, and divert themselves with curious sports, including Krickett."

The game thereafter accompanied the Englishman everywhere. Soldiers, sailors, traders and missionaries left it as a strange legacy in many lands. The Light Division played a game at Lisbon before the battle of Busaco. Some of the British secretariat enjoyed it on the Prater during the Congress of Vienna. The game was played in Corfu during the British protectorate, and in Odessa of all places in 1881. Cricket clubs were formed over one hundred years ago in Geneva and Oslo; and Philadelphia has suffered from an English reputation ever since it first got together a cricket team. The Dutch and the Danes have become particularly proficient.

Thus cricket was sent overseas as a silent ambassador of the English way of life, and certainly it fulfilled that function well, being totally incomprehensible to most foreigners, and utterly infuriating when comprehended. Thus the player who sets his mind upon making a large score, or taking many wickets for his side, is never allowed to enjoy his triumph. It would not be "cricket." He is doomed, by the

Village cricket.

very nature of the game, to frustration or a hollow triumph. The most successful of all cricketers, in the purely statistical sense, were the Englishman Dr. W. G. Grace and the Australian Sir Don Bradman, but neither really made the grade. The one was regarded as something of a bounder because he smacked the ball too hard over the pavilion roof, and the other was regarded as a typical machine-like Australian, just intent on scoring runs at all costs. (Which, by God, he did!)

Cricket is to be played not for the runs but for the sake of the game. The cricketer must play for the pure enjoyment of the sport, or condemn himself to embitterment. Thus he must learn to govern himself —and others.

Cricket was devised by aristocrats in the first place, and it is essentially the chivalrous sport of Christian knights brought up-to-date. The English public schools nurtured it. There is a story about the school Uppingham and its famous headmaster Thring. The story goes that a young and very keen assistant master, eager to ram some grammatical point into the leaking little minds of his class, kept them in two minutes over time, that is a little beyond midday. The headmaster encountered him, a menacing figure. "Now, look here, young man," he roared, "we must come to an understanding about this: is it to be cricket or is it to be books?"

The public schoolboys took the game to India, and the princes of that land became highly proficient at it. But the aristocratic cricketers did not all have titles. Someone has recounted how he found a group of dead end kids playing cricket in a narrow London street. They had what appeared to be a leg of a chair for a bat, and their ball was a stone. But the spectator observed to his horror that a baby was sitting in the road among the players, and was directly in the line of the bowler. He hurried forward and grabbed the baby just as the stone came hurtling towards him. "Hi, mister, what are you doing?" shouted an indignant urchin. "He's our wicket!"

The Lytteltons were a typical English aristocratic family, and perhaps the most famous member was the Hon. Alfred Lyttelton. On several occasions he kept wicket for England, but he was also a brilliant batsman, very popular with the spectators; and he was a good bowler. The outstanding feat of his cricketing career was performed during the match between England and Australia at the Oval amid the drab London slums in 1884. Until recently it was remembered as clearly in the Pall Mall clubs as if it had been the day before. England was in a difficult position. Young and impudent Australia had made 532 runs for six wickets; it was a blazing day; and every member of the

English eleven save Lyttelton, the wicketkeeper, had bowled themselves silly. As a desperate last resort the English captain, Lord Harris, called upon the wicketkeeper (who was not expected to undertake this job). With a useless fast bowler at the other end of the pitch, Lyttelton kept on his pads, and proceeded to bowl lazy, slow lobs. He dismissed the four remaining Australian batsmen, Midwinter, Blackham, Spofforth and Boyle, for only eight runs.

This Alfred Lyttelton was the most popular batsman of his time because of his supreme contempt for even the most dangerous bowling. He hit out like a man, even if it cost him his wicket; and his peers would say proudly: "Alfred is a sportsman. He thinks of the game, not the score."

Neville was the brother of Alfred. He had a short cricketing career, but scored over 800 runs with eight "centuries" during that time. Another brother, the Rev. the Hon. Edward Lyttelton, D.D., a famous churchman, won an even more sensational fame by twice "catching out" the redoubtable Dr. W. G. Grace, the best all-round cricketer England had produced. People would walk fifty miles to watch Grace play.

Yet another of the Lyttelton brothers, Robert Henry, wrote a popular book on cricket, and the eldest brother, who became Lord Cobham, had a son who played for Eton and Worcestershire and a grandson, the Hon. C. J. Lyttelton, who was a very distinguished player.

The poet Byron was a member of the Harrow team in the first Eton-Harrow match in 1805.

It should be noted that it was the real English—not the Scots, Welsh or Irish—who loved this extraordinary, irrational game. And as the British overseas territories were developed it was chiefly in two places that cricket took firm root, Australia and the West Indies.

Thus the most famous cricketer was reared in the Australian bush. He learned to play by throwing an old golf ball at the brick part of a disused tank a few yards away, then trying his best to hit the ball, on the rebound, with a crude bat fashioned from the limb of a gum tree. That boy was Bradman.

He has said himself: "I was never coached; I was never told how to hold a bat. I was my own teacher, and the first bat I ever used was the limb of a gum tree. No boy lived near enough to my house to join me in a game, and as often as not I was left to play alone."

Bradman was not only the world's most successful batsman, he was also superb as a fieldsman, that neglected art of waiting in the distance for catches to come. How did he acquire this art? According to his own version, in intervals of the batting practice aforementioned, he would stand a short distance from a fence, and throw a golf ball hard, to rebound from a given spot on the rounded rail. He was kept up to the mark by the knowledge that if he did not hit the correct spot the ball would glance off at an angle, and he would have to go and look for it. But when the ball hit the correct spot it would come straight back into his hands. A thousand times a day, in the gruelling sun.

The youngster went to a local school. He was selected for the principal football team, represented the school at tennis, and in athletics he won the 100 yards, 220 yards, and the quarter and half mile championships. While he was still in the junior school, Bradman was selected to play in the senior cricket team, and carried his bat (not out) for 55 runs at the age of eleven. The following year he scored his first century, 115 not out, from a total score for the side of only 156.

When Bradman was thirteen, his father—a carpenter—took him to Sydney, where he saw a first-class match on the Sydney cricket ground. "I shall never be satisfied until I play on this ground," said the boy; and his father smiled. But Bradman was there, as a member of the Australian side, only a few years later. At seventeen years of age he scored 300 runs, a record, against a local team. At twenty he was in the national team; and thereafter he broke most cricketing records. He became a national hero. There even developed an Australian version of the Lord's Prayer, which ended: "For ours is the Harbour, the Bridge, and the Bradman, Amen."

West Indian Negroes similarly became superb cricketers, due again perhaps to the bright climate and hard pitches: and out of this fact, and the Australian miracle, came the virtual end of England. It was bad enough to be defeated continually at football, athletics, boxing, table tennis and bridge by lesser breeds without the law, but when slim and prancing Negroes demonstrated it was not only crude, uncoached Australians who could teach the Old Country how to play cricket, of all games, then all was over.

As said the ineffable cricket was developed not just as a game but as a national religion. The rules had been carefully devised to make the game as dull as possible and completely infuriating to an ambitious man. It was intended to civilize savages and bring out the Christian best in the huskiest of brutes. The sporting spirit was what counted, not the silvered trophy at the end.

But the Australians, playing only to win, were soon the overall winners; and the West Indians, playing for fun, were similarly able to make the stodgy English cricketers look silly.

Did England realize then that for a long time she had been hopelessly wrong?

The English sportsman had been taught, above all things, to "play fair." He had been discouraged from specializing selfishly, and the "all-rounder" was regarded as the most complete man. But this team spirit meant the suppression of individualism and the ultimate reversion of the noblest of savages to his squalid and mechanical, ant-hill beginnings. The system was to train character even more than muscle. When players were chosen to represent England in international competitions they were actually picked not just for skill but also for their high principles and good manners: above all the capacity both to win and to lose "gracefully."

It had been mistakenly assumed that man had advanced from the level of the brute beast and that a new, basically-Christian order called "civilization" had been effectively and permanently imposed upon the human race. Even the most advanced English thinkers of the 20th century believed this, the poor dears as especially represented by that supreme mixed-up kid of the period, Bertrand Russell, who wrote:

> We need a morality based upon love of life, upon pleasure in growth and positive achievement. . . . A man should be regarded as "good" if he is happy, expansive, generous and glad when others are happy. . . . A man who acquires a fortune by cruelty or exploitation should be regarded as at present we regard what is called an "immoral" man and he should be so regarded even if he goes to church regularly.

So primarily Russell was just one more English public schoolboy. He had been taught to "play the game" and to despise the "thruster," the "freshman."

This English spirit survived the punishments of the two world wars and might even have endured after what should have been the ultimate lesson of the Nazi concentration camps. Maybe it might have persisted in spite of sporting defeats by such as the Australians, West Indians and the football "wops." But it could not last in the face of the nuclear threat.

The final world game started to be played when Russia built nuclear bombs as big as America's. The English knew then, or should have known, that all the philosophies were wrong save the creed that might is right. They had built their own national strength on the basis of that creed. They had crushed rivals in decisive battles, the Armada, Blenheim, Waterloo. Their worldwide colonies had been created at the point of a gun. And the best man in any game was really the man who played the hardest, the cleverest and the most decisively. After that a magnanimous victor could afford to give the other fellow another chance, but he could not afford to let him win or he himself was lost.

The English began to fail when they deliberately tried to win with a hand tied behind the back, just to show off. They failed completely when that doctrine was encouraged by the priests to the point when the best prizes at a school sports day—true, this—were given to those who came last in the races. Thereafter, as Bertrand Russell so blandly proclaimed, it became actually immoral to win. Therefore England had increasingly and always to lose.

The schools would have been better to have taught the English young of the 19th and 20th centuries not how to play football and cricket for "the sake of the game" but how to play to win. To that end it would have been necessary for them to have initiated classes not only in muscle-building and karate, but also in permissible fouling and judicious cheating. Could they not see that achievement in a jungle universe was primarily the product of brute force allied to extreme cunning and tactical skill, and that the victor who did not beat his breast like an ape at the end was a bloody hypocrite who deserved to have the victory snatched from him by those who knew that he must be basically weak?

All the same England's brave effort to disturb the balance of nature and to impose her own sporting ethic upon the world and herself was a marvellous curiosity, and can still be savored in its last days by a percipient visitor.

In London, for example, he should lose no opportunity of attending one of the great Association football matches, at such a typical ground as Highbury. He will watch a game played like a gigantic set of chess. Perhaps by the end a goal or two will have been scored. More likely not, because the refinement of this pastime is that it should produce as few positive results as possible. It was developed as a game, do not forget, for the express purpose of preventing little boys from becoming domineering men. Thus it can be very beautiful, the ballet-like movements of the colorful players on the great green pitch, the advancements between forwards with the ball passed regularly between them, the abortive shot at goal and the high-jumping save of the jerseyed goal-keeper.

But the great crowd is murmuring and eventually the first bottles will be thrown. The real, basic England is still there and stirring. It cannot stand much more of this frustration and wants blood. It is still the Roman crowd of the ampitheatres.

A visitor will come away from that game with the disturbing knowledge that he has been present at the funeral of a wonderful but inutterably stupid idea. He will know that tomorrow those football players will probably be armed with knives. They will have to be.

Then he could travel down through the rolling shires to a great English public school, preferably on a Saturday afternoon. In summer. Just a few spectators will be present here, sitting on wooden forms or lying on the grass around an emerald pitch whereon slim young men in white flannels engage in an extraordinary ritual. This consists of throwing a ball in an exceedingly awkward fashion at one of them who stands before three sticks stuck in the ground. With any luck he manages to hit that ball with a bat upon which he has been rather ineffectually leaning forward. If he does indeed contrive to give the ball a real whack there will be a low murmur from the spectators, like a ripple of embarrassment around a ring of eunuchs, and perhaps someone will be courageous enough to utter, but not shout the words out aloud: "Well played, sir!"

Then the play is submerged in the sunshine and all is quiet and quite uneventful for bee-buzzing hours it seems. Practically nothing happens.

There was actually one rebel Englishman named Larwood. He went out to Australia and threw the ball in such a way that it almost killed some of his opponents. At last England beat the Australians thanks to him, but only at the cost of a major diplomatic incident and nearly the end of the British Empire overnight. It was so obviously not cricket.

Or pause in most villages of the south at weekends and watch the locals play. There are husky publicans in braces and farm workers with bulging muscles and prim clerks in horn-rims, and their antics cause much mysterious amusement to sophisticated spectators. But rarely is there any "unsporting" behavior, and if there is the community digests and expels it quickly. Winning is not what counts, only the ritual of the game as such.

The best mountaineers in the world were Englishmen so long as they had the monopoly. But once the others had their chance to climb they quickly overtook the English. Germans and Americans in particular put what amounted to scaffolding up unscaleable faces and clam-

Hounds ready for the hunt, outside the inevitable pub.

bered up and down like flies. The English muttered and said "Anyone could have done that," but they had lost their preeminence.

Thus the only hope for the English if they want to make a comeback in the world is to forget what Dr. Arnold taught at Rugby and to remember that in the ultimate conflict "anything goes."

A good start could be made by making bridge a compulsory game at schools. Not only is it good for arithmetic and general mental agility, but it is completely and utterly unsporting. No one says "Pick that card up and play another one. You made a mistake." Everyone plays just to win and uses every method to that end—every method that cannot actually be exposed as cheating. For that reason the "best" English are not very good at it; and the masters come from modern peoples who have learnt in the school of real life.

10

Pedigree

The basic fact to remember about England is that until quite recently she was the most powerful and richest country in the world. When she lost these advantages by her own folly she retained at least some of the trappings of her former pride, and those comprise the "best" of this land for people who like the best. The great country houses may be hollow shells but often the magnificent outer structures remain to titillate the tastebuds of connoisseurs in national achievement. The sporting spirit has been disproved as a way of getting places but can still be studied with delight on the village green. Do not expect fashionable crowds on the Brighton promenades anymore, but the Regency façades continue to gleam in the bleak sunshine there and the rude postcards and slot machines remain as charming relics of a rumbustious way of life now largely gone.

In order to cater for the big 19th century money England evolved some highly skilled luxury industries, and here again the outer shell remains, albeit in rapidly diminishing form, where the creative demand has largely vanished.

Thus in men's clothing there are still English specialists without world compare, headed by the tailors of Savile Row in London, and the environs of Savile Row. Dignified craftsmen not only cut each suit individually from the cloth, but sew the suit together by hand. The mark of their work is a complete marriage of the suit to the man, plus an indefinable aptness and "quietness" of style, and, of course, the crude broadness and slight irregularity of the visible stitches. It is at the time of writing still possible to walk down Savile Row and glance into the basements and see, through the windows, these last survivors

Foxhunting: A morning meet in Wiltshire.

of the true tailors as they sit cross-legged on their tables, sewing.

Very soon these old firms will vanish, or change their methods. Not only do the ambitious children of the craftsmen prefer to convert their fathers' business to mass-production tailoring, wherein there is greater turnover and higher social status—such a modern tailor can stay in his lush office all day and never touch a needle and thread himself—but property "developers" steadily seduce these inheritors and the proud Row itself gradually becomes a characterless thorough-fare of commercial blocks that are far too expensive for shopkeepers to inhabit.

Meanwhile, however, a few of the once-prolific hand tailors do remain, here and elsewhere in the West End; and it will be found if they are visited that the clothing they make, and their methods, are quite unique in an increasingly cheap and nasty world.

Also there are still a few of the hosiers, shirtmakers and fashioners of silk cravats that once occupied every second shop in the St. James's area, and just one or two of the hand bootmakers and hatters that formerly flourished hereabouts.

Until now it has been possible for a man to clothe himself more elegantly in London than anywhere else in the world. This has been essentially the masculine capital. London has never been able to make feminine clothes like Paris. In spite of their provocative skirts English-women and their dressmakers have never had the clothes sense of French and American women and of the great Parisian couturiers (who, like the men's tailors of London are unique but a fast-vanishing breed).

Londoners have subconsciously made a very desperate effort to re-tain their masculine sartorial preeminence, through the phenomenon known universally as "Carnaby Street." This has attempted to elevate the extreme and vulgar fashions of suddenly overpaid apprentices into a new, chic mode. It has been in effect a species of fancy dress, with a strong Bronx flavor always. At the same time enterprising drapers in the King's Road of Chelsea applied the same principles to the clothing of young women, with all-revealing skirts as the master stroke when all else really failed. The depths to which England had sunk were plumbed at this time by travel advertisements in foreign countries that could recommend London only as a kind of latter-day mass-production whorehouse. Naturally most men liked it very much, as they have always liked prostitutes. It is, however, an old saying that while men are attracted to bad girls they are rarely foolish enough to marry them.

So it was unlikely that either the Carnaby Street or King's Road extravagances would permanently give London a sartorial attraction to replace the dying glories of Savile Row and St. James's. The new modes were startling and might even be chic, but they were not "pedigree."

The word "pedigree" means "of a known and ancient line of des-cent." The tailors of Savile Row made their men's suits exactly ac-cording to a formula used by their antecedents for many generations, a proved, almost perfect formula. Their products were classical in the same sense as works of art that had passed the test of time. It would be necessary for the Carnaby Street and King's Road methods to be followed for at least a hundred years before they could achieve that degree of perfection and receive that final accolade. Perhaps they might be followed for a hundred years. But they haven't been yet.

Curiously enough England did originate, in the pedigree sense, at least one essential of completely modern fashion, namely artificial silk as used for stockings.

The curious story begins over three hundred years ago, when an

Englishman named Dr. Robert Hooke wrote that he had discovered "a pretty kind of artificial stuff which might make a glutinous composition better than silk." But textile manufacturers were fully occupied in succeeding centuries with other English inventions—the new machines for spinning and weaving of cotton and wool, the fabrication of blankets named after Thomas Blanket of Bristol, of worsted material named after the village of Worsted in Norfolk, and of tweed from the Scottish river valley of that name. Artificial silk had to wait —for the electric lightbulb.

This was first made by Joseph Swan, an Englishman, but not until he had endured many disappointments. The difficulty was to find a material that could be used for filaments in the bulbs. Eventually he tried collodion, a sticky substance made from gun-cotton; and it was instantly successful. The filaments were made by forcing collodion through small holes and so producing threads. In 1885 Swan exhibited these in London as the first strands of artificial silk.

But still a way had not been found of making good yarn from the threads; and women had still to be content with stockings and clothes made of wool and cotton, all save the few who could afford real silk. Thus they had less glamor but larger families, and the true modern age could not begin.

Collodion was expensive, and could be spun and woven only after laborious processes.

One day two more Englishmen, C. F. Cross and E. J. Bevan, while following up Swan's discoveries, began to consider the properties of the potato. They considered in particular the cellulose that formed the solid framework of the tuber. Could not that be used instead of collodion? The two inventors experimented for a time, and at length they produced an excellent, tough filament. Very soon the trade became interested, and money was put up for further experiments.

It was found that a thread could be produced in large quantities not only from potatoes, but also from woodpulp and many waste materials. But there was still one great difficulty. The machines used for spinning cotton and wool fibers into durable thread were too clumsy for the delicate cellulose, and an entirely new instrument would be needed, unlike anything that had been devised before.

So another two Englishmen, C. H. Stearn and C. F. Topham, worked long hours in a small laboratory to construct the key tool of the modern artificial silk industry, a mechanical spinner to twist the hanging filaments of cellulose by centrifugal force. The new clothing era had begun.

It was interrupted by the first world war, during which the original artificial silk factory was engaged in making "dope" for airplane wings. But immediately after that war the factory started to supply women all over the world with the threads to make the glittering fabrics that they had previously been unable to afford. Licenses to use the new machines were taken out by industrialists in other lands. Came the depression and the second world war—and afterwards it was primarily those foreign industrialists who developed what poor old England had started. America, Germany, France, Italy, Japan, Switzerland—they all romped ahead while England was struggling with herself. Englishmen "sportingly" said "The more the merrier. We believe in free trade, which made us wealthy when we imposed the freedom with our gunboats." America specifically developed the spinning of what became known as nylon, opening the first factory in 1940 when the pilots of the Royal Air Force were fighting the Battle of Britain, which they won but England lost.

The legend is that Gandhi once said Indians could easily throw out the British if only they could eat roast beef.

Actually the British left India of their own accord just at the time when their eating habits changed. They were forced by poverty and over-population to eat increasingly out of cans, and to absorb frozen lamb from New Zealand and home-grown cross-bred cow meat instead of the former good bull meat from the Argentine (that had been based on the pedigree blood of English and Scottish cattle).

Hitherto these British breeds, the Hereford, the Shorthorn, the Aberdeen-Angus, the Devon, the Sussex and the Lincoln Red, not to mention the Galloway, the Highland and the Red Poll, had not only produced the world's finest eating beef but had fathered and mothered the great herds of all the major meat-producing countries.

The cattle of America's Wild West almost all came from England originally, and specifically from Herefordshire and the Welsh border countries—the white-faced and gentle-mannered Hereford—together with Shorthorns from the north of England. They were taken across in sailing ships and pioneer steam freighters right through the 19th century: and a hundred years later it was still necessary for American cattlemen regularly to visit the livestock sales in England to buy fresh young bulls and females for thousands of dollars. This was because the breeds tended to lose potency and character after a few generations in the new environment.

There has always been something in the chemical qualities of the soil of the British Isles that produces consistently a finer flesh than almost anywhere else; and at the same time the skills of British pedigree breeders have never shipped well. In the Americas it has been a matter of mass production of herds and of grazing virgin grasses down to the dust-bowl level. In Australia and Africa it has been a matter of struggling with extremes of climate. The English and Scottish cattle breeders inherited not only a deep soil constantly enriched by mixed farming, but also a tradition of putting quality first and turning the nose up at quantity production.

One of the greatest of the Hereford breeders was H. R. Griffiths of lovely, sleepy Tarrington on the red soil amid the hop gardens and with the black-and-white half-timbered farmhouses still comfortably inhabited after hundreds of years. He was a wispy, sensitive man who was not ashamed to say that he liked to try to write poetry; and when the present author asked him if he had been satisfied with his life he replied: "Well, I haven't done much but I have at least straightened the hind leg of the Hereford."

Really dedicated breeders like Griffiths, and Eyton, and that aristocratic Quincey whose eccentricities have already been described, literally converted the Hereford from a sturdy and rangy beast of burden—it pulled the wagons along the muddy roads in olden days—to a blocky animal made almost wholly of good beef and sweetening bone, with that lovely yellow fat from the red soil. Also they almost completely eliminated bad temperament from the breed, until a huge Hereford bull could be led around the show ring by a little child. These breeders liked money—who doesn't?—but they liked perfection more, and few of them made the real fortunes or acquired the honors that they deserved. What they had done was purely to improve an animal for eating, but, if their contemporaries had applied the same principles to human breeding instead of to atom bombs might not the world have become a happier and safer place?

The Herefords also went to the great plains of South America, and the prairies of Canada, and were partly responsible eventually for establishing the infant beef industries of Australia, New Zealand and South Africa. Finally they were imported into eastern European countries such as Yugoslavia and Rumania, and even into Russia, where their progeny would grow into great herds and improve the diet of the people (and make them increasingly discontented with their lot? As Gandhi said?).

The Hereford when compared with the indigenous beef animals of other countries is the best for pedigree points and for quick yields at comparatively low cost. But in England it is regarded as the mass-production beast by comparison with the two great Scottish breeds, the Aberdeen-Angus and the Scotch Shorthorn. These last proliferate in England itself, and exports of the Scottish cattle from English farms have added the cream to many overseas herds. The very best of beef comes from their descendants. Only the Charollais of France can be regarded as a competitor, but the meat of the animal is less firm and tasty than that of the Hereford even, and it is well-known that when the French offer a good steak it is usually over-sweet horse flesh.

Unfortunately, as already said, the British breeds tend to lose quality after a few generations abroad; and it is true that nowhere in the world can such fine meat be eaten as in the British Isles. European and American steaks look good but often have no taste at all compared with the best in Britain. But: note. It must be the best. The new poverty of the country has taken the people back to where they were two hundred years before, eaters of cow and pig meat and various farinaceous messes. The visitor must patronize an important butcher or restaurant to find the real good English meat that is now largely reserved for him as a privileged class.

Nor would the wonderful, unique cattle continue to be bred if it were not for the pride and public spirit of wealthy farmers. Small peasant farmers sometimes win big prizes with beautiful Herefords and Aberdeen-Anguses, but the blood line of these has been nurtured with the money of rich enthusiasts. There is not and there never has been any real money in producing the best in any department of life. Quality has ever been a byproduct of money made from conquest or cheap, large-scale trading. If the world wants good meat it must first allow farmers to make a lot of money in other ways.

This is specially demonstrated by the unfortunate case of the British fishing industry. As the beef of these islands tastes better than the meat from any other part of the globe, so does the fish: and in both cases the flavor probably comes from a happy combination of climate and skill in handling. But whereas the cattle have continued to improve thanks to the work of rich farmers, the fish have remained the same as throughout the centuries. Even their handling has not greatly advanced. As a result the visitor cannot always be recommended to eat fish while in England. In many cases it will not only be of poor quality but also in bad condition. This should have been quite unnecessary, but that is another story.

Superb milk can be drunk in England, if carefully ordered. This is because English Jersey and Guernsey cattle have the same fine quality as the great beef breeds. The connoisseur should demand this thick, yellow-tinted milk, and will never forget the experience of drinking it. The greatest dairying industry of the world is that of New Zealand, and it is based on the Jersey cow. There are much more than 100,000 Jersey breeders in the United States alone.

A unique quality is also to be found in the English-bred dog. A great number of breeds have been brought to perfection in this country by people who have the careful English flair for handling animals and who, on the whole but of course not always, can be trusted. If a man should still have his suits made to his measure in England he should also buy his dog there, always remembering, however, that there are fashions in breeds as in clothes, and that often a breed is ruined by an extreme effort to conform with fashion. Nevertheless the modern dog is peculiarly an English phenomenon. It is to be found elsewhere but only in England as a privileged being whom most people love more than they do themselves and their children.

This country has also given many famous breeds of sheep to humanity, from the Leicester as developed first by that great 18th-century agriculturalist Robert Bakewell, to the wonderful chubby Southdown of Kent and Sussex. Australia, New Zealand and South Africa supply most of the world's wool and mutton from sheep whose blood originally came from the British Isles (save for the Merino that originally came from Spain but was a very inadequate beast until developed by Australian breeders of English descent).

Similarly English research has produced some of the best strains of wheat, starting with the work over a hundred years ago of Hallett of Brighton (he demonstrated that a single seed of wheat could be made to produce no fewer than 94 separate stems) and culminating in researches at the experimental farm of the Cambridge School of Agriculture which almost doubled mankind's yield of daily bread.

England has always been regarded as the finest wheat-growing country. Her average yield of 31½ bushels to the acre is still unequalled. Sir Rowland H. Biffen, at Cambridge, produced the famous Yeoman wheat, which can yield 96 bushels. Then he contrived to breed the strain which is immune from the disease of rust. Such work as this cannot be measured in terms of national pride; it is the benefit of humanity. The Rothamsted Experimental Station in England created the modern science of the soil. But agricultural education as such began in England. The first chair of agriculture and rural economy was established at Oxford in 1796 (although of course Edinburgh had led the way with a similar institution six years before that).

Yet the enthusiastic tourist must be warned that if the roast beef of old England is increasingly difficult to find then English bread after all this superb experimentation with wheat is perhaps the least edible in the world to all but Englishmen. It has been increasingly made to suit the taste of the largest number, which is inevitably a debased and low taste: for a soft, underbaked loaf from flour that has been chemically treated to remove all color and taste (and most of the vitamins in the process). If the very best of France has until recently been its bread then this has certainly been the very worst of England.

The medieval rites of so-called chivalry that produced the English sporting spirit where also responsible for the equally remarkable English cart horse. Heavy chargers were required to carry the armored knights in clashing battles and in tournaments. They were bred heavy for the purpose, these horses, and became the ancestors of such noble breeds as the Shire and the Suffolk Punch, not to mention the Clydesdale in Scotland. Afterwards the hunter, the Yorkshire Coach, the Hanoverian and the Hackney were bred for riding and for pulling road vehicles at speed. Then, in the early years of the 18th century, just three Arab horses were imported from the Middle East, and out of them proceeded the great English bloodstock industry. The English descendants of those original Arabs, thanks to careful breeding and the effect of climate and soil on constitution, bone and general development, can hopelessly outmatch the best horse to be found in the desert lands today. English horse breeding (and its offshoot in the colony of Ireland) has supplied the modern world with the wherewithal to lose money to the bookmakers everywhere. The annual bloodstock sales at Newmarket still turnover millions of dollars. "A horse! A horse! My kingdom for a horse!" cried an unfortunate monarch once; and he would still be advised to go to England for it.

"I think your policemen are wonderful," was once almost a mating call of American film stars when they visited London, to be compared for significance only with the more indigenous plaint in Hollywood which was summed up in the immortal words "Come up and see me sometimes, baby."

It all happened because an English politician named Sir Robert Peel wanted to make his name in 1822 as Home Secretary, that is, minister in charge of law and order within the realm. He had found on assuming office that law and order scarcely existed. Crime was so Chicago-rife in England at that time that it was difficult to know what to do with the criminals. They were confined in old ships on the river

Thames and elsewhere, and they were executed by the thousand, or shipped overseas to such ethnological garbage cans as Australia. Their offences were often trivial, but even the death penalty or Australia did not deter these petty highwaymen, stealers of handkerchiefs, poachers of preserved game, forgers, burglars and deserters from the army and navy. The population was increasing rapidly thanks to the Industrial Revolution, and this crime problem was serious. Sir Robert examined it coolly. He found that the police consisted very much of undisciplined ruffians who were themselves criminals, using corruption and violence for its own sake. They were imperfectly organized, almost unpaid, and had no self-respect.

The police reforms of Peel principally involved better pay, proper uniforms and the use of disciplined as against individual force to frighten and round up villains. It is true that Peel more or less disarmed his police, and that he used the death penalty only for murder and high treason, but his success was really due to the same kind of careful organization and improvement of the status of his operatives that later enabled an Edgar Hoover to create the great F.B.I.

Half England said Sir Robert was mad; and it was predicted that such a wave of crime would mount from the gutters as might envelop and extinguish all the free institutions of the country.

Crime in England began to diminish from the day that the new police forces were inaugurated. The "bobbies," so-called after the Christian name of their founder, became actually popular with the rough people, popular as no law enforcement agents or soldiery ever had been before. Soon the newspapers were printing anecdotes of their humanity as individuals; and eventually the London policeman in particular became so tame in the national eye that he could be pictured escorting little children and ducks across the road, holding up all the traffic for this purpose.

Much was continually made of the fact that the only weapon carried by an English policeman was a wooden baton. It was felt by many people in the great sheltered days of this rich country that the true secret of crime enforcement was thus turning the other cheek and not opposing force to force but using sweet reason and friendly persuasion. Alas it was soon found in the more realistic days of the later 20th century that the policemen had not needed guns because the criminals of the sheltered era did not carry them either. Once the villains started to shoot freely the ancient policy had to be changed; and at this time of writing the English police are increasingly equipped to kill if necessary, or at least to incapacitate totally with such weapons as tear gas.

All the same they are still pedigree products of the best in English civilization, primarily for their superb organization from New Scotland Yard and for their quiet efficiency and phlegmatic temperament. Anyone who wants to save England from anarchy or communist revolution tomorrow will have to rely primarily upon those unique police.

Another outstanding quality production of the English in their days of 20th-century decline is antiques. The word itself is an English invention. In most other countries save English-influenced America, it is "antiquities." The pretense is still maintained in those countries that such items of furniture, silver, ceramics and sculptural and pictorial art are relics from the far-distant past. But the English term "antique" might be defined as a euphemism for something that can pass as old with a majority of antique dealers and collectors. Anyone who has read in French that extraordinary work of André Mailfert's entitled *Au Pays des Antiquaires* will know that the manufacture of "antiques" has always been a basic industry of man, as widespread and ancient as the making of clothes. Mailfert in France between the wars not only achieved supreme success as a faker but was the first of his calling ever to write down the facts honestly about it.

Mailfert was another Rousseau in that his chief literary aim was to tell the whole truth and gain lasting fame from it. The remarkable feature of his work is that it had absolutely no effect upon the suckers, who when they read him believed that what he said applied to many "antiques" but definitely not to theirs. It seems that one of the deepest desires of man has always been to possess what other men lack, and especially to possess what has been regarded as valuable for a long, long time.

Over 2000 years ago Rome was a city where rich men were swindled by people who made and sold to them what were purported to be ancient Greek and Tuscan antiquities. Workshops on the same sites in Rome today swindle the same kind of people with articles, newly made by them, which are purported to be ancient Roman (and Greek and Tuscan) antiquities. Only perhaps the term "swindle" is in itself erroneous. Can a man be swindled when subconsciously he wants to be?

The same applied to the "reliquaries" of the Middle Ages. These were items connected with Jesus Christ and the early days of the Christian church, manufactured wholesale by clever fakers, and sold to people who wanted to be tricked. Enough wood from the true cross was distributed in this way to make a great forest of such crosses covering all Asia. Spots of martyred blood, bones, pieces of shrouds, even teeth were cunningly devised and distributed across Europe by the same kind of people who later traded as antique dealers.

Often the fakers were organized by princes of the church; and the rear parts of cathedrals frequently accommodated the craftsmen who made the relics. The cathedral of Lausanne in Switzerland eventually had a printing and a coin press for making fake money, the ultimate in this kind of ecclesiastical commerce.

The hand craftsmen of England were chiefly concerned, right up to the 18th century, with making weapons for soldiers. This was essentially a primitive, military civilization. The most common name in England was Smith, and the Smiths mainly made swords. It was not until the 18th century that wealthy Englishmen suddenly realized there was money and social status in collecting old articles, and they found them chiefly in Italy during Grand Tours. Englishmen then went to Italy to buy what they hoped was old in the same way as Americans today visit England. The clever Italians did their best for them, hammering away at marbles day and night.

But in the 19th century the new rich classes of England, opulent with the money made from the Industrial Revolution, began to take an interest in their own artistic past. It gradually became the cult to furnish neo-Gothic monstrosity mansions with articles that might have been old, and these articles were increasingly made by craftsmen whose markets for new goods had been taken over by the mass-production machines. The great cabinetmakers, potters and silversmiths— even the pictorial artists—found that they could no longer make a living out of new work. So they increasingly became fakers of the old.

In the 20th century so much mock-old furniture, china, silver and other artistic articles were sold in England as to support an enormous home and export industry. It could not have been genuinely old because the English population prior to the 19th century consisted only of a few millions of people, most of whom possessed only a few sticks of furniture. Chippendale would have needed a hundred pairs of hands to have made all the chairs and cabinets attributed to him in later days. Hester Bateman the woman silversmith would have needed a thousand pairs of hands to have made all the coffee pots later sold with her mark.

This was not reprehensible. It was just natural. The superb craftsmen could not compete with the machines in the 19th century; and rich people wanted to be duped. In an increasingly cheap and nasty age it was the universal desire of people with good taste to surround themselves with objects of beauty and mounting value. The fakers evolved in response to an understandable demand. They were the product of a declining civilization.

Metaphorical tears have continually trickled down stupid cheeks at the thought of England in the 20th century as a happy home being sold up to satisfy the American and Swiss creditors. Periodical outcries would protest against the immense exports of English antiques and other works of art. The country was becoming just a vast second-hand shop, patriots would complain. These people genuinely believed that their ancestors had stocked their houses with objects of beauty which were now being sold to pay war debts.

But most of the so-called antiques that were exported from England during the 20th century were made in England during the 20th century.

This did not apply just to simple articles of furniture. Often these were made of basically genuine materials, such as old church pews and cut-down pieces of clumsy peasant furniture. The woods were also taken from ancient beams and floors. The cleverest and ultimately the

Royal Crescent, Bath, a masterpiece of English 18th-century domestic architecture.

most valuable fakes were of small and complicated articles such as French-style clocks and snuffboxes of rich materials and so-called Old Master pictures, even period clothing and early automobiles. One factory concerned itself wholly with the making of very ancient fire-arms which could not be faulted in any way, so precise was the attention paid by the fakers to period details and the use of genuinely old materials. Another man specialized in the making of Tompion bracket clocks, and another in the printing of Speed and Blaue maps on hand-made paper of 17th-century type.

A certain collector said: "I have no wish to be swindled so I will buy only what it would not be worthwhile to fake." He bought old farm implements and even farm workers' torn and worn-out boots, which, although he did not know it, were being manufactured in dozens each week by a near-genius of Birmingham.

One of these latter-day Benvenuto Cellinis told the author that a man should never pay more for a so-called antique than he would have to pay for the same article new. That was its true value, he said, in terms of material, labor and profit. He himself got little more than that value for his work and the true killings were made by the antique dealers who bought from him, dealers who had all sorts of devices for forcing up prices, such as the "ring" or "knock-out" at auction sales where the goods were planted.

This, of course, was not true. The value of an "antique" is not its cost of production plus reasonable profit but the price it ultimately fetches in the marketplace. A man need never feel he has been "swindled" when he buys an "antique" so long as he has bought it from an important dealer and holds on to his signed receipt, which is a guarantee of "age" and "authenticity."

Thus a great industry has been created, and not only has it brought valuable foreign exchange to a struggling England but also it has greatly enriched the world with the beautiful products of fine hand craftsmen. If those fakers had offered their goods as new they would rarely have sold them. The world that allows genuine artists to starve makes fortunes for those who trade in forgeries of the work of genuine artists by genuine artists.

So one of the very best offerings of England is the "Chelsea" china, the "Hepplewhite" furniture, the 19th-century "genre" paintings, the "Batterseas" and "Bilston" enamels, the pot-lids, warming-pans, "Ravenscroft" glass, "Victorian" silver and sporting prints and rare editions of "old" books to be found in the charming antique shops. These shops proliferate especially in the nicer parts of London and in pleas-

The narrow "Lanes" of Brighton with a typical antique shop.

ant villages and towns where there are convenient hotels and interesting evening walks. Prices always seem quite reasonable by comparison with European countries thanks to progressive devaluations of the pound sterling, and quality is superb by comparison with the Continental equivalent.

This is because the English dealers honestly want to appear to be selling a genuine antique. They are immensely proud of their reputation as traders, and belong to a snob association which does its very best to whiten their sepulchres. They will take great pains to point out where an article is "wrong." They will say: "The cornice has been restored here and there, and the handles are of course new."

But they will never speak like the Swiss dealer who took the author round his premises and said: "You are an expert so there is no need for me to tell you that everything here is new."

In Europe the fakers are clever enough but something prevents them from completing the job nearly always. They do not, save in certain French cases such as that of the great Mailfert, take the trouble to give their fakes the true "patina" of age. It is uncomfortable to visit most European antique shops because the articles displayed are so obviously not genuine.

England's genius is in polishing and dirtying and breaking and weathering and it finally flowers in the wishful thinking of the antique dealer himself, who, like all habitual liars, comes himself to believe in his lies. This is a great achievement, only to be compared with that of certain religions and of sincere Russian communists and of American Rotarians. The fake has become genuine as mind once became matter.

11

Cathedral

The present chapter would once have come first and not last in a book of this kind. It is a measure of the revolution in men's thinking that towards the end of the 20th century the initial target for the tourist in England is not the remarkable cathedrals of that country. In former times the visitor just made the round of those cathedrals and left it at that. Today there is even something repellent about a cathedral. It represents a monstrous link with a past that failed. That past failed because it produced not only the cathedrals but also us. The country houses can still be admired. It is possible to sentimentalize over them and to laugh at them lovingly. The church buildings not only made fools of us for far too long; they also made us the fools that we are. That is how truly modern man thinks.

Truly modern man can scarcely see the beauties of the ecclesiastical architecture and interior trimmings, so rebellious does he feel when the ponderous doors are opened and the musty smell comes out. His emotion is too strong for his reason.

Yet a completely unbiased observer would agree that in a catalogue of the best products of the English those strong towers and soaring spires, those delicate screens and flying buttresses would have to be placed first. They might be products of an outmoded philosophy but they are unique in all the world, and represent more consolidated beauty than any other collection of buildings in any other country.

Chartres and Notre-Dame and half-destroyed Reims and some others in France might be comparable with those of England, but France has neither the numbers nor the sweet simplicity. German types such as Cologne are dark and frightening by comparison, and the Italian variety is ruined by the excesses of the counter-Reformation, the baroque embellishment, the neo-classical pillars and domes, the candles and pilgrim booths and the incense.

If England has more strikes and fogs per head of population than other countries, she certainly has more cathedrals, whose geographical distribution nicely determines the relative cultural backgrounds of the various regions. Thus the London counties—Essex, Middlesex, Surrey and Kent—have per head of population only a few cathedrals by comparison with the deep-soiled counties of the Midlands and the west of England. Great Lancashire is inferior to Yorkshire and West-morland and Cumberland are largely wastelands in spite of red Carlisle.

A cathedral is the chief church of a bishop's diocese; and any town in which a cathedral is situated, no matter how small, must auto-matically be called a city. Time and time again the building dominates the people and the town, and only ceases to have that overbearing kind of character when a real city, such as London or Manchester, has grown up around it.

A cathedral is a crenellated ship of stone riding the sea of the roll-ing hills and yellow cornlands. It is a condensed mass of all the medieval arts and crafts, and, until Manhattan, it represented the greatest achievement of man as an architect. Yet, like a Hollywood film of the most fruitful period, it was never the artistic inspiration of a single man. It was the work of a constantly changing team over a very long period.

The first period was the Saxon, usually dated about 700 to 1060 A.D. Round-headed emigrants from Germany erected crude copies of what they imagined were Roman palaces in order to glorify their new Roman god of the Christian church. Door and window spaces were small with simple triangular or rounded tops and little ornamentation. Towers were squat and the little churches nestled into the land like animals seeking protection. To a modern purist they are the nicest of all English ecclesiastical buildings still, but a sensitive man can perceive how the idea of the building did proceed originally from the great Roman villa, which was designed to keep its inmates cool in a hot country and to overawe weekend visitors with its vast Oriental proportions and echoing aisles. The ancient Romans, like the modern Americans, thought big, and the great English cathedral is the medieval Englishman's idea of how they lived.

But there are no English Saxon cathedrals as such. Many of the great buildings rest on Saxon foundations and have features still of that early period, such as wonderful Lincoln which summons the faithful from far and wide to its dominating hill. This might well be the finest and most beautiful of English cathedrals, and should perhaps be visited first. The surrounding country is flat but rich. The city of Lincoln is old and crowded and mounts to the enormous pile of the cathedral in steps and stairs of all periods dating back to the Roman occupation, when Lincoln was great *Lindum Colonia*. There is a 12th-century Jew's House on the way up, and the antique dealers are still there. The dominating pile of the cathedral itself has some useful hotels around. It was begun in the 11th century but contains work of many succeeding centuries. Its remarkable position is such that the Greek origin of the word "cathedral" applies perfectly: a seat, and in this case a bishop's throne high above his people.

The proudest bishops came over with William the Conqueror, and were usually his relatives. The true cathedral is therefore a Norman invention as such, the ultimate in churches to make the most money and wield the greatest power. And the Normans, supreme as builders till they were finally beaten by New Yorkers, just took the simple, squat Saxon style and blew it up. They worked chiefly from about 1066 till 1190 and they used great cylindrical pillars, very thick stone walls, semi-circular arches above doors and windows, which would be lavishly decorated.

Canterbury in Kent has the most representative of English cathedrals. Not only is it exquisitely beautiful but it contains examples of all the main building styles from Norman to late Perpendicular. The choir, the Trinity Chapel, the nave and the Bell Harry Tower display classic examples of transitional-Norman and Perpendicular work. That choir, where the rosy-cheeked little devils so pipingly sing, contains the tombs of the Black Prince and of Henry IV. Then Stephen Langton, the politician-archbishop who forced Magna Carta out of King John in the 13th century, lies a heap of bones in the Warriors' Chapel, and the mosaic glass of St. Thomas's Chapel dates back to the same period and is the finest in the world.

The original murder in the cathedral took place here. Thomas Becket was another archbishop with ideas above his station. He foolishly supported his Pope against his King and was killed for it, neatly in the north-west transept, and thereafter was canonized and made such a martyr that even the King who sent the assassins had to come and do penance. A deep depression in the stone pavement shows where pilgrims to the shrine knelt and knelt. And St. Augustine's chair is still there. He was not the popular writer of that name but the Roman Benedictine missionary who was sent to England to convert the natives to Christianity in 597. He became the first archbishop of Canterbury with the proceeds; and to this day that archbishop is the head of the Church of England, although for a long time past he has been able to afford to live in London.

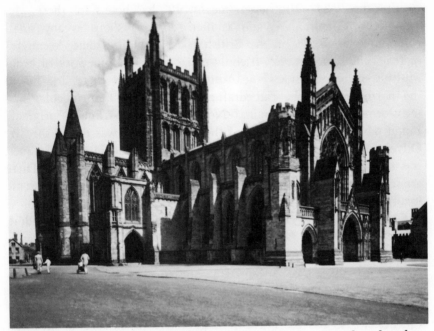

Hereford Cathedral was largely built by the Normans but has been strongly Saxon-influenced in its bleak simplicity.

Another cathedral chiefly built by the Normans, and similarly containing features from later periods, is that of Hereford, a town and county that must be visited if the true England is to be known. Here the Saxon influence is marked in the excessive plainness and crouching quality of the design. One of the greatest early maps is the Mappa Mundi on the wall of the south transept; and there are not only rare MSS but also chained books in the library.

This quiet city of Hereford strangely has many historical associations with the entertainments industry. David Garrick was born there, and Nell Gwynne is still celebrated in these farming thoroughfares, also Sarah Siddons.

Winchester Cathedral also dates back to the beginning of the

Norman style and is a masterpiece of what is popularly known as Gothic. In certain respects it is the largest cathedral of its type in the world, and it dominates a small city which again displays most features of the history of England, from King Alfred (who made the place his capital) to one of the oldest of public schools, founded by William of Wykeham in 1382, another of the millionaire bishops (whose scholars have since, ironically, becoming equally adept at soaking the rich). Winchester, meanwhile, has hotels for those who can sleep through noise, and as many antique shops as any small community of its size in the British Isles, including some "restorers" of real genius. It is a nice, friendly place, set in a framework of beautifully spoilt countryside. Jane Austen elected to die there, and lies in the north aisle of the cathedral nave (superbly Perpendicular and transformed from the original Norman). King Arthur's "original" round table is in the remains of the castle, which was demolished by Oliver Cromwell, but of course, like most genuine English antiques, is a superb reproduction by a local craftsman (13th century). There are also many small churches of rare historical interest and some lovely timber-framed houses.

Chichester, not so far away, has the characteristic Sussex cathedral, again mainly Norman and early, with a strangely detached bell tower. Romanesque sculptures inside dispute with Saxon slabs and 14th-century misericords for antiquarian interest. (A misericord here is a shelf under a hinged seat in a choir, as against, elsewhere, a monastic apartment in which indulgences were given and probably taken.) Chichester also has the finest of market crosses, situated in the dead center of the little city where all the traffic swirls. It has stood there, as beautiful as a king's crown made of stone, for over five hundred years.

For more early Norman work it is now necessary to go north up the eastern side of England. Ely in Cambridgeshire is little more than a magnificent cathedral of the period, Norman and also Perpendicular. Special features are the octagonal lantern tower, the Prior's Door and the Lady Chapel. But Norwich, capital of Norfolk, is a town of renown where one of the finest of the world's cathedrals of the early period has never succeeded in dominating the inhabitants completely. Many of these inhabitants, being Quakers who ostensibly despise money, have made so much of it that the financiers of the place have become famous, and the rich prelates of the diocese have been somewhat overshadowed.

But Norwich Cathedral has a magnificent spire, and the Norman nave is supported by stone vaulting embellished with 328 bosses to illustrate biblical history. Nurse Cavell's grave is outside the east end, and nearby the house of Cotman the Norwich School painter can be visited. The Guildhall exhibits a Spanish admiral's sword presented by Horatio Nelson (who was a local boy), and Sir Thomas Browne, whose *Religio Medici* contains some of the finest English prose ever written, lies buried in St. Peter Mancroft Church in Upper Market Place. George Borrow was another perfect writer of English: he has a house to commemorate him; while John Crome's favorite seat and table can be seen in the Rifleman Inn. "Old Crome" was a humble house painter who became the unique artist of the damp landscape. The old Grammar School in Norwich was attended not only by Nelson and Borrow but also by that John Brooke who became the self-governing Rajah of Sarawak. The Pauls made splendid machinery here and the Colmans more or less invented mustard.

Peterborough, farther northwest, is largely a drab town of industry, but has one of the most magnificent of all the Norman cathedrals. The west front, of early English date, is an architectural beauty beyond compare. Up the coast road to the north is that Boston which, more than any other town, gave us America. The 15th-century Old Guildhall can be visited, where some of the Pilgrim Fathers plotted in prison. St. Botolph's Church has not only the famous "Boston Stump" lantern tower, but also a tablet commemorating no fewer than five local rascals who became Governors of Massachusetts.

The next stop is York, wherein the Minster is one more delectable cathedral, Norman but always added to. Certain features belong to the Early English period and others to the Decorated, while the final style known as Perpendicular has its marks here also. But York has become throughout the ages almost too true to be good. It is filled with historic relics but also with traffic and lusty workers. It is another essentially Quaker city like Norwich, and as such tries to have the best of two worlds, the sacred and the profane, which of course is the way hypocrites are made.

The Friends' Burial Ground in Carr Lane has the grave of John Woolman, the 18th-century American Quaker. The Merchant Adventurers' Hall in Fosgate recalls how Yorkshiremen always did their best to make money from colonies, and in so doing, helped to create the modern American world. After all, the greatest of cities is no longer New Amsterdam but is New York.

And St. Peter's School at York is probably the oldest in the world. It was started some 1300 years ago. Guy Fawkes and three other of the Gunpowder Plot conspirators learnt at this school how to be rebels. Poor men, they probably had the right ideas even at that period, but unfortunately lacked the technical equipment to carry them out.

The combination of cathedrals and strong men is remarkably potent in the world of affairs. A famous antique dealer of York, who had made a fortune from speaking with a golden tongue to customers, was involved in several scandals but would often take an hour off to sit in the great Minster, meditating.

When the curious visitor proceeds to the *Ultima Thule* of these parts, which is called Durham, he will experience the true beginnings of England's best architecture. The town is grim and so is the climate, and the cathedral is built like a red-stained Norman castle. It started as a Saxon church. The nave is pure Norman. Here lies buried no less a representative Englishman of more than 1200 years ago than the Venerable Bede. When the rest of humanity was engaged in still more squalid pursuits he devoted his sheltered days to historical research. Then he wrote down his findings in the light and urbane style which became the mark of the best English scholarship. And he invented the way we still date our letters.

The cathedrals survived the Reformation and the split with Rome. The great buildings of the various monastic orders did not, and they can be visited only as ruins. But what ruins! There are none quite so lovely anywhere in Europe. In Yorkshire alone there are many, ranging from Bolton Abbey to Fountains, and from Jervaulx Abbey to Rievaulx. Fountains Abbey dates from the 12th century, appears suddenly in fair Studley Royal Park, and is the best standing survivor, architecturally, of the age when monks were men. Rievaulx, grey-walled and Cistercian, looks like the cathedrals will appear after the final bombing, even nobler in death than in life.

The second architectural style was and is the Early English, dated usually from about 1186 to 1280, and it is the simplest form of Gothic building, light and graceful in style with pointed arches. The windows and doors are long and narrow with lancet heads. Pillars become slender and are sometimes surrounded by detached shafts. The west front of Ripon Cathedral in Yorkshire is absolutely typical (and Ripon is a nice little town with much of its history still unspoilt). In the crypt is a place where women were taken to test their chastity. This must have provided as much fun for the ecclesiastics as it was fundamentally a waste of time and energy. Maybe there is some con-

Fountains Abbey in Yorkshire goes back to the twelfth century.

nection between this and the Ripon custom of the "Wakeman's Horn," blown each night at 9 P.M. apparently to arouse the citizens at a time when they would normally have gone to bed to sleep. "Horn-blower" and "Bellman" are old city constables of Ripon. (Newby Hall nearby should be visited as a splendid Adam house, exhibiting Gobelin tapestries and much classical statuary.)

These ruins of Bolton Abbey are over 800 years old.

Away over on the western side of the Pennines, near the Scottish border, is Carlisle, a city of red sandstone and not much else save another rare example of the Early English type of cathedral. The Norman nave is where Sir Walter Scott got married to Charlotte Carpenter, whose house may be seen at 81 Castle Street. And there is a memorial tablet on the outside wall of the Congregational Church in Lowther Street to, of all people, President Woodrow Wilson.

The Town Hall, Carlisle, is a very pretty early-18th-century building, almost perfect of its style.

Wells, right down in distant Somerset, has a cathedral built along the same distinctive Early English lines as that of Carlisle, but infinitely more beautiful because of the different stone. Moreover the characteristic gaunt west front is brightened by many sculptured figures, depicting what seemed to be history in the 13th century. The inverted arches that support the central tower of this edifice are quite unique.

But the finest of all Early English-type cathedrals, and certainly the best Gothic church in existence, is that of Salisbury in Wiltshire. The county consists largely of chalk downs with many relics of prehistoric man. Across the rolling distances the great cathedral spire rises like a summons to immortality. Its 404 feet makes it the highest in England. The somewhat dour Early English style is mitigated by the sheer size of the place and by its situation in a very charming "close" of the period, a little self-contained town for ecclesiastics. There are marble columns inside and many interesting monuments. Salisbury offers ancient inns and historical oddities (such as "Ye Halle of John Halle," dating from the 15th century but restored by Pugin in 1834 and latterly the entrance to the Gaumont Cinema).

Stonehenge on Salisbury Plain is the oldest building in England, belonging to the early Bronze Age, and might have been the first of all the cathedrals, a temple perhaps to the sun god. Druids still assemble there on the longest day of the year to observe the phenomenon of the rising sun as marked by the Hele Stone, but they no longer use the huge Slaughter Stone for human sacrifices, and the chief problem hereabouts in modern times is preventing vandals from defacing or making off with the trilithons (sarsens capped by lintels). There are still thirty of these large stones in the outside circle. The inner ring and "horseshoe" of traditionally "foreign" stones presents the nicest problem, as it has been deduced that the massive materials were

Salisbury, possibly the most beautiful Gothic cathedral in Christendom.

brought from Prescelly Mountains in distant Pembrokeshire across the broad Bristol Channel.

The Decorated period of church architecture, from say 1272 to about 1380, is precisely that, an elaboration of previous styles with such additions as extra lights and traceries to the larger windows, and sculptured foliage on the capitals of longer and more slender columns. The effect is of greater spaciousness and splendor, and Exeter has the cathedral principally built in the new style. The west front is a lovely mass of tracery around an enormous window. The unique transeptal towers balance the composition perfectly. The vaulting of the nave inside carries the eye to heaven, and the bishop's throne is a very early piece of carved oak furniture, constructed entirely without nails. The "close" around the cathedral has many ancient buildings in which new tricks are played. Number 16 has a Roman bath and well and other relics in the basement.

After the Decorated period came the final Perpendicular style (from roughly 1380 till 1550). The builders by now had realized that vertical, straight lines produced not only the greatest beauty but also the most spiritual inspiration. Like silk stockings these last masterpieces of Gothic art were designed to attract the eye upwards; and such details as windows were given parallel mounting mullions. Pugin, the 19th-century plagiarist, got most of his ideas from Perpendicular cathedrals such as great Gloucester in particular. This was one of the few arts that did not gutter out in decadence. Even the special decorations of the last period, such as fan-tracery on vaults and roofs, and shields and the like over arched doorways, did not detract from the basic simple perfection of the grand design.

It is generally considered that the Perpendicular style was born when the rich diocese of Gloucester wanted to improve its originally Norman cathedral. The main tower was built in the 15th century and is one of the few cathedral towers that are not made to look squat by the immense edifice below. The shrine-tomb of Edward II is inside, and the east light is provided by the largest stained glass window that has survived so long. There are flying ribs under the central tower, and the choir and transept are rib-vaulted. In the Norman chapter-house of this cathedral the original Domesday Book was partly compiled—William's catalogue of his conquest and the beginning of the reign of the civil servant in England. There is a triforium or whispering-passage, and medieval encaustic tiles: and Gloucester outside is a mess but still until recently retained several ancient inns. The Bell was curiously the birthplace of the 18th-century preacher George Whitefield, a founder of Methodism, but the wonderful Renaissance overmantel in this pub is probably of equal importance today. The Fleece has a wistaria older than much of America, which seasonably tints the side of the cobbled coach courtyard with watery blue, and an underground bar called the "Monk's Retreat," although from what battle is not known. The New Inn was thus called because it was one of the oldest in England, originally a 15th-century pilgrim's hostelry. (Today some of these inns may be disappearing forever in a typical municipal scheme of "improvement.")

W. E. Henley's birthplace is in Gloucester, although the time is long since past when it meant anything to anybody; and the Hoare's House in Hare Lane has nothing to do with licensed prostitution but commemorates an early American family. Visitors can similarly drool over the first Sunday School ever, as established by the local man Robert Raikes.

Another interesting Perpendicular cathedral is in, of all places, Manchester, wholly begrimed and hemmed in by the industrial and commercial squalor of the city. The characteristic soaring lines are there, and inside the great feature is woodwork, in the roofs and the finely carved choir stalls and screens. The "Father Smith" organ is famous, and the Arras tapestry, the brass chandeliers in the choir, and the 18th-century ironwork which abounds.

Do not despise Manchester. It is ugly but first in so much. The oldest railway station in the world can still be visited in a goods yard, and a timberyard in Collier Street, of central Deansgate, has a fragment of wall which once belonged to the original Roman "Mancunium." One of the world's most valuable collection of books is the John Rylands Library, occupying Champneys' extraordinary piece of Gothic *pastiche* in Deansgate. There is the Platt Gallery of English Costume, apt in a city that made its fortune from textiles, and the Portico Library contains very rare first editions. Richard Cobden, who touchingly thought that England could afford "free trade," once lived in County Court, Quay Street, and the Grammar School, founded in 1515, still gets better academic results than any other scholastic institution of England. The oldest free library in Europe is part of Chetham's Hospital, another school (developed from the philanthropist Humphrey Cheetham's original Blue Coat school for poor boys). The fine Central Library occupies an extraordinary circular building, and the City Art Gallery contains a fortune for invaders. The Royal Exchange is the largest building in the world used for exchange purposes, and of course Manchester's Smithfield is one of the largest food markets in the world. Even Granada Television had the first studios in Europe built specifically for television; and dear Victoria Station has one of the longest railway platforms in the world.

The "Perpendicular" style ended the cathedral in its true Gothic form, but the architectural method known as Renaissance (about 1550 to 1700) produced in St. Paul's, London, at least one masterpiece in its own right. This was what an Englishman, Christopher Wren, thought the Romans invented: entablatures, columns and fussy clas-

Liverpool Metropolitan Cathedral: our contribution.

The modern rebuilding of bombed Coventry Cathedral.

sical details beneath a huge dome. The details of the design can be coldly repellent, but the overall effect in this special case is wholly magnificent, and there is no other cathedral exactly like it anywhere. Only St. Peter's at Rome can be compared with St. Paul's, and if St. Peter's is grander it is messier and not half so nicely proportioned.

Strangely enough, it took another sooty and essentially unlovely great city of England, Liverpool, to attempt the building of two 20th-century cathedrals, one for the Protestant diocese as started by Sir Giles Gilbert Scott in 1904, and the other begun for the Catholics in the 1930s by Lutyens. Both are unfinished at the time of writing and this is probably just as well. They, like the great half-building at Guildford in Surrey, and the modern rebuilding of bombed Coventry Cathedral, are already monuments to an age that specializes in the ruin, which is inherent in an essentially diseased civilization.

Similarly to describe the thousands of ancient churches in England would take a book many times the length of this one. And it would be a hollow task, as all these buildings are no more than sepulchres now. It is interesting and salutary to visit graveyards but it does not make a cheerful holiday. That is why ecclesiastical architecture has been relegated to the end of a book that has striven to accentuate what a foreigner will most enjoy in England: the living idiosyncracies that still remain for loving study.

Index

233